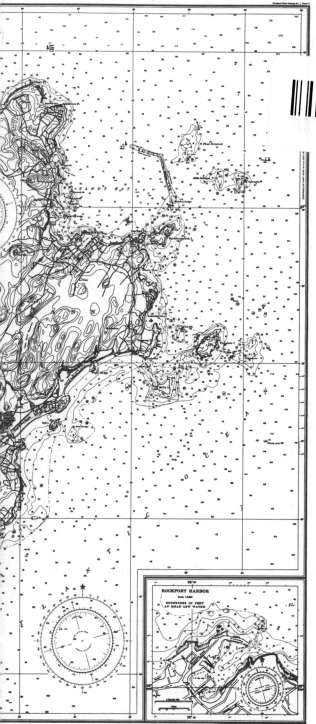

CAPE ANN

*National Oceanic and
Atmospheric Administration,
United States Department
of Commerce*

OLSON'S PUSH

The "Grand Peregrination" by ship.
Two eagles fly round the earth in opposite directions, indicating that
it is an odyssey in search of wholeness.—Maier, *Viatorium* (1651)

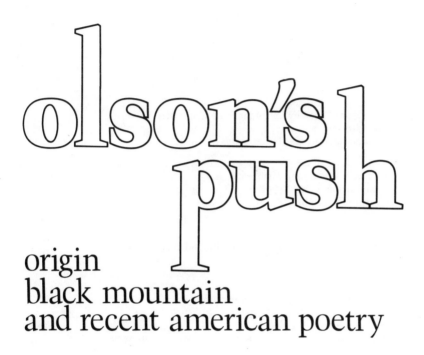

olson's push

origin
black mountain
and recent american poetry

SHERMAN PAUL

LOUISIANA STATE UNIVERSITY PRESS
Baton Rouge and London

Design: Dwight Agner
Typeface: VIP Trump Mediaeval
Composition: G & S Typesetters, Inc.
Printing and binding: Kingsport Press

LIBRARY OF CONGRESS CATALOGING IN PUBLICATION DATA

Paul, Sherman.
  Olson's push.

  Includes bibliographical references and index.
    1. Olson, Charles, 1910–1970—Criticism and
interpretation.   I. Title.
PS3529.L655Z84   811'.5'4   78–6694
ISBN 0–8071–0461–2

Acknowledgments

The author gratefully acknowledges the following for quoted material from the works of Charles Olson:

Archaeologist of Morning. Copyright © 1970 by Charles Olson; Viking Press, Inc., the estate of Charles Olson, and Cape Goliard Press.

The Maximus Poems: Vol. I, copyright © 1960 by Charles Olson, Jargon/Corinth Books; Vol. II, copyright © 1968 by Charles Olson, Cape Goliard/Grossman; Vol. III, copyright © 1975 by the estate of Charles Olson, Viking Press, Inc.; Vols. IV, V, VI, copyright © 1968 by Charles Olson; Grossman, the estate of Charles Olson, and Cape Goliard Press.

Letters for Origin. Copyright © 1969 by Charles Olson, Viking Press, Inc.

Selected Writings. Copyright © 1966 by Charles Olson, New Directions Publishing Corporation.

Mayan Letters. Copyright © 1966 by Charles Olson, New Directions Publishing Corporation and Jonathan Cape Ltd., on behalf of the estate of Charles Olson.

Unpublished material from Charles Olson's papers in the Literary Manuscripts Collection of the University of Connecticut Library, copyright © 1978 by the University of Connecticut.

Diagram on page 195 from Henri Frankfort, *The Intellectual Adventure of Ancient Man,* copyright © 1946 by University of Chicago Press.

For W. H. Rueckert & M. R. Stern
polis is this

Every one has some interest in the
advent of the poet, and no one knows
how much it may concern him.

EMERSON

Contents

Preface

NO ONE knew better than Olson that even though writing is single and solitary it depends upon the collective effort of others. Working on him has made me especially aware of this and of the polis that comes into existence when others generously help. How could I have begun at all without such necessary guides as George F. Butterick and Albert Glover's *A Bibliography of Works by Charles Olson*, Butterick's annotations of *The Maximus Poems*, and Butterick's journal, *Olson: The Journal of the Charles Olson Archives*? How could I have managed without the texts edited by Don Allen, George Butterick, Ann Charters, Robert Creeley, Albert Glover, so many of them published by Don Allen? Without the essays and materials in John Taggart's *MAPS*; in the Olson issue of *Boundary 2* edited by Matthew Corrigan? Without the Archives at the University of Connecticut Library, the headquarters of Olson scholarship, so ably directed by George Butterick? Without the "intelligence" of John Cech, who kept me informed and often supplied me with books; of Jody Swilky, Alan Nagel, Carol Kyle, and Michael Joyce who did similar offices; of Stavros Deligiorgis, whose learning and knowledge of Olson was ready resource? Without the many articles and dissertations, and my students and our seminars; yes, and *that* seminar, years ago, got up by Barrett Watten as an "action studies" in which we read "West" and some of *The Maximus Poems*?

Even writing a book requires the kind of fostering and sustaining that makes possible literary movements such as the recent one in which Olson figures. It is truly an event in the seamless web of events. And so debts like mine are large and endless, never fully acknowledged or paid. Let me at least note several: to the Department of English, the Research Council, and the Graduate College of the University of Iowa for financial support; to the Library of the University of Iowa, the Beinecke Library of Yale University, and the Special Collections of the University of Connecticut Library—and Richard Schimmelpfeng, its director—for their services; to Harriet and Milton Stern for their hospitality during a long lovely stay at Storrs; to William H. Rueckert for his brilliant position papers on literature, history, ecology, and criticism; to Lynn Swigart for his photograph of Ten Pound Island and E. Hyde Cox of the Cape Ann Historical Association for procuring the print of the Fitz Hugh Lane painting; to Lynn Swigart, James Ballowe, Douglas Wilson, and Austin Warren for the necessary and frequent community of letters and visits; to Con Merker for typing the manuscript; to Leslie Phillabaum, Lloyd G. Lyman, Beverly Jarrett, Martha Hall, and Dwight Agner for their most generous and expert services of negotiation, editing, and design; and to Jim, my wife, who, sharing the work, again made it possible.

Introduction: *Archaeologist of Morning*

THIS INTRODUCTION is brief because the essay that follows is itself introductory, one of the first of a necessary and large critical endeavor. Its subject, Olson's *push*, to use his own emphatic and often self-characterizing word, is important. This may be gauged by the fact that anyone wishing to understand recent poetry and writing—postmodernism, literature since World War II—has sooner or later to come to him. He is a central figure, a "vortex," rightly compared with Ezra Pound, one of his masters in a preceding generation. As Paul Blackburn, a poet of Olson's generation, puts it:

> We have had our gene-
> ration of innovators, 19
> 15 & the rest.
> What Pound and Williams & Moore have done
> is in the air, is, perhaps, the air.
> Let the species now give rise to a few
> masters
> (since the fields are open
> and the air cleared) [1]

Blackburn—his own poem is an instance of what it asserts—refers to the generation of 1915, the generation of modernists that included not only Pound, Williams, and Moore, but Eliot, Joyce, Lawrence, and Yeats. And he refers to his own generation, the postmodernists, whose advent may be marked by the publication in 1950 of Olson's "Projective Verse," an essay comparable in importance to Pound's early essays and notes on poetry ("A Retrospect") and Eliot's "Tradition and the Individual Talent." Blackburn mentions only those of the earlier gen-

eration of poets whom his generation finds useful; he does not
mention Eliot, the dominant figure in poetry and criticism
between the wars and, with Auden, the literary master of
another generation, the generation immediately preceding his.
He remarks that *now* the "fields are open" (an allusion to
Robert Duncan's *The Opening of the Field* and to the *field* or
open poetics fostered by Olson) and that the air is cleared.
He takes for granted that any reader of his poem will know
that what was cleared, or clearing, by 1950, was the formalist
(New Critical) closed conception of the poem and with it a
cosmology and epistemology of the kind that underlay
symbolism—a cosmology and epistemology cleared away for
Olson and others of his generation by the new physics and
geometries, and notably by Whitehead's *Process and Reality*
(process is reality).[2]

As Blackburn's version of this literary history indicates,
there was a hiatus during the years between the wars and the
"advances" of the innovators, especially Pound and Williams,
were not carried forward until Olson and the writers of his
generation recovered that ground and began to build on it. This
recovery and redirection of the poetic tradition—and it reaches
back beyond Pound and Williams to Emerson and Whitman—
is one measure of the importance of Olson's work. It is part of
a new sally of the human spirit, and Olson had a commanding
role in it because he was, by age, a member of the second
generation and, by literary practice, a member of the third, or
Blackburn's, generation. No one has seen as well as Robert
Duncan how much this matters. In a letter to Olson, in which
he worked out relationships between writer-and-writing and
phases of history, he placed Olson not so much between the
wars as in respect to them:

> Born in 1910, sd. Charles Olson was conceived,
> born, and nursed; but also initiated into
> childhood—learned to walk and talk

"before the war" [World War I] the last
possible member of a creative family that we
now sketch as having its *time* from 1882
[when Joyce was born]–1914: and its *type*
in the poem [*The Cantos, The Waste Land, Ulysses*]
that organizes time and space to "include
history"....

But *Maximus* is not only like the world-poem
[such as those cited above and others like
Paterson], it is also the first of a different
type.

Duncan means that *Maximus*, Olson's major work, is of a
different type because Olson also belongs to another generation: "You were the oldest one could have been (a boy of 9 to
10) to have been also a child in the period 1919–1929." And
one of the unquestionable things his scheme brings out is that
wars, early and late, have much to do with his work:

you	1910–1914	"pre-War"
	1914–1918	FIRST WORLD WAR
me	1919–1929	the "illusion" of peace and prosperity
Denise Levertov		
Creeley	1930–1940	the disillusion of depression and war-preparation
	1940–1945	SECOND WORLD WAR
	1945–on	the state of War economy with the idea of world destruction[3]

Olson's world poem differs because its object, in the face of
world destruction, is ecological: to give us again "an actual
earth of value...."

I cannot answer for Blackburn whether Olson is one of the
masters he is looking for, though there is evidence enough in
the testimony of poets of his generation—Duncan said that
Olson was one of the poets he had to study, a "Big Fire Source"
—to suggest that he is.[4] Unquestionably someone so generative

and generous made a difference. And mastery—there is time
to come to conclusions about that when the work is better
known—need not now be the measure of the importance of all
he helped to set in motion. Olson's accomplishment as a poet
includes *The Maximus Poems*, one of the recent long poems
worthy to stand with *The Cantos* and *Paterson*, and a number
of remarkable poems in the collection *Archaeologist of
Morning*. This title—archaeologist of morning—is the best and
all-inclusive name for his work, whether as poet, literary
promoter à la Pound (of *Origin* and *Black Mountain Review*,
the primary little magazines of the 1950s), educator (rector of
Black Mountain College), and scholar–teacher–thinker-at-
large (Emerson's American Scholar). For Olson, in all of these
ways, was determined to recover beginnings, the origins of
new possibilities. His push involved the double work of the
great intellectual effort since romanticism—that of recon-
ceiving the nature of the cosmos and the nature of man, to the
end not only of overcoming our estrangement from the familiar
world (he frequently quotes Heraclitus' "Man is estranged from
that with which he is most familiar") but, as was not always
the case in earlier attempts to do this, of restoring the humility,
care, and letting-be necessary to its very existence. According
to Olson (and others: Heidegger, for example), estrangement
and dominance began with the redefinition of *logos* in the time
of Socrates. Both, accordingly, are phenomena of western
civilization, and their rectification calls in question the very
basis of its discourse and humanist habits of thoughts. This is
enough to indicate the magnitude and centrality of Olson's
concern(s)—concerns that involved, among other things, his
reconsideration of history and tradition, mythology, poetry
(especially its physiology, its oral impulse, its nature as act),
place and *polis*; concerns that he brought together in an
ecological vision (image of the world) that expresses ultimate
concern.

Key to Abbreviations of Books
and Manuscripts by Charles Olson

AM   *Archaeologist of Morning* (London: Cape Goliard Press, in association with Grossman Publishers, 1970). Unless indicated, all of Olson's poems, other than *The Maximus Poems*, are from this collection.

AP   *Additional Prose: A Bibliography on America, Proprioception & Other Notes & Essays*, ed. by George F. Butterick (Bolinas: Four Seasons Foundation, 1974).

ARCHIVES   Charles Olson Archives, University of Connecticut Library, Storrs.

BED   *A Bibliography on America for Ed Dorn* (San Francisco: Four Seasons Foundation, 1964).

CM   *Causal Mythology*, ed. by Donald Allen (San Francisco: Four Seasons Foundation, 1969).

CMI   *Call Me Ishmael: A Study of Melville* (San Francisco: City Lights Books, n.d. [1947]).

CO & EP   *Charles Olson & Ezra Pound: An Encounter at St. Elizabeths*, ed. by Catherine Seelye (New York: Grossman Publishers/Viking Press, 1975).

HU   *Human Universe and Other Essays*, ed. by Donald Allen (New York: Grove Press, 1967).

LFO   *Letters for Origin: 1950–1955*, ed. by Albert Glover (London: Cape Goliard, in association with Grossman Publishers, 1969).

MAX.   *The Maximus Poems*.
          I. *The Maximus Poems* (New York: Jargon/Corinth Books, 1960).
          II: *Maximus Poems IV, V, VI* (London: Cape Goliard, in association with Grossman Publishers, 1968).
          III: *The Maximus Poems: Volume Three*, ed. by Charles

Boer and George F. Butterick (New York: Grossman Publishers/Viking Press, 1975).

ML   *Mayan Letters*, ed. by Robert Creeley (London: Jonathan
Cape, 1968).

NOTEBOOKS   Charles Olson Archives, University of Connecticut
Library, Storrs.

O   *Olson: The Journal of the Charles Olson Archives*, ed.
by George F. Butterick, published by the University of
Connecticut Library.

P   *Proprioception* (San Francisco: Four Seasons Foundation, 1965).

PT   *Poetry and Truth: The Beloit Lectures and Poems*,
trans. and ed. by George F. Butterick (San Francisco:
Four Seasons Foundation, 1971).

RB   *Reading at Berkeley*, trans. by Zoe Brown (San Francisco: Coyote, 1966).

SVH   *The Special View of History*, ed. by Ann Charters
(Berkeley: Oyez, 1970).

SW   *Selected Writings of Charles Olson*, ed. by Robert
Creeley (New York: New Directions, 1966).

OLSON'S PUSH

The Will to Change: Clearing Away the Junk of History [1]

"IF YOU DON'T know Kingfishers," Olson wrote Cid Corman just before leaving Yucatan in July, 1951, "you don't have a starter!" [2] This poem, clearly, had been his, and he used it later to open *The Distances* (1960), the first collection of his poems issued by a trade publisher. "The Kingfishers" is one of the longest and most accomplished of the early poems, of special importance for Olson because it is, like some other poems of his emergence, a position poem. For him it had prefaced the trip to Yucatan; it set the conditions tested there and, accordingly, made that watershed experience the ground upon which he could continue to build his work. This is probably the reason for his reminding Corman of it at this time. He felt vindicated, for when he had written the poem two years earlier, in Washington, his career as a poet had only begun, was still uncertain and in need of just such declarative poems—cries of emergence. Only by announcing his position could he make a start, and what is notable in the early poems—and essays—is the extent to which he feels and responds to this necessity, finds in it the initiative act.

Temperament has much to do with it. Olson's essential stance is resistant, as Robert Creeley recognized when, in editing Olson's writing, he placed "The Resistance" first. In this brief essay, Olson takes up his body, his house, his citadel, and resists a besieging death. Not only is time the enemy ("the way my time is quantitative," he explains in "The Story of an Olson, and Bad Thing," "and must, thus, be turned into space") but the environing world, or the pressure he feels it exerts on him. In "Maximus to Gloucester, Letter 27 [withheld]," he says

that the "geography/ . . . leans in/ on me" and that he must
compel it "backwards"—and in reading this poem on the NET
program devoted to him, he grandly enacts this deliverance by
pushing out and fully extending his arms. It's the "smother" he
resists, as the frantic conclusion of "The Story of an Olson"
tells us: "to breathe, to breathe!" is what he wants. And this
may help us understand how much the need for breath as a
resistant force informs his conception of projective verse, why
breathing (declaration) is the initial act and in that time of
general death a cry of birth.[3]

   We must not forget the war in any calculation of Olson's
work. His choice of the vocation of poet is clearly a response
to it even though the decision was delayed by other anxieties
and uncertainties. He had all the credentials, and his career
had all the signs of precocity. But he came to poetry late. He
had published as early as 1938, having, with Edward Dahlberg's
help, placed "Lear and Moby-Dick" in *Twice A Year*; and in
the following year he had been awarded a Guggenheim Fellowship to continue his work on Melville. Dahlberg had opened
his way to the literary world—and, later, would open the way
to Black Mountain College. But Olson wrote his first poems in
1940, at the age of thirty, and did not decide for poetry until
1945, when, having gladly served in political offices under
Roosevelt, he turned in disgust from Truman's politics ("merchandise men," he said in *The Maximus Poems*, "who get to be
President/ after winning, age 12,/ cereal ad/ prizes").[4] Even so,
his emergence was protracted and difficult because it involved
a more than usual concern with the fathers: the need to make
peace with his own father, whose recognition and approval the
orphaned son asks in the epigraph to *Call Me Ishmael*, his first
important work, completed at this time; and the need to reject
surrogate fathers, Dahlberg, his first mentor, and Ezra Pound,
whom he was then attending at St. Elizabeths Hospital, and to
find others, less demanding and awesome and more immedi-

ately useful, like William Carlos Williams and Carl Sauer.[5]

Dahlberg's impress is clear enough in *Call Me Ishmael*, and he is acknowledged there, the break with him having already begun. As for his own father, who died in 1935 and had not forgiven his son's refusal of a suitcase, Olson expressed his love and confessed his guilt in *The Post Office*, a memoir of his father written early in 1948, about the time of his break with Pound.[6] And as for Pound, who was always his "master" and to whom his debt is incalculable, the break, extending over the two years Olson visited Pound at St. Elizabeths, is recorded in *Charles Olson & Ezra Pound*, Olson's account of what in a genuine sense was for him an encounter, not only cause for rejection but imperative to change his own life and go a different way.[7]

Of course such reconciliations and rejections, prompted by profound psychic need, are never conclusive. They persist in Olson's work, are among its most characteristic motifs, rejection especially, as in his mythic examples of the diorite stone and of Typhon battling Zeus, examples expressing not only the rebelliousness of the son but a self-action (*tropos*) hostile and resistant to all imposition. (Olson's democratic sentiment, so sorely tried by Pound, has deeper sources than his identification with minorities and immigrants.) So for Olson at this time reconciliation and rejection were only enabling actions necessary to emergence, and, as the repudiation of Pound in so many subsequent poems shows, he still needed to resist in order to clear and keep his way.

By the time Olson finished "The Kingfishers," on July 20, 1949, he had entered fully on his career. Some of his poems had been published (in respectable popular magazines: *Harpers Monthly*, *Harpers Bazaar*, *Atlantic Monthly*). *Call Me Ishmael* had appeared as well as *Y & X*, a foldover of five poems by Olson and five drawings by Corrado Cagli, issued by Caresse Crosby

at the Black Sun Press—one of the most prestigious imprints
in modern letters, showing the extent of his connections and
his connection, burdensome, he later admitted, to "that generation," the generation of Joyce, Lawrence, and Pound.[8] He had
also received another Guggenheim Fellowship, had lectured on
art and poetry, and had begun to teach at Black Mountain College. But beginning at the top did not make beginning any
easier.

How did he begin? Modestly, with small poems (for him),
and, inevitably, in debt, nowhere so far along as in the prose
of *Call Me Ishmael*. The earliest poems—"Lower Field—
Enniscorthy," "A Lion upon the Floor," "Troilus," "Only the
Red Fox, Only the Crow," "Pacific Lament," "In the Hills
South of Capernaum, Port," "Name-Day Night"—are chiefly
exercises, somewhat stiff and formal, mostly in tutelage to
Williams and Pound, and still dependent on Elizabethan music
and "metaphysical" discourse. These poems often strain in a
"poetic" way and sometimes lack the charged emotion Pound
asks of poetry. Olson is concerned, as he would always be, with
the visual shape of the poem, with its format (he appreciated
graphics, having collaborated with Ben Shahn) and with its
design (to use Frank O'Hara's distinction between design and
form, outer appearance—"shape of content"—and inner movement).[9] "A Lion upon the Floor," for example, is both visually
and aurally fugal, working out a congenial theme from Yeats's
last letter, "The abstract is not life and everywhere draws out
its contradictions. You can refute Hegel but not the Saint or the
Song of Sixpence." (Olson knew Yeats well enough to adopt his
voice in "This Is Yeats Speaking," an eloquent statement of
the complex issues of Pound's "treason.") And he is concerned
with what is notably his:[10] play of syllable, close music, movement, and aural/oral quality, though his utterance is formal—
and often didactic—bearing the marks of early forensic experience.

For all the indebtedness, the poems still address his occasions—indebtedness being very much a part of them. "Lower
Field—Enniscorthy" is an exercise in attention, the first requisite of stance, where the direct presentation of things in the
landscape is marred by a simile ("sheep like soldiers/ black
leggings . . .") evoked by the memory of "dark sheep in the drill
field" which Olson had copied out from the manuscript of
Pound's first *Pisan Canto* (LXXIV). The concluding lines ("over
all/ the sun") may also derive from Pound by way of a poem
Olson admitted he had "stolen" from him, "A Translation,"
which contains the lines "look to a constant renovation LOOK
to/ as each new day/ look: the sun!" Such borrowing troubled
Olson, who reported that he had told Pound that "it was the
only time I had rifled him, directly, anyhow." But it hardly
comprises a debt as large as the Imagist incentive of this poem
or the incentive, taken from Williams, to attend the landscape,
literally that portion of the earth one sees, one's *field*. In this
poem, originally called "Field notes," Olson is unsuccessful,
still outside the field, an "I" not yet an "eye." Nevertheless he
is at his major work, locating himself and living in a physical
world of things, and we will remember this when, at the end of
his life, he tells of his devotion to "the Father Plant & Day-
Sun of/ life he Helios *L* to quote pater," pater here being Pound.[11]

The early poems insist on natural physical being and resistance to death, and poetry is the option in behalf of them. Fuller being: the life of the body, the senses, gusto, love; location
in the world: ground, roots, salt; new attentions—these are his
demands. Olson also looks for models, to his friends, the Greek
dancers of "Name-Day Night"; to Jesus, whose words he transposes to his own ends in "In the Hills South of Capernaum,
Port." For he would bravely face death (and "multiply/ by life
its shortcoming"), and he would be perfect—have no double
allegiance ("be clear too concerning treasures and/or masters/
any double allegiance")—would take "the natural for base/

assume [his] nature as a bird his or the grass," and teach "as
one having [spiritual] authority." He would find in poetry a
way to do this, and a way to reject the world of power and
abstraction without yielding his public concerns. And so, with
all this for his burden, the early poems are evidence of difficult
beginning: to begin by resisting the world and by enacting
radical change, tasks compounded in the poems by resistance
to his masters and by the need to find new poetic means. Perhaps this is the reason the poems are small and stiff. They work
against themselves, as he too worked against himself, their
energy not yet liberated, free to enter the "open" of larger
forms. "It is a mere son I've been till now," Olson noted in
1948, when the break with Pound prompted him to review his
indebtedness and lack of self-reliance: "The way I have leaned
on each of men mentioned [John Finch, a classmate; Melville,
Dahlberg, Cagli, Pound] for direction of work, decisions, gone
to them to prime the pump. In each case, however, the love
has been covert, & the work posed as my own. The price I have
paid is the *resistance* to them, which has racked me—the
pathetic struggle to keep my own ego above their water." [12]

Y & X (1948) also exhibits this struggle and the resolution of
what Olson at this time felt were "unresolved 'amours'" with
Cagli and Pound. [13] He has certainly gone to Cagli to prime the
pump. Two poems, "The Moebius Strip" (in an early version
called "To Corrado Cagli," published on the occasion of an
exhibition of the painter's work) and "Trinacria," refer to
Cagli's drawings and are interesting chiefly for the sense of
reality they inspired, Olson's recognition of a world-in-motion
where outside is inside and militant resistance is the requisite
stance. Other poems—"The K" and "La Préface"—allude to
Cagli by way of tarot, which he taught Olson, and celebrate
their friendship. [14] Now Cagli, whom Olson met in 1940 (the
meeting is recalled in "La Préface": "It was May, precise date,

1940. I had air my lungs could breathe"), was a refugee from
Pound's adopted country, Fascist Italy. Pound had known him
there and, in conversation with Olson, maintained that Cagli
was a Zionist and had stopped painting him when he learned of
Pound's opposition to the movement. This falsehood angered
Olson, and his anger may be fully measured by his recollection
at Berkeley, stirred undoubtedly by his last meeting with
Pound at Spoleto in 1965, of the importance to him of the two
men—Cagli and Creeley—who had been his contemporaries,
that is, partners in his emergence and the emergence of a new
generation.[15] For that emergence, after all, was what Olson's
association with Cagli in the publication of *Y & X* declared by
rejecting Pound.

Of the five poems in *Y & X*, three deal explicitly with problems of emergence. "The K," among Olson's very earliest
poems and the best among them—the "go-away poem" he said
was written just after the Inauguration in 1945—is his "answer."[16] It asserts his need to become the "tumescent I," to
live fully and not in fear of his family's "fatal male small span,"
and to retain in poetry his primary interest in "the affairs
of men."[17] "The Green Man" (originally entitled "In Praise of
the Fool") is a furious song declaring allegiance to his new
vocation—

> Follow, fool, your stick and bag
> and each furious cloud.
> Let those who want to, chase a king.

—allegiance to the vocation he felt Pound had betrayed, the
real treason about which he wrote at this time:

> Jongleur, now jangled
> And was your wish
> a mere need to ring
> and sing
> be cap and bells
> to a king?[18]

And "La Préface," preface indeed: the finest poem up to this
time, used to preface *Y & X* and *In Cold Hell, In Thicket*, the
large collection Creeley published and Corman issued as
Origin #8 in 1953, where it is followed by "The Kingfishers." [19]
No other poem by Olson responds so directly to World War II
and so clearly tells us that his work originates in the moral
collapse of western civilization—tells us that history, which
he measures here in terms of Altamira Cave and Buchenwald,
has made him a counteragent in combat with it. The poem is
as important to his work as "The Second Coming" is to Yeats's,
and Yeats's poem is recalled in it in the concluding lines, "The
Babe/ the Howling Babe," though the birth Olson speaks for is
altogether different, as different as life and death, from the
birth Yeats feared. [20] Olson did not know the war at firsthand,
but Pound and Cagli did. And both had responded to it: Pound
in perhaps the greatest of the *Cantos*, those on his internment
at Pisa, and Cagli in a series of powerful drawings of Buchenwald. The primacy of Buchenwald as evidence of moral enormity is obvious in Olson's documentary presentation. It stands
for the "l'univers concentrationnaire," the death to which the
humanist enterprise of abstraction, power, and ego has contributed, for the fact that changes everything and demands the
new birth he speaks of again in "The Story of an Olson, and
Bad Thing"—that "at the old stand, there, now, they sell/ gold
from teeth, / & from burned bones, fertilizers." It is the fact
that calls for the "root act," the resistance he takes up in "The
Resistance," where he implicates Eliot in the debacle of our
time: "When man is reduced to so much fat for soup, super-
phosphate for soil, fillings and shoes for sale, he has, to begin
again, one answer, one point of resistance to such fragmenta-
tion, one organized ground, a ground he comes to by a way the
precise contrary of the cross, of spirit in the old sense, in old
mouths."

Yes, he has to begin again, and this beginning is what the

poem announces. Cagli and Olson, born in 1910, are "the new born," "the radical, the root, he and I"—a new generation whose task is a "new Osiris, Odysseus ship." And the task begins with a rejection of Pound, not only the Fascist but the poet, rejection, clearly, whose deepest ground is history rather than spite or anxiety of influence. The limbs of the dismembered Osiris that Olson will gather will not be those that in his beginning Pound gathered in *The New Age*.[21] To use Pound's poetics to other ends, as Olson does in this Poundian poem, is the first proof. Nor will his "Odysseus ship" be Pound's. For Pound's Odyssey, begun by Homer and taken up by Dante, had been concluded, according to Olson, by Ahab. It was the voyage of humanism, he told Creeley in *Mayan Letters*—"humanism is (homer) coming in, and (melville) going out"—and in Pound's case, he believed, it was wholly retrospective and useless.[22]

"The Kingfishers" is also a Poundian poem, and Pound is   II
everywhere in it. The issue upon which it turns is Pound's particular faith in historical renewal, a faith for Olson that forecloses the future and demands that he open it not only by hunting among stones—by becoming an archaeologist of morning—but by an attack on Pound nothing less than destructive. It is as if he took the mandate for the poem from Williams' *The Wedge* (1944), where writing is said to be "war or part of it, merely a different sector of the field," and had already endorsed Williams' belief in the creative necessity of destruction that he himself later expressed in "La Torre": "To destroy/ is start again// to let breath in. . . ."[23] His task, like that of the "elder" poets (Pound, Eliot, Williams) who figure in the poem, involves the crisis of civilization, and like them, though of another generation, he is a poet of culture, a poet burdened by history.[24] This is why the need to act, to

enter on the work of beginning again, is the personal crux of
the poem.

Olson does not disguise but honors his debt to Pound in
"The Kingfishers." The ideogrammic form immediately tells
us to whom he has gone to school.[25] And Pound speaks in the
poem, is given voice, is recognized as "guide" and "kin" and
acknowledged for his courage (in words Olson takes from the
preface to *Guide to Kulchur* and makes his own: "I commit
myself, and,/ given my freedom, I'd be a cad/ if I didn't . . .").
Olson does not treat Pound in the mean-spirited parodic
fashion of "Issue, Mood" and "I, Mencius, Pupil of the Master . . ." but undertakes again the trial of Pound he had proposed when Pound was brought to Washington. He judges
Pound on the basis of his entire work and makes clear that he
is not, as he had Yeats say, one of the passive young men who
remained silent concerning what "you have taken from him
. . . the advances we [the elder writers] made for you."[26]

When Olson begins the poem with the memorable proposition rallying his generation, "What does not change/ is the will
to change," he has Pound—and his associates—already in
mind. For Pound is an exception to this rule, a reactionary who,
Olson believed, feared "anything forward" and built his career
on "remembering," on "nostalgia."[27] The slash that scores this
line also calls up Pound, and by way of the similarly scored
question that Olson poses Pound at the end of the poem ("shall
you uncover honey/ where maggots are?") tells us that at the
start Olson is thinking of the *Pisan Cantos*. He is thinking
particularly of

> Thus Ben and la Clara *a Milano*
>   by the heels at Milano
> That maggots shd/ eat the dead bullock

—and thinking, as the entire verse indicates, of Pound's faith
in fascism and its inextricable connection with the great liter-

ary labor of gathering "from the air," as Pound says in these *Cantos*, "a live tradition. . . ."[28]

The opening line, set off by itself, is, as often with Olson, a text for meditation, containing the poem that activity of thought unfolds. Ideogrammic form enables this activity, permits the poet to explore the field of thought, to cluster and hold in tension the many elements cast up by thought in its movement. It is an open form permitting the poet, as Allen Ginsberg says, to score the development of his ideas, their "exfoliation, on the page organically, showing the shape [and shapeliness] of thought. . . ."[29] Such form exposes thought, and when we enter the poem and become participants in its activity, as we must, we discover that what makes it a large (and important) poem is the extent of its field, the number of elements that in fact comprise it and, finally, meaningfully cohere and bring the poem to resolution, not only to closure but to the decision to act. For the poem, above all, is an action, as most of those who have exegeted it forget, and what matters is the movement of thought that makes it "a starter," that moves Olson to further action.[30]

The proposition from Heraclitus with which Olson begins his meditation is also a summons to action. The will to change, asserted here, is itself changeless; it is the permanent motive of history because it is the moving force in men and women, *tropos*, the urge of self-action; and it is the will Olson possesses and later attributes to all men and women in the conception of "actual willful man." Olson stresses this in his emendation of Heraclitus' Fragment 83: *Metabállon anapaúete*, "Change alone is unchanging," as Davenport has it, or "It rests by changing," as G. S. Kirk has it.[31] Good etymologist that he was—hunting among the roots of words as an archaeologist hunts among stones—he noted in *metabállon*, as Davenport points out, the idea of willfulness, *bállo* (I throw) and recognized its kinship to *boúlomai* (I will).[32] Thus we have "What does not change/ is the will to change," which, in Olson's context, is not so much a proposition about the flux of nature as about history. Nor even so is it, as Davenport claims, the beginning of a meditation on ruins in the tradition of the late eighteenth and nineteenth centuries, a conjecture owing more to Davenport's desire to introduce into the field of Olson's poem Neruda's recently published *The Heights of Macchu Picchu* than to that tradition itself, with its cultivation of the picturesque and a sensibility moved to pleasant melancholy by the ideas of transience and mutability.[33]

Of course where the Heraclitean theme is most notably present in contemporary literature is in Eliot's *Four Quartets* (1940–1942), the poem immediately evoked by Olson's proposition and by his title, which recalls the Kingfisher in "Burnt Norton" and perhaps, by Kenneth Burkean twist, the Fisher King of *The Waste Land*. Olson knew well enough the passage from "Burnt Norton" ("After the kingfisher's wing/ Has answered light to light, and is silent, the light is still/ At the still point of the turning world") to offer a secular version of his own at the conclusion of "At Yorktown" ("a bird wheels// and time is a shine caught blue/ from a martin's/ back").[34] Certainly, he has Eliot—Pound mentions "the Possum" at the beginning of *The Pisan Cantos*—very much in mind and, especially in respect to Christianity and, by extension, European tradition, challenges him too. This is confirmed by the recollection, narrated in the remainder of the introductory section, of a traditionalist intellectual whose distraction is caused by erosion of tradition and discontinuity of culture.

When the poet awakens after the party he subsequently recounts, he does not immediately remember Fernand's surprising talk of the kingfishers but the difficulty he had in caging his parakeets, live birds, whom he hopes to mate, birds that may indicate a vital interest in Mexico, as well as prompt his memory of the kingfishers. *Then* he remembers Fernand—

and a situation that requires glossing in order to fully appreciate its weight. Albers, of course, is Josef Albers, painter and teacher at the Bauhaus, whom John Rice, the founder of Black Mountain College, had brought there, one of the eminent émigrés of the 1930s, who did so much as rector in the second period of the college to determine its direction and give it a European flavor.[35] He had hired Olson, who began teaching there in 1948; and since Olson always spoke warmly and respectfully of Albers, it may be assumed that the disapproval he feels is not directed at him but at a type of intellectual to be found at Black Mountain, though not necessarily nor exclusively there. (Nothing definitely places the occasion at Black Mountain.) Now Fernand, who except for his French given name remains unidentified, "had talked lispingly of Albers and Angkor Vat," a recollection judging him both in "lispingly" (M. L. Rosenthal considers him "effete") and for the ease with which he moves from contemporary artist to Cambodian ruin.[36] In this he reminds us of Malraux, the European intellectual *par excellence*, who had adventured among the ruins in *The Royal Way* and treated art synchronically in *The Psychology of Art*, while the sentence as a whole, with its echo of the women who "come and go/ Talking of Michelangelo" reminds us of Prufrock. And the description of Fernand's retreat—"sliding along the wall of the night, losing himself/ in some crack of the ruins"—judges him even more severely by recasting in this context Edmund Wilson's contemptuous remark about traditionalist intellectuals who "crawl into cracks to avoid disaster."[37] But finally what astonishes Olson and contributes most to his censure is Fernand's familiarity with the kingfisher, not with its significance in his own culture but in the very Mayan-Aztec culture Olson has begun to study. Fernand remembers the trade in feathers, valued for their ceremonial use, and the sacrificial pool at Chichen Itza into which messengers in feathered headdress, bearing messages for the

gods, were drowned (dispatched!). By evoking the latter in
"The pool is slime,"[38] he tells the despair he feels at loss of
tradition. This is genuine, and it is moving. But it is not his
tradition, and only a far-fetched example of such loss. Nor has
he turned from his culture to another, as Olson has, under the
necessity of actively beginning again.

These verses tell us that Olson opposes all that Fernand represents. They comment ironically on the text, for intellectuals
like Fernand lack the will to change. Both Fernand and Olson
acknowledge the Heraclitean flux, the lapse in time of the
meaning and force of tradition, the decline and fall of civilizations. But Fernand is a dilettante who despairs and loses himself in the past ("night . . ./ some crack of the ruins") where
Olson, concerned chiefly with the present *use* of the past,
wishes to meet inevitable change with his own will to change.
In the Whiteheadean terms in which he later treats this theme,
he wishes to participate in process, to be "actual willful man"
in the history that opens before us because the past belongs to
the present field and contributes to the occasions of ceaseless
creation.

The distinction here between European and American is
stereotypical, but it is a familiar distinction in American
thought and should be noted if only to indicate Olson's lineage
and the importance of his theme. "Our age is retrospective. It
builds the sepulchres of the fathers," Emerson had protested in·
Nature (1836). And nearer our own time, there is Williams,
who set himself against Eliot in similar terms and believed,
as Kenneth Burke observed, that the counterpart of Culture is
contact.[39] Perhaps the distinction might be put in archaeologist of mourning and archaeologist of morning.

To say, as Olson does in the continuing meditation, that "I
thought of the E on the stone, and of what Mao said," is to re-
state the initial text, to give it particularity, and, as we shall

see, to put digging (archaeology) and acting together. The statement joins a past and present event, something lost in history (as our first effort to gloss "the E on the stone" perhaps instructs us) and something very much present; and both, we learn, are related to the life of nations, to civilizations, one of the West, the other of the East.

The "E on the stone" (I quote Davenport, who has glossed it with exceptional fulness)—the E "is the epsilon carved on the omphalos, or navel stone, at the oracle of Delphi in Boiotia." Yet it may not be an epsilon; it may be a mystical Pythagorean symbol, or the symbol of Delphi, of the center of the world, one end of the world's axis. For though it is clear that the E once had meaning of vital importance, its meaning has been lost, was lost, in fact, by Plutarch's time (second century A.D.), as Plutarch's essay, "The E at Delphi," with its several interpretations of the symbol, indicates.[40] Olson says in a later section of the poem that in the distant, difficult-to-recover past, "the E/ cut so rudely on the oldest stone/ sounded otherwise,/ was differently heard. . . ." Here "so rudely" and the attribution of sound remind us of the nightingale "so rudely forced" of *The Waste Land*, a bird whose mythical meaning, like the kingfisher's, has been lost. So the "oldest stone," to use the subsequent line of Eliot's poem, is a withered stump of time, not an origin but a gravestone—a comment on the Apollonian tradition that began at Delphi.[41] Still Olson's thought of the stone might include remembrance of its discovery in this century by François Coubry, a French archaeologist, and in this way point toward his own "hunt among stones," his way of recovering origins, of bringing the distant past into the present and so beginning anew, a nonviolent way, moreover, to be contrasted with, and preferred to, Mao's revolutionary way.

This does not mean that Olson impugned Mao's recently successful revolution or endorsed Pound's view of Mao, in the first *Pisan Canto*, as "a snotty barbarian ignorant of T'ang history. . . ." Nothing in the poem suggests this, and Olson's quotation from a contemporary speech of Mao's affirms his own belief in the need to act and begin again: "The light of the dawn is before us. Let us rise up and act," a motto for an archaeologist of morning. Davenport clusters Mao with war, with Cortes and the conquistadores who destroyed Mexican civilization, and in respect to what he calls the "unwilled change of war" (I prefer the term "unnatural violence") he is probably right. But when we consider Olson's antipathy to Madame Chiang Kaishek—"that international doll," he says in Letter 8 of *The Maximus Poems*—and his approving remembrance of Mao's following the course that he felt had been followed at Black Mountain College—that is, the retreat from an empty mandarin civilization described in *All Men Are Brothers*—we conclude otherwise.[42] Mao is an example of the very thing Olson advises: he does not (necessarily or wholly) destroy civilization, as Davenport claims, but renews it by going outside its traditions, in this instance by bringing western thought (Marxism) to bear on the East. Again, this does not mean that Olson is a Marxist or sanguine about revolution, though he thought, as he later told Creeley, that "Mao makes Mexico certain."[43] What Olson approves is stance and method.

This conclusion is justified by the counterpoint and logic of hope and despair, present and past, of

> la lumiere"
>> *but* the kingfisher
> de l'aurore"
>> *but* the kingfisher flew west
> est devant nous!
>> he got the color of his breast
>> from the heat of the setting sun![44]

These lines skillfully accomplish the association of the Christian legend of how the kingfisher acquired its reddish

breast and the present decline of the West. They make us
realize that from the East, as Mao sees it, the setting sun is
a rising sun, "l'aurore" that gives him hope.[45] Read according
to the prescriptions of "Projective Verse," the dropped, inset
lines about the kingfisher suggest subordination, which also
seems to be confirmed by the way in which Mao's words
frame this section. And Mao's words, "The light of the dawn is
before us" (resumed later in the poem by "The light is in the
east") have an authority whose force Pound, certainly, would
have recognized because they render the ideography of the concluding example

Sun   Rises (in the) East

in Fenollosa's *The Chinese Written Character as a Medium
for Poetry*.[46]

In this verse, the closing lines ("he got the color of his breast/
from the heat of the setting sun!") serve nicely to make the
transition to the subsequent scientific description of the kingfisher because, in the poem's brief calculus, the kingfisher,
with its Christian associations, replaces the Delphic stone and
enables Olson, in discounting the bird's legends, to repudiate
Christianity. And Eliot. Olson, as we saw in "The Resistance,"
believes that Christianity is cause not cure of the waste land
(the sterility of the West), that, as Maxine Combs puts it, "the
kingfisher . . . will [not] cure the Fisher King."

Now we should no more be surprised to find a transposition
from the article on kingfishers in the *Encyclopaedia Britannica*
(11th edition) than to find Mao's words. Ideogram is collage.
And Olson *read* encyclopaedias—and dictionaries. This was
part of his morning work. They were the first things he turned
to when he began digging. In "Starting fr where you are. . . ,"
a guide for students at Black Mountain College, he charted

the procedure he followed; and of significance in explaining
the use of such materials in the poem, is his insistence on
exactness and seeing for oneself—"And cf. (see)." Scholarship
is digging, seeing for oneself; the metaphor is archeological,
and archeology is method, not reliance on history (writing
about) but the digging up of actual evidence, things themselves.[47] In turning from legend to fact, Olson, accordingly,
has already begun to hunt among stones in search of an answer
to the question he will pose at the end.

Where he had used legend at the start to suggest the connection between Christianity and the decline of the West, he now
discounts legend to the same end. The scientific description he
employs shows that the actual character of the kingfisher has
nothing to do with the legends about it. "The legends are/
legends"—and they are introduced by their negation, the negative cancelling the legends in the very statement of them: the
bird does not indicate a favoring wind, does not avert the
thunderbolt, does not bring the halcyon days. Olson has already noted the feebleness of its feet (in the *Britannica* their
comparative functionlessness is stressed), and now, describing
its nesting habits—the nest, Combs says, is the specific Christian among otherwise pagan allusions—he further depreciates
the legendary bird. The fact of the matter is that it builds its
nest on "rejectamenta," and as the young are reared it becomes
a "nest of excrement and decayed fish . . ./ a dripping, fetid
mass." This description is almost exactly that of the source,
but the disposition is artful and in keeping with the spirit that
moved Olson to omit "pretty" before "cup-shaped structure. . . ." The concluding phrase ("a dripping, fetid mass") is
conspicuously placed in relation to what precedes it and to the
words of Mao that follow. This supports Maxine Combs's
claim that Olson (a lapsed Catholic) is intentionally punning
on "Mass." And it recalls "The pool is slime," which provides
one of the links to the next section and, by way of its place in

an image-cluster of putrescence (slime, fetid mass, rot, maggots), shows us that the answer Olson has begun to discover
will be negative.

Again the poem moves forward (or circles, since this is the way
of meditative exploration) by restating the text. "What does
not change/ is the will to change" becomes "When the attentions change/ the jungle// leaps in"—the slight alteration, the
break after "jungle," owing to Olson's wish to enact the leap.
New attentions, with their virtue of changing things, may
point back to Mao, for whom they were coincident with the
will to change, or to Angkor Vat, where they were coincident
with the historical change that permitted the jungle to re-
assert itself. One is active, the other passive; and nature, as
much as Mao, is a "conqueror," her natural violence—of the
rhythm of life itself, destructive yet creative—regenerative
where war is not. Davenport says that these lines call up
Canto xx, where Pound recognizes the jungle ("HO BIOS")
as the "Basis of renewal, renewals"—a passage, incidentally,
supporting Olson's rejection of the notion of chaos-as-void.[48]
I would add, for evident reasons of theme and form, Williams'
The Wedge, a book Olson certainly turned to for the prefatory
statement on the relation of individual speech to intrinsic form
and undoubtedly appreciated for the affirmation of poetic
office in its opening poem:

> —through metaphor to reconcile
> the people and the stones.
> Compose. (No ideas
> but in things) Invent!
> Saxifrage is my flower that splits
> the rocks.

Preeminently the poet of attention, Williams expected the
poet to do the salutary destructive-creative work proposed by
Olson in his poem.

The other way, the way of unnatural violence, is presented in "that other conqueror" who "so resembles ourselves. . . ." He may be Mao, he may be Cortes, as the subsequent verses suggest; but the point of these verses is that the other way is contrary to all human good. The Delphic stone, mentioned in this context, speaks, via Eliot's nightingale, for irreparable violation, incalculable loss; and it probably stands in for glyphs which, being phonetic as well as ideographic, were "heard." In this way the meditation moves easily to Olson's primary example of war and destruction of civilization, Cortes' conquest of Mexico.

Olson's source is William Prescott's great history.[49] From it he takes the fragments he transposes and paraphrases so effectively, fragments of that drama of the beginning (the gifts of feathers and gold Montezuma gave Cortes) and of the end (the massacre at Cholula, among others).[50] The disposition of the verses suggests that the Mexican use of treasure ("as, in another time, were treasures used") was consonant with peace, with "the use/ of tilled fields," where Cortes' use was not. (*Use* is already an important measure of value for Olson.) This contrast sufficiently explains why "The pool is slime." For "all now is war," Olson says in a consummate verse that speaks also for his own time, and not so much for loss of tradition as for loss of polis and productive work:

> And now all is war
> where so lately there was peace
> and the sweet brotherhood, the use
> of tilled fields.[51]

War (of death and dying) provides the transition to the concluding section of Part I. Here the theme of change is most fully developed in Heraclitean terms. Davenport notes that "Not one death but many" also derives from *The Heights of Macchu Picchu* ("y no una muerte, sino muchas muertes").

This long poem, which he says resembles and inspired "The Kingfishers," is relevant here because it treats another conquest and the living death of a subject people—even though the line cited is used by Neruda to speak of a present urban rather than a past agricultural situation and Olson's argument immediately turns elsewhere.[52] It turns to Heraclitus because it is directed to Eliot who found in Incarnation a way of transcending the flux of time and disclaiming the responsibility of history. Here Olson transposes material from Ammonius' speech in Plutarch's "The E at Delphi." Most of us are familiar with some of it, at least with "Into the same river no man steps twice," though we may not appreciate the central and profound issues that for Olson are at stake in it.

These issues are cosmological and historical, and relate directly to Olson's concern with action. The views so briefly presented here are treated more fully later in *The Special View of History*, where Olson grounds them in Whitehead, whose work he had finally discovered for himself. This is to say that Whitehead confirmed the basic view of reality Olson had already acquired from, among others, Pound and Fenollosa—which, in turn, explains why Eliot, not Pound, figures here.

Ammonius' explanation of Heraclitus' famous saying renders Whiteheadean process: "at the same instant it [any living substance] both settles into its place and forsakes its place; 'it is coming and going.'" An event is a node of the process, in process. Reality is process, "is change," Olson says, "presents/ no more than itself. . . ." It is

> . . . the birth of air, is
> the birth of water, is
> a state between
> the origin and
> the end, between
> birth and the beginning of
> another fetid nest

This passage, though marked by Olson's rhythm, parodies Eliot and, by recalling in "fetid nest" the earlier repudiation of Christianity, mocks him.[53]

But what is the human bearing of a process world? How does one stand in respect to it? For one thing, if living is dying, we have, having died many times in living through the ages of man, "a ridiculous fear of one death" (Ammonius)—a lesson not lost on Olson, who had been moved by fear of death to live in the totality of things. For another thing, stance, that we stand in the process ("in that crashing water," he says in "Adamo Me . . .") and deal with it with the virtue that Keats called negative capability:

> And the too strong grasping of it,
> when it is pressed together and condensed,
> loses it

As Olson says, paraphrasing Keats at the beginning of "Equal, That Is, to the Real Itself," "I do better to stay in the condition of things." For he wishes not to transcend history (the flux of events) but enter it, and use it.

This is possible because history for him is "not accumulation but change." History is not simple addition, the merely linear causality assumed by those who read its course as inevitable decline and accordingly prefer the past to the present, a view Pound expresses in *Hugh Selwyn Mauberley*:

> All things are a flowing,
> Sage Heracleitus says;
> But a tawdry cheapness
> Shall outlast our days.

On the contrary, since history is process its course is never single, never inevitable, and never foreclosed. Process opens possibility, and history is always prospective, never limited by origin, which, in any case, may be recovered, not cyclically (as in Eliade) but spatially, in the fullness of time. This is what

"feed-back" proves, and why Olson considers it "the law" of
history. For feedback, as Olson learned from Norbert Wiener's
recently published book on cybernetics, is a means of correc-
tion, the use of knowledge of past events to foster change in an
on-going process. Applied to history, it underwrites the cogni-
tive motive and the more familiar notion of a usable past; and
it explains what at first may seem curious in Olson—his lively
interest in the immediate present and the distant past.[54]

Feedback assumes process. As the juxtaposition of scientific
material on systems-control and "discrete or continuous sequence" from Wiener tells us, it is an idea in keeping with the
notion of Heraclitean flux, and with Olson's view that "the
structures of the real are flexible, quanta do dissolve, all does
flow." It is also in keeping with the ideas of field and of active
participation within it ("man, in the midst of it, knowing well
how he was folded in, as well as how suddenly and strikingly
he could extend himself").[55] So it tasks us, as the conclusion of
Olson's meditation tasks him, to become an agent of change,
"This very thing you are."

The percussive rhythm and force as well as insistence of this
section brings the meditation back to Pound, the most conspicuous presence of Section II and, with Rimbaud, of Section
III. Enjoined to act, Olson ponders the difficulties of taking
action in the waste land of the West.

Now Olson's thought does not begin as before on the level
of proposition. The initial fragments are inset and indicate
both its interior movement and (as in the shape of all that
follows) the agitation accompanying it. The fragments concern
Mexican burial and baptismal ceremonies and the evidence
sometimes adduced to prove the Asian origin of Amerindian
culture. Associations of death and life (regeneration), sun and
west, East and West pick up previous insistences—may even
for Olson recall the summons of "La Préface"—and bring him

to the unavoidable issue: "The light is in the east [not necessarily the Orient, but the east of his horizon]. Yes. And we
must rise, act. Yet. . . ." He has made Mao's words his own,
the correlative of "This very thing you are"; but the difficulty
of acting is recognized in "Yet," which hovers at the end of the
line, balancing "Yes," modifying its affirmation.

The sense of Western civilization rendered in what follows
is essentially Pound's—the Pound of *The Pisan Cantos*, who,
witness of World War II, describes himself, Odysseus the way-
farer, as "a man on whom the sun has gone down."[56] He is
Olson's Virgil, the "guide" leading the younger poet through
the hell civilization has become, teaching him his way of enduring it, to "regard the light, contemplate/ the flower ["that
longest-lasting rose"]" and to follow the wisdom of Confucius.[57] Olson transposes from the initial *Pisan Canto* the
lines of the *Analects* Pound himself had paraphrased ("what
whiteness will you add to this whiteness,/ what candor?") and
takes from Pound "pudor" and "pejorocracy," the latter the
word with which he expresses disgust in the first volume of
The Maximus Poems. And what he says there of Gloucester
he might well say of civilization at large: "love is not easy . . .//
now that pejorocracy is here."

It is not easy to act in a state of revulsion, in the state of
dismay expressed in this section of the poem. Mexico itself, to
which it is clear Olson is turning, offers the usual testimony of
unnatural violence, testimony of wanton bloodshed on the
part of Cortes, who justified his acts in terms of Christian
abhorrence at human sacrifice, and was justified in turn by
Prescott. But Olson does not excuse "the excuser"—he does
not approve Prescott's heroic portrait of Cortes—and cites
against him the attempt to extenuate human sacrifice by
noting its existence in other civilizations. The lines from
Marco Polo's account of the cannibalism of the Chinese and

Japanese ("la piu saporita et migliore/ che si possa truovar al mondo": the most savory and best that can be found in the world) are conspicuously used by Olson after the manner of Pound, and perhaps to instruct him. For the deep indentation of these lines does not indicate subordination so much as intensity of thought and feeling; they remind us of "First Fact" in *Call Me Ishmael*, of the cannibalism reported there, of human extremity, extremes. The meditation pivots on them and moves on to put in question not Pound's fealty but insufficiently grounded, too easily achieved vision.

It is not that Pound didn't look long and hard enough but that he didn't, Olson believes, look long and hard enough at what is hidden, under, below—and hence could "uncover honey/ where maggots are. . . ." For Olson the extremes are not related to each other in the paradoxical religious way suggested by the biblical allusion of this line.[58] They are contraries (in Blake's sense), and to "contemplate/ the flower" is, he tellingly puns, to contemplate also "whence it arose," the dark ground of generation and the dialectical nature of change:

> with what violence benevolence is bought
> what cost in gesture justice brings
> what wrongs domestic rights involve
> . . . .[59]

Here, as often in Olson's work, anaphora contributes to percussive effect. But also note the assonance of "violence" and "benevolence" and the consonance of "gesture" and "justice," both enacting the dialectical change expressed in "is brought" and "brings," themselves verbal rhymes. Note also that the concluding verses have a similar structure of three long and two short lines, the latter tightly, forcefully closing the verse, and that the second verse reverses the relation of terms in the first so that the dark rather than the light element emerges from the process:

> what pudor pejorocracy affronts
> how awe, night-rest and neighborhood can rot
> what breeds where dirtiness is law
> what crawls
> below

In the initial lines Olson speaks with Pound's words and, as Davenport points out, with those of Shakespeare's Timon. The conjunction may be significant when one considers what Olson is doing in this poem and his comment on *Timon of Athens* in *Call Me Ishmael* ("what gave *Timon* its special intensity was that Timon was undone by friends").[60] Stirring beneath these lines—or "crawl[ing]/ below"—to adapt Olson's phrase— is an act of rejection, and Timon's speech (IV, I) was probably memorable because it awakened Olson's guilt over fathers (the passage tells of a son's injury to his father and the consequent loss of civil good). Olson's own behavior, accordingly, accounts for the unusual bitterness expressed here, for the collocation of "rot," "breeds," and "crawls," the putrescence that answers "shall you uncover honey/ where maggots are?"

The negative answer to this question also answers in the negative the imperative to action at the beginning of this section. And in this context Mao's words become Pound's as well, those moving words near the end of *The Pisan Cantos* where he says, "to have done instead of not doing/ this is not vanity . . .// error is all in the not done,/ all in the diffidence that faltered." So the movement of this section is downward, away from the summons of light, and in it Olson is temporarily overcome by what, in *The Maximus Poems*, he calls the "underpart."

The concluding section of "The Kingfishers" is short, visually tidy, almost regular in its quatrains. The verses are carved. In them Olson speaks in a manner reminiscent of Pound. The first person, hitherto little used, is now conspicuous; the sentences are strongly declarative. The prominent "I" recalls "The K," where the poet answers assertively ("Take, then, my answer") and explains the tidal movement that works through ebb to the "tumescent I." And "The K" is relevant also because the poet in it is concerned with new attentions ("Our attention is simpler") and with contact with a familiar world ("The salts and minerals of earth return"). In these verses Olson overcomes the despair of the previous section and directly, conclusively answers Pound.

The initial lines ("I am no Greek, hath not th' advantage./ And of course, no Roman") do not, I think, deny Olson's learning in the classics—he gave a tutorial in the Greeks at Black Mountain College—but disclaim allegiance to the classical tradition.[61] Pound, of course, having taken Odysseus for a persona, was an eminent poet of (in) that tradition.[62] But Olson's kinship, as he goes on to explain—and exemplify—is not with Pound's tradition but with his courage. It may be, he says, that not standing within the classical tradition is a "disadvantage" —especially in regard to "beauty," which Pound said, in a refrain Olson copied from *The Pisan Cantos*, "is difficult."[63] Nevertheless, Olson has stepped outside this tradition and taken other risks, and has found another model in Rimbaud, one of his great moderns (with Melville, Dostoevski, and Lawrence) and, incidentally, a forebear to whom Pound himself once turned.

That Olson puts Rimbaud against Pound, who early recognized his modernity and made him known in translation, is easily explained. Olson is not attacking Pound's defense of antisymbolist art but his restricted tradition. The lines he cites from *Une Saison en enfer* reject that tradition in the profoundest way. When he says that his hunger (taste) is only for earth and stones, he declares for the familiar world he feels Pound's tradition imperils. The best gloss here is Olson's remark in

The Special View of History: "It is this which Heraclitus
meant when he laid down the law which was vitiated by
Socrates and only restored by Rimbaud: that man is estranged
from that [with] which he is most familiar." So Heraclitus
enters the poem in another way and provides the end towards
which Olson directs the will to change. Olson refuses "the
generalizing time" Socrates initiated—Western civilization,
Europe, the classical tradition—and he stands with Rimbaud
not only because he shares his "taste" for something besides
"beauty," but because he is about to follow his example of
going outside the European tradition.[64]

Backwards and outside. This was Olson's advice to students
in the Greek tutorial when they confronted Homer and the
other great writers who appeared later in the fifth century
B.C.: "take both backwards and outside em, not get caught in
that culture trap of taking them forwards, as tho all that we
are depends on em."[65] He himself went back to the Sumerians
and Hittites and outside to the Mayans, thereby escaping the
"Western Box" in which he felt Pound was trapped. He appreciated the methodology of *The Cantos* because it created a
space-field, "turned time into what we must now have, space
& its live air"; but he found *The Cantos* useless because "after
1917," as he later told Creeley, "the materials he [Pound] had
found useful are not at all of use." For Olson the first World
War marked the end of "Yurrup (West, Cento, Renaissance)";
that tradition was played out, offered no feedback, and nothing
useful, no honey, he believed, would emerge from its rot, from
fascism.[66]

Pound therefore was no longer a guide to culture. So breaking with Pound, Olson turns to Mexico. This is how I read
"I have interested myself/ in what was slain in the sun. . . ."[67]
Here Olson will hunt among stones in order to recover, as in
fact he did, some valuable lessons of renewal. One lesson was
that there were people who were not estranged from the famil-

iar, who lived in the physical world and knew how to attend it closely, to make it a "human universe." Another was the realization that since time does not alter the fact that they were like us, there is no "history." In the enthusiasm of his discovery of the Mayan world, the only "history" Olson acknowledged was the "*second time*. . . ."[68] This does not mean that he transcends history. Instead it tells us what his preparatory poem declares: that civilizations decline when there is no will to change; that the decline of civilization is not necessarily followed by the rise of another—only the agency of "actual willful men" opens that possibility; and that there is ground for hope and reason to act because all history is present and what linear history and restricted tradition have denied us is still there to be used.[69]

On the Way to the Fathers TWO

Some time towards the end of 1950, it was in December I think, but the letter isn't dated, I heard that Charles Olson was off to Yucatan. A sudden 'fluke'—the availability of some retirement money owed him from past work as a mail carrier—gave him enough for the trip, 'not much but a couple of hundred, sufficient, to go, GO be, THERE . . . '. By February I had got another letter, 'have just this minute opened this machine in this house lerma. . . . ' From that time on I heard from him regularly, and so was witness to one of the most incisive experiences ever recorded. Obviously it is very simple to call it that, that is, what then happened, and what Olson made of his surroundings and himself. Otherwise, it is necessary to remember that Olson had already been moving in this direction, back to a point of origin which would be capable of extending 'history' in a new and more usable sense. In his book on Melville, Call Me Ishmael, he had made the statement, 'we are the last first people . . .'; and in his poetry, most clearly in The Kingfishers, there was constant emphasis on the need to break with the too simple westernisms of a 'greek culture'.[1]

Actually, Olson didn't get away as planned. His mother's sudden illness called him home—she died on Christmas day—and he didn't leave for Yucatan until mid-January 1951. Because of this delay, he had ready for Cid Corman all the material—even "The Moon is the Number 18," his funeral poem—for the first issue of *Origin*, which featured him. Leaving with all in order, he was indeed on the way. In the preceding months he had instructed Corman and thereby helped to shape a magazine that would become the single most important vehicle for the poets coming to prominence in the 1950s—the "some others" to whom he alludes at the end of his letter to Grover

Smith.[2] He had prepared confirmation for himself, and this, conjoined with his experience of *origins* in Yucatan and his immediate return to Black Mountain College, where he helped to bring the curriculum into closer accord with his views, energized him for the rest of the decade, the most productive and remarkable of his career. In *Origin* and in *The Black Mountain Review*, which he established later with Creeley as editor, and in the college, he had reliable outlets that demanded his work. As he told Corman, "The thing is, because *Origin* exists, I write better, I write more. . . ." He also had, as never before or afterward, the "collective" he desired, both the magazine, which he spoke of as "my place," and the college, which, significantly, was a place common to both him and the Indian ("think of the Indian eyes have seen/ this same thing . . .") and an intimate community ('"It was a polis," sd his friend, "no wonder/ you wanted to take part in its/ creation"').[3]

Creeley helps us understand this incredible push when he reminds us of Olson's momentum, of the fact that he was already in motion. Of this the work itself is the most impressive measure. A good third of the poems collected in *Archaeologist of Morning* were written by July, 1951, when he returned from Yucatan, and among his most important prose pieces, "Human Universe" and "Apollonius of Tyana," were written immediately after. As early as *Call Me Ishmael*, he knew the direction he would take, and before he left for Yucatan he not only had sufficiently cleared the way of his fathers but had worked through to the essential position and the directives that would enable him to return to the way of the fathers. ("Der Weg stirbt," he said, posing the problem in—and of—the "Human Universe.") The signature of this wonderful realization—and of the characteristic generosity that accompanied it—is Olson's insistence, in teaching both Cid Corman and Rainer Maria Gerhardt, that he is giving them a present.

"Please *hear* me," he implores, when telling Corman how an American writer must begin, "I am giving you a present."[4] And he knew that Corman, already the beneficiary of previous letters, would also feel the weight of that sentence because it is conspicuously reiterated in the poem to Gerhardt ("To Gerhardt, there, among Europe's things. . . .") that he had published in *Origin*. In that poem of fathers and sons as well as in his relation to Corman, Olson becomes a father because he has something valuable to give, and he gives it as fathers should, as the fathers he had found willingly did.

The present Olson bestows is nothing less than the present that modernism had tried to recover: the thing Williams said, long before in *Spring and All*, that one never dares to know, "the exact moment that he is," the life he is indeed living; this, and its necessary social complement, a "culture of immediate references," as he referred to place in "The American Background."[5] The present is the present world, the actual familiar world of things from which, Olson reminds us in using Heraclitus' words, we have for too long been estranged; it is also presence. The present is a "human universe," the possibility opened again by modern science (and the sciences of man) and confirmed for him in Yucatan by the extant ways of the Maya.

Among the earliest indications of Olson's interest in restoring the present is the intuition of space in *Call Me Ishmael* and his concern with space (as against time) as a present totality of things and as *topos* (geography, ground, earth). Another sign is the book on the human body Olson mentioned in talking over his projects with Pound at St. Elizabeths—his desire to write "the fable of organs," to give us "the BODY [as] the first and simplest and most unthought of fact of a human life." Olson never wrote this book, but he suggested its insistences in "The Resistance" and in *Proprioception* ("what happens within us") and assimilated its ideas in the body of his work, in all that respects function, the dynamic and kinetic (in dance, for example), and in his theory of verse where the physiological is one of the notable emphases.[6]

Olson did not press these inquiries because the occasion to which he responded at the time of his emergence was the immediate one of his situation as a poet and the situation of poetry. The "kick-off piece," as he called it in his first letter to Creeley, was "Projective Verse," an essay that in the interval between its acceptance and publication benefited from their almost daily correspondence.[7] *Topos* figures in it as field, the place of the poet's activity, but more prominent (in terms of his own later formula) are *tropos* and *typos*, matters of self-action and imprinting, registering one's force. Admittedly brief and limited, this essay, like some of Williams' critical essays, was a declaration, for himself and others, enabling him to keep to the advance. "A man," he told Creeley, "god damn well has to come up with his own lang., syntax and song both"; and this, a central issue of projective verse, "THIS IS THE BATTLE." The battle, of course, had been going on for a long time but at this particular moment had subsided: the forties and early fifties, on the evidence of many poets starting out then, were a bad time, marked, as Olson says in his essay, by "reaction," by the desire "to return verse to inherited forms of cadence and rime."[8] This is why he begins the essay, "Verse now, 1950, if it is to go ahead, if it is to be of *essential* use." And why an essay, which one assumes from its obscure publication would not be widely noticed, proved to be a tocsin.

Of essays written in "presentation" prose ("not written," Olson explained, "but thrust"), "Projective Verse" is the least presentational and combative.[9] The voice that speaks here is unassuming—consonant with Olson's admission of dogmatism and acknowledgment of the merits of the adversary, of Eliot's speech-force and notable line and of the debt owed to closed forms of verse ("how much . . . each of us owes to the nonprojective, and will continue to owe, as both go alongside each other"). Olson is aware of debts. He notes the precedent work, chiefly of Pound and Williams, but also of Cummings and Crane, and wishes now to bring them forward and, fully recognizing them, to advance their work, move beyond them. When irritated with Corman's judging the music of *Maximus* against the measures of Pound and Williams, he spoke of the elder poets as "inferior predecessors"; but he does not so consider them here (or elsewhere)—rather, in Pasternak's truer phrase, as "beloved predecessors"—and to read the essay in the light of a later ill-considered remark is itself ill-considered.[10]

That "Projective Verse" has so many precedents is one measure of its importance; that it made a difference in the literary situation, had results where a book like Karl Shapiro's *Essay on Rime* (1945) did not, is another. Olson knew the precedents and might have fully acknowledged them had he not been concerned, as he always was, with use. He knew that his work depended not only on Pound and Williams—he mentions them immediately in the opening paragraph—but on their predecessors, on Coleridge (for "Form as Proceding") and Emerson (for "meter-making argument": intrinsic form) and Whitman (for free verse).[11] The battle he was resuming, he knew, had begun with the romantic revolution in poetry; many had been enlisted in it, more recently D. H. Lawrence, whose essay, "Poetry of the Present," is even briefer than but as challenging as his own, and Ernest Fenollosa, whose essay, *The Chinese Written Character as a Medium for Poetry*, provided the basis of what, in "Projective Verse," is most distinctly his own.[12]

Before writing "Projective Verse," Olson addressed the theory and practice of verse in "ABCs."[13] These poems take their title from Pound's valuable primer, *ABC of Reading*, and are declarations/demonstrations both acknowledging and advancing beyond indebtedness, replacing ABC with T(opos),

T(ropos), T(ypos). Olson considers many problems—in fact the number of problems distinguish the initial poem, where spatial form answers to his awareness of having all things present at once in the act of writing. The trouble with the inherited forms, and with writing as against speech, is that the linearity of these forms ("you must/ stand in line") is not equal to the speed and complexity of experience (or event). "Speech," he says, "is as swift as synapse. . . ." [14] And that is the difficulty, for the synapse of word and association, which he exemplifies here, not only takes (he fears) a lifetime to master but brings into the field of the poem the content of a lifetime's experience, from the tenement in Worcester he lived in as a boy to last night's erotic dream. Speech neither waits nor recognizes boundaries; of the body, proprioception is involved: "Interiors/ and their registration. . . ." So, instead of "The word forms/ on the left" of prescriptive forms, he proposes "Words, form/ but the extension of/ content," a formal principle of "Projective Verse." And that principle, clearly, rallies the others with which he concludes:

> Style, est verbum
> The word
> is image, and the reverend reverse is
> Eliot
> Pound
> is verse

The first declaration in behalf of the word is also an etymological tribute to Fenollosa's insistence on the verbal (process) character of language. The last, verbally playful and caustic toward Eliot in its preferment of Pound, brilliantly recognizes a central and profound issue of modern art: the issue of image vs. symbol, of a poetry of reality, that Pound, from the time he proposed imagism, did so much to champion. [15]

"ABCs (2)" pursues the theme of proprioception ("Interiors/

and their registration") and brings us to the tropic center of
Olson's work, to the recognition that poetry is not impersonal
but inevitably moved by the twistings and turnings of the self,
the unknown, hidden self revealed in dreams and nightmare.
Poetry, as he later told Corman, originates "at the heart of
us—where it hurts," in the dark wood, the cold hell he knew
so well and explored in "In Cold Hell, In Thicket," a poem
from whose anxiety the trip to Yucatan relieved him.[16] Like
this poem, which is not closed off by capitalization or punctua-
tion, poetry is extensive with experience, admits no boundaries; and like the rushing tidal river he mentions, or the
"crashing/ water" of "Adamo Me," it is full of risk and demands skill (and control: the line recalls Eliot), a matter, truly,
of life and death:

> And the boat,
> how he swerves it to avoid the yelping rocks
> where the tidal river rushes[17]

The image of steering the boat, used in other poems of emergence, tells the difficulty Olson felt, the emotional confusion
he risked, in entering the field, the totality of things.[18] And the
verse at the center of the poem, enclosed by it—

> one sd:
>
> > of rhythm is image
> > of image is knowing
> > of knowing there is
> > a construct

—tells us that risk is necessary because what it provides is
both fundamental and initiatory. Olson told Corman that "he
who has rhythm has the universe"; that is, that he is not outside the process, outside reality, as in the symbolist universe
founded on idealism, but in it, answering to it in himsclf, and
that the image, accordingly, is not of the thing, it is the thing.
And he told Duncan, "He who controls rhythm/ controls"—

controls by following the logic of creation, of construction, formulated here.[19]

This instruction in the conditions of making poems (poetic activity), Olson said later, was passed to him in a dream by the "fathers." But fathers, he admitted in *Poetry and Truth*, was actually father, "the leading poet alive in the world," Pound.[20] And Pound—and Williams—are the poets whose *work* he dismisses in "ABCs (3—for Rimbaud)," which the title as well as the poem itself tells us is best read in connection with "The Kingfishers." Olson's fierce rejection of them—and this applies also to his scrutiny of *The Cantos* and *Paterson* in the letters he wrote from Yucatan to Creeley and Corman—is the measure of his distress before the task set him by the poetics of the previous poems. For among the totality of things in which he finds himself are the things of contemporary society that distress him. And who—

> Who
> can beat that life
> into form, who
> is so hopeful—who
> has mislead us?

And even so, grant that *The Cantos* and *Paterson* have beaten that life into form: "To have what back?" This poem has the agitated form of what is thrown up as well as thrown together (the poem as *conjecture*: Olson's substitute for beating things into form) and its judgment, particularly of Pound, partakes of its extremity.[21]

Pound/ is verse. This is evident in Olson's practice. And also evident is Williams' belief that movement in verse, which is characterized by speech, is "a physical more than a literary character," and that "each speech having its own character the poetry it engenders will be peculiar to that speech also in its own intrinsic form."[22] ("... a man ... has to come up with his

abling the resistance that is so much a part of Olson's sense of being-in-the/world. "When I also speak of PV as propellant," he told Vincent Ferrini, in a letter of this time, "I think of the man as his own muzzle—and charge."[30]

Olson owes more to Fenollosa than the ground of a poetics of self-action. Probably by way of Pound he took over the conception of the poem as "a high energy-construct." But very much his own is the application to the poem of Fenollosa's idea of the transference of energy. Olson acknowledges Fenollosa's account of the sentence as a "flash of lightning," as necessarily following the syntax of process, the natural order of cause and effect; and the representation of this natural syntax clarifies his valuable appropriations:

Fenollosa

term	*transference*	*term*
from	*of*	*to*
which	*force*	*which*
agent	*act*	*object*
Farmer	*pounds*	*rice*
[subject]	[verb]	[object]

Olson

poet	poem	reader

For Olson the poet is agent, "subject from which the act *starts*" (*actual willful man*, as he says later in *The Special View of History*); the poem has all the force of the verb, the essential element of "the universal form of action in nature," the embodiment of "the very *stroke* of the act"; and the reader, like the object, is "the receiver of the impact."[31] It is important to note that the reader is now essential, that transference of energy means that Olson wants to communicate directly, without loss of speech-force—hence, his use of letters. Furthermore, the structure of the poem, which is more complex than that of the sentence, corresponds, as much as the structure of

the sentence, to the process nature of the world. "Every element in an open poem," Olson says, "must be taken up in the
kinetic of the poem just as solidly as we are accustomed to
take what we call the objects of reality; and . . . those elements
are to be seen as creating the tensions of a poem just as totally
as do those other objects create what we know as the world."[32]
The poem, in Whiteheadean terms, is an event, has that structure; and since the poet's action in the field of the poem is one
with his action in the field of reality, he who possesses rhythm
may indeed be said to possess the universe and this art of
enactment may be, as Olson later claimed, "the only twin life
has—its only valid metaphysic."[33]

There are still other appropriations of fundamental importance. Olson not only found in Fenollosa an account of reality
as process that preceded and prepared for his discovery of
Whitehead's *Process and Reality*, he found the faith in the
order of nature that underprops and distinguishes his work.
For Fenollosa, as for Emerson upon whom he levies, the meta-
phorical nature and growth of language bespeaks both process
and order ("speech grew, following slowly the intricate maze
of nature's suggestions and affinities"). For them, as Fenollosa
says, "the prehistoric poets who created language discovered
the whole harmonious framework of nature, they sang out her
processes in their hymns"—as Olson may be said to do in "The
Praises," a position poem of this time, much concerned with
pre-Socratic philosophy, that declares his basic trust in the
universe. Fenollosa, moreover, appreciated the primitive poets
who, in Emerson's words, fastened words to visible things,
and, as he says, adding to Emerson's remarks on relations,
employ metaphors that follow the "objective lines of relations
in nature herself." And these primitive poets who "created
language" ("poetry, language and the care of myth," Fenollosa
notes, "grew up together") "agreed with science and not with
logic" because they too "got at the things." Both science and

poetry—modern thinkers and primitive poets: their conjunction is significant for Olson—recover the familiar world of
particular things. Their common enemy, reviled by Fenollosa,
is logic ("this European logic," "the inveterate logic of classification") which prohibits, he claims, the representation of
"change . . . or any kind of growth." This logic provides the
foundation of what Olson calls the "old discourse." And the
"new discourse" he opposes to it not only turns, as Fenollosa
proposes, from the abuse and tyranny of abstractions to things
but accommodates the functions and interactions and inter-
penetrations of things, takes into account the fact that nature
(process) "has no grammar," and permits language to "inter-
play as nature interplays."[34]

Surely one may say, with Martin Pops, that Fenollosa's *The
Chinese Written Character as a Medium for Poetry* "silently
undergirds" Olson's "Projective Verse"; even say, more
boldly, that at this time its ideas and insistences, spirit and
faith are of more importance to his project than those of any
other single text. But this is only another way of saying what,
even at this point, should be clear: that a poetics that matters
involves, as Kenneth Burke says, "a theory of reality, a psychology, and an ethics"; that "Projective Verse" proposes
Olson's project.[35]

Olson reminds us of this at the start by noting the two-part
division of the essay and the primacy of stance toward reality:
"what stance toward reality brings such verse into being." And
though in this essay he only suggests his theory of reality,
enough is said to show that it makes a radical difference.
"Field" names process reality, and is the ground of the poem.
The poet's activity in the one is the model of his activity in
the other. And what most concerns Olson here, in view of a
universe of things in which we too are only things, is ethical:
that we stand in and use nature humbly, that we rid ourselves,
as many romantic and modern poets failed to do, of "the lyrical

interference of the individual as ego, [as] 'subject,'" that we yield the imagination as a power that imposes shape and acquire instead the imaginative sympathy of Keats' "Negative Capability." This is the essential "projective act." According to Olson, it permits the poet to participate in the field and liberates his forms ("his shapes will make their own way").[36]

"Negative Capability" enters the essay only by way of Olson's reference to Keats and his disparagement of the "Egotistical Sublime." It is a major concept in Olson's thought, connected with ideas he does not entertain here: risk, nakedness. These ideas, as much as anything, arouse opposition to his thought, to "the changing sense of life" that, Robert Duncan says, accompanies "a changing aesthetic." When Duncan, for example, mentions "Projective Verse" in "Towards an Open Universe"—his title makes explicit an assumption of open verse—it is in regard to "exposed, open form." Open verse involves exposure and risk because, as Duncan says elsewhere in response to Frost's notion of verse-making as a game of tennis, "the counterpart of free [open] verse may be free thought and free movement" and the poet may not be a tennis player but an "explorer."[37] Open form involves "unbound thinking" (Williams' phrase) because the poet who thinks with his poem by living in his occasion frees himself from rules and preconceptions; he *is* open, open as Lawrence says he must be ("This opening, and this alone, is the essential act of attention, the essential poetic and vital act"), and lives in the present, in that moment in which we truly live.[38]

The glories of open verse are also its dangers. Olson knew the dangers, as his poems testify, but welcomed risk and sought nakedness. That he did not mention them in this essay may be accounted for by his basic trust and the fact, made explicit in *The Special View of History*, that for him chaos held no terrors, not at least as long as he was able to act. Two sentences may explain this: "What Keats proposes as Negative Capability is the readmission of the familiar" (from *The Special View of History*) and "nothing is so marvellous as to be alone in the phenomenal world, which is raging, and yet apart" (from Lawrence's *The Man Who Died*, cited by Olson in his "Notes on Lawrence & the Real").[39] Olson's debt to Lawrence is primary but too large to be tallied here.[40] It is enough to note in the foreword to *Fantasia of the Unconscious* how much is resonant with Olson and becomes programmatic in him. And it is enough to note, as relevant to "Projective Verse," the preface to Harry Crosby's book, already referred to, and "Poetry of the Present," which introduced an American edition of Lawrence's poems.

From the first essay, in which Lawrence sets the new poetry of attention against poesy (symbolism) and recalls us gladly to chaos, these sentences are especially noteworthy: "The desire for chaos is the breath of their [poets now] poetry. The fear of chaos is in their parade of forms and technique. . . . the grand chaos is all alive, and everlasting. From it we draw the breath of life. If we shut ourselves off from it, we stifle. . . ."[41] The second essay is a richer source, again contrasting a finished poetry (closed: "fixed, set, static") against a poetry of the instant, in process—a poetry even freer than *vers libre*. "There must be mutation," Lawrence says, "swifter than iridescence, haste, not rest, come-and-go, not fixity, inconclusiveness, immediacy, the quality of life itself, without denouement or close. There must be the rapid momentaneous association of things which meet and pass on the forever incalculable journey of creation: everything left in its own rapid, fluid relationship with the rest of things." And who exemplifies such poetry? such "direct utterance from the instant, whole man"? Only Whitman, whom Olson never gives such prominence but whom he read carefully early and late; Whitman, with his "carnal self," with the "insurgent naked throb" of his utterance. Lawrence speaks the language of self-act, of projective

verse, and his finest example is one that Olson never forgot:
"The law must come new each time from within. The bird is
on the wing in the winds, flexible to every breath, a living
spark in the storm, its very flickering depending upon its
supreme mutability and power of change." Olson remembered,
in "A Round & A Canon," the chii-mi whose recovery and
flight and incredible "inside strength" he brilliantly described
in *Mayan Letters*—the bird in "his own world, his own careful
context, those/ balances." In this poem, Olson assimilates
dancer and bird, and sees in the mobile equilibrium of the
bird—of self-in-world—the great vital act, the thing to be
achieved in (by) projective verse.[42]

Olson's reply to Grover Smith follows "Projective Verse" in
Human Universe, an edition of Olson's essays edited by
Donald Allen. That's as it should be. For Olson's letter, published in 1954, is a coda to the "kick-off piece" and much of
the work it inspired. In "exposing, this Smith," Olson succinctly puts a central issue of his poetics—joins it because
Smith "keeps readers from the advance in discourse which
Pound & Williams, and Crane, after his lights, led the rest of us
on to."[43] Smith, he feels, too easily dismisses the forty-year
work of these poets, and by asking poets to employ rational
patterns of discourse, by "imposing old discourse on a group of
men who are still working toward the new . . . depresses the
whole of the American push to find out an alternative discourse to the inherited one . . . [that is] try, by some other
means than 'pattern' and the 'rational,' to cause discourse to
cover . . . the real." Olson identifies Smith with Eliot, with
"cultural colonialism" and "Reaction." The old discourse ("the
inherited one") not only began with the Greeks, who imposed
idea on act, but is "implicit in the language from Chaucer to
Browning." It is—and remains for Eliot and Smith—the ratio-
nale of English verse.[44]

The issue of old vs. new discourse, or more extensively an old humanism vs. a new humanism, is not a provincial one of England vs. America.[45] It is an issue of modernism, of the present culture of the West, as Olson knew. Nevertheless, and not without reason, Olson at this time treats it narrowly in the familiar terms of the American quarrel with England—with Europe. In a letter to Vincent Ferrini (a kick-off piece in *Origin* #1) he advises his Gloucester friend to renew language by listening to the speech of the people in the street rather than "to read *anything* of the Europeans." The advice is Williams', but Olson makes it his own by linking it with a directive of his work: ". . . we are the last first people (he sd). And that means discovery, anew, of speech." And by way of explanation he adds "there would have been no excuse for my doing the PV ["Projective Verse"] piece, if, around us, there was anything but too . . . much anglo-american verse."[46]

The publication of this and other letters in the first issue of *Origin* was a victory for the very program Olson refers to in it, and as document tells of Olson's effort to instruct all concerned, not just Ferrini, in its significance. In October, 1950, he had begun the correspondence with Cid Corman (collected in *Letters for Origin*) that contributed so much to the distinctive quality of the magazine. Even before the letter to Ferrini, he had, with characteristic energy, immediately followed an introductory letter to Corman with a much longer one expressing his views. ("I put myself into that long letter to you on a mag-today, spent hours making it, hours I might have put into verse or into, say, an article like the PRO-VERSE thing," Olson complained when Corman did not take up quickly enough the ideas with which he had been overwhelmed.)[47] This correspondence, like that with Creeley in the *Mayan Letters*, enables us to witness an experience equally incisive— in fact, since many of these letters were written in Yucatan, their incandescence also shares the discovery of that origin.

In them, as Ferrini says, we encounter Olson ("LETTERS FOR ORIGIN are more Charles than anything he has ever written"): "he grabs you by the ear with one hand on your shoulder and his breath pounding away." Understandably for Ferrini, who, like Corman, was also overwhelmed, someone to be taught, brought around, more, say, than Creeley.[48] And as important, in the letters we encounter Olson making a push: exemplifying and elaborating the principles of "Projective Verse," giving them an American footing, indeed making them American.

The personal reasons for Olson's American stand do not necessarily invalidate it. His sense of being an American, for example, was provoked by Ezra Pound whose WASP hauteur offended him. The son of immigrants, and himself a governmental official who had been charged with their interests, he did not appreciate the exclusion so nicely, genteelly told, in an anecdote of his visits to Pound. Asked by an old Philadelphia lady who had known Pound all of his life if he, Olson, were English, he had replied, "My father was Swedish and my mother Irish, which makes me very American. She looks up at me [he reports], and says, 'Then you must have a sense of humor!'"[49] Olson identified with the Portuguese fishermen of Gloucester; and in a letter to Corman instructing him in the initial requisite of projective verse—that one must speak of "ONE'S SELF AND ONE'S RELATIONS" because "We Americans have nothing but our personal details"—he said that this applied "especially [to] us, us heteros of these States & tenements, as I am, as you are."[50] The debt to Whitman acknowledged here reminds us that Dahlberg, Olson's first mentor, was a "bottom dog" who, in introducing him to the Stieglitz circle and in writing about Randolph Bourne in *Do These Bones Live* (1941), gave him the cultural ground of the "American moment," an American tradition to oppose to that of Pound and Eliot. And how much that tradition was opposed is perhaps indicated in Eliot's refusal of *Call Me Ishmael* as "too American a book."[51]

Olson's American stand does not involve the American cele-bration the early evidence of which distressed him. Nor is it, as he told Corman at the outset, "a matter of jingoism." It follows instead from an assessment of Culture and from the desire to found a culture on "new premises of experience." In estimating the value of Olson's push, we must be as acutely aware of the cultural situation as he was and remember that his stand represents a major shift in attention, a concern, as he explains to Corman, with the "going reality," with the "reality con-temporary to us, here, in the States."[52] His undertaking is not, as similar undertakings have often been in our literary history, a simple nationalistic one. What he takes from Emerson is the romantic element in American thought appreciated by San-tayana: the primacy of experience. And what he repudiates is not merely servility to tradition so much as a tradition no longer adequate to reality. Olson wants a new discourse that will cover the real—reality as we now experience it and under-stand it: as the mathematicians, physicists, poets, and philos-ophers have now construed it for us. And with this—the grand aim of all his work—he wants a new culture, or rather, know-ing the enormous task, to initiate it, to begin to provide "the kind of grounding on which that culture of Europe rested rests is now buried in." When Corman, following the practice of little magazines, wished to include " 'foreign' material," Olson reminded him that a European writer has an advantage an American writer lacks, that "grounding": he "stands on SCHOLARSHIP of his people (as well as a clear tradition back thru the Latin to the Greek and on back)"; he stands on com-mon ground with his readers and has the confidence such culture provides ("culture is confidence," he told Creeley), or, in terms applicable to himself, he can breathe—"a culture breathes, takes breath for granted, as men do" and does so because "such breath has been worked for, millenniums." This confidence, this ease, is not however the American writer's privilege. Those writers—and magazines—that assume it is, Olson insists, are "backtrailing . . . culture scratching!"[53]

Olson tried to turn Corman from "the whole dull business of CULTURE" to the more demanding work of fronting present reality and using the new, notably American, scholarship to prepare the soil of a new culture. Of *work*, the epigraph he provided was sufficient reminder: "o my sone, rise from thy bed . . ./ work what is wise"; of intent, the various names considered for the magazine—"The Spring and The Source," "re Source" (also resource), "Origin." He tried to win Corman by depicting the literary situation—by making it a critical situation—and reminding him of previous coups: of Emerson's *Dial*, the *Little Review*, the *English Review*. And knowing as well the current little magazines, among them such recent entrants as the *Hudson Review*, *Poetry New York*, and *Nine*, he defined his radical conception of *Origin* against the last, the British magazine *Nine*.[54]

Considering its cultural pretentiousness, he could not have chosen better—nor for personal reasons of importance to him. Peter Russell, editor of *Nine*, stood to Pound as Corman (Olson hoped) to Olson. Russell was the dutiful son Olson refused to be, an editor and publisher, who at this time was promoting Pound, not the poet whose prosodic advances Olson furthered so much as the economist, translator, guardian of tradition. *Nine*, endorsed by Eliot, appeared in 1949, with the declared purpose of recalling writers to their cultural inheritance, to a tradition broader than that proposed by F. R. Leavis or found in "insidious modernism," the whole tradition of European literature from Homer to the present day. The American poets it published in an issue on contemporary poetry were John Crowe Ransom and Allen Tate; its distinguishing feature was

translation, defended on the grounds of establishing creative
contact with the past.[55]

Clearly, *Nine* was not concerned with what Olson meant by
the going reality of the present. It exemplified, for Olson, the
closed field of Culture (exclusively art, of taste) and the political power of Culture in the service of reaction. By publishing
translations of the Latin poets, it did more than establish
contact with the past: it restored the equation of Rome and
London and with it the culture of Elizabethan mercantilism,
of which, Olson added in his explanation to Corman, "NINE
is as precise a new assertion as is Winston Churchill of feudal
politics." Later on, Olson ridiculed Russell and pointed out the
danger of Russell's work—and so helps us see why, in asking
Corman to consider the purposes of *Origin* in terms of Eliot's
"Tradition and the Individual Talent" ("where are we at this
40 yr end of that essay . . . ?"), he had chosen the right text.
"The *Nine* boys (now shrunk to one little Peter)," he wrote in
reviewing Ernst Robert Curtius' *European Literature and the
Latin Middle Ages*, "were Trojan-English, that is to say . . .
their schoolboy Renaissance was only more of the Aeneid. But
it turns out it is as Mr. Churchill is. Europe is one genealogy,
Curtius is at the pains the politicians are, to prove. Homer to
Goethe. And Stefan George's is the vision."[56] When Olson
responds to *Europe* and puts America against it, he has in mind
the implementation of Eliot's essay: the creation by critics and
historians of "one genealogy," the "mind of Europe" that Eliot
had extolled and given the independent and complete status of
an "ideal order." This is the conception of tradition Peter
Russell echoes in his editorial statement: "The whole tradition . . . behind us, immemorially old"—a tradition the individual talent can do little to modify and is asked instead to
serve by using the inherited materials to make "new assem-
blies of all the past."[57]

"Culture (history when it is Europeanised)" has often been

an instrument of imperialism, both dominating and controlling, and in its contemporary assertion is very much like the cartels whose struggle during the last war to close (rationalize) the economic system to their benefit is a major aspect of history brilliantly treated in Pynchon's *Gravity's Rainbow*.[58] To this formidable Culture, this hegemony of the past, Olson opposes the "present." The O of *Origin*, he told Corman, stood for "open"; the magazine was not a "*champ clos* (!) of taste alone" but a field of force, the energy with which it replaces taste the result of the participant activity of the man who fronts present reality. The task of *Origin* was *to open*, to admit what had been left out, the scholarship, for example, of such contemporary Americans as Carl Sauer, Frederick Jackson Merk, Norbert Wiener—proof that "the American PUSH is not at all all machines & engineers"—and the literature of what, culturally speaking, is a third world, of Sumer, Maya, the American Indian.[59]

Though Corman never fully met this demand to use the magazine as resource, he followed Olson's most important instruction: to compose the magazine in the projective way of composing poems, to center a single issue in a single writer whose work, presumably, fronts present reality (he does this, among others, with Olson, Creeley, and Blackburn) and in doing this to compose nondeductivity by "discontinuity . . . field, fragment, grit & vulgarity." As Olson told Ferrini, "when traditions go, the DISCONTINUOUS becomes the greener place." So here. Collage. Olson asked Corman to take some forty pages of a writer's work (the whole front of it in its characteristic variety, including, Olson insisted, letters, his notable form) and compose it, along with the work of others, by means of "juxtaposition, correlation, interaction." He asked Corman to do what Mayan glyphs happily confirmed for him: compose in terms of a central human figure, "build by a man, instead of by, (as per usual), ABSTRACTIONS."[60]

The result, so remarkably achieved in *Origin* #1, is a composite portrait of Olson, who, understandably, was enthusiastic about Corman's editorial work: "the fullest satisfaction i have ever had from print, lad, the fullest." He was especially impressed (gratified) by "how, the whole thing is, IS. How it sets itself out there, straight"; or, as he put it in a follow-up letter in which instruction for future issues tells the pleasure of his recognition in this one, by "how much energy . . . he [has] got in, to make a thing stand on its own feet as, a force, in, the fields of force which surround everyone of us, of which we, too, are forces: to stand FORTH." The language here, as he immediately realized, belongs to "Projective Verse." Corman had enacted in the field of the magazine the drama of *topos*, *tropos*, *typos*. And since Olson's references invite it, it may be said of this American push to open Culture that the heteros of these States had put down the homos of Europe. In the words of "The Gate and the Center," printed in this issue, they had begun to recover "the primordial & phallic energies and methodologies which . . . make it possible for man, that participant thing, to take up, straight, nature's, live nature's force."[61]

"Well, by 1951 *Origin* arrived, and its first issue had such a blockbuster of Olson that I had to come off it." That's how Robert Duncan remembered it twenty years later. "Projective Verse" had excited him because it confirmed his practice, but Olson's blockbuster had won his allegiance to him as a poet and a father.[62]

How did Olson stand forth, at the beginning of his career? How did Corman (the "chore-/ agos") present him, dance the manuscripts, or, in another kinetic metaphor of Olson's, weave them, using the work of others—anonymous, except for identification at the very start—to "relieve" him and set him in relief?[63] First, by exclusions, by choosing to hold over for the next issue material that might present another face of Olson

and weaken his push. He followed Olson's advice in not printing "Issue, Mood," a poem so direct in attack and parodic of
Pound that Olson himself does not appear justified so much as
petty; and by doing this Corman also effectively removed
Pound's powerful presence.[64] He did not, it seems, exclude
"The Escaped Cock: Notes on Lawrence & the Real" because
it evokes Lawrence's presence, though nothing that calls attention to Olson's predecessors is used in a way comparable to
Creeley's "Hart Crane," printed here; the notes *are* notes, not
readily accessible, and some of what they say gets said in other
material. As for "A Po-sy, A Po-sy," it is not a very good poem,
the work of Olson-the-vaudevillian and gagman, a presump-
tive anti-Culture vulgarian.

Then Corman opened *Origin* with a twelve-page block of
Olson: with the initial *Maximus* poem, a letter to Ferrini, and
a "song," "Adamo Me." In the first, "I, Maximus of Gloucester, to You," Olson comes forward as Maximus, in his role
of teacher and culture-hero concerned with his city and his
people, with the creation of form (polis and poem), with act
and the redemption of "pejorocracy." The poem itself enacts
the weaving of materials exemplified in *Origin*, calls up the
precedent long poems of Pound, Williams, Crane, and Eliot
(countervailing *Four Quartets*, a poem treating Cape Ann), and
works to affirmation, to an open field of possibility, of creative
opportunity and renewal. Olson fronts present reality, his own
immediate space, and especially significant for this issue and
his conception of *Origin*, it is the reality and space of New
England. ("I think you," he later told Corman, "as well as all
of us New Englanders [Creeley, Blackburn, Eigner, Ferrini] . . .
are only parts of a Landsgeist that has now, again [he had
evoked Emerson's *The Dial*], reasserted itself.")[65] The projective, public speech of this letter becomes private speech in the
letter to Ferrini. This letter, beginning with the need for "resistance," complements and explains the assertive role of Maxi-

mus in the preceding poem. Its language is similarly projective; and in it, even though Olson sometimes eases into what
might be called a conversation of poets (the letter represents
that important matrix and necessity of his work), he is still
the teacher, clearly the authority. In the interests of an American poetry, he instructs Ferrini in some essentials of "Projective Verse" (which enters the magazine also in the bibliographical footnote Corman appends). He tells him—it is a
touchstone—that "we have to kick sentences in the face here,
if we are to express the going reality." 66 "Adamo Me" is also
assertive, a song of the self rejecting both Pound and Eliot.
The title, adapted from Canto XLV, becomes Olson's defiant
signature, and the method, and much of what Olson says, is
parodic of *The Waste Land*, especially of the episode in the
rose garden. Olson celebrates life over death (a victory not
easily gained, as "The Story of an Olson, and Bad Thing" will
soon remind us) and refuses the bribes of Pound's beauty and
Eliot's eternity, here conjoined. He accepts the human condition in respect to natural physical existence, the raging
phenomenal world, sea, tide, sand. He glorifies sexuality and
proposes the stance of living in the living, of exposing oneself
to and momently capturing beauty and love from the flux
of life.

The poems in the twelve-page block that follows are of lesser
scale and force than Olson's. They nicely include a poem by
Ferrini (the correspondent in this issue, not Creeley who might
have been used) and a translation (yes!) of Catullus by Corman. Most of the work, offsetting Olson's, is nonprojective.
Some poems are in quatrains, one is a sonnet; the basic measure is iambic pentameter, occasionally rhymed. The cadences
are familiar but the voice of these poems is conversational,
in keeping with instructive passages, in French, cited by
Corman, on the sound and music of spoken language (Corman
was concerned with this throughout the run of the magazine).

None of these poems is pretentious, all involve personal occasions, and, significantly, in keeping with the insistence of "I, Maximus of Gloucester, to You," some have a local character. "Creatures like Chameleons" treats the faded culture of Massachusetts, "A Ruined Power Dam" local history, and "Some Musicians Play" presents reality.[67]

Olson next appears in prose-verse, with "The Story of an Olson, and Bad Thing." As the title indicates, this is more personal—biographical—than the previous poems. It turns on his father's death (his mother's death will be treated later), his own encounter with the "Enemie," and the immediate death-ridden culture: the private and public occasions of his "resistance" and desire to renew life by restoring the human business of living ("the business we're here for"). This "story" balances "Adamo Me" in size and connects with it in theme, a fact pointed up by framing it with poems by Catullus. And after an interval equal in size, which includes a long poem by William Bronk and a letter from Williams to Creeley—these writers are closer to Olson than the earlier ones, and Williams' letter is a manifesto on the need to purify the language of the "stinking dead, usages of the past" as assertive as Olson's to Ferrini—Olson appears again in "The Gate & the Center."

In this essay in presentation prose Olson is the Culture-outlaw and pedagogue. (The poet, he had told Corman, is the only pedagogue left, the only one to be trusted; pedagogue and scholar, for him, oppose "academics" and redefine Emerson's American Scholar.) The Culture-outlaw, outrageously assertive and swashbuckling, treats Culture and its heroes irreverently, and what he says of "Old Stink Sock [Socrates]" and the "primes in our speech" picks up the earlier declarations of Williams. The pedagogue provides the scholarship (the names of scholars, he had explained to Corman when he submitted the essay, are "images of force not taken up"); he indicates

the resources that might enable us to recover origins.[68] He is
at his bridgework. The essay, the keynote of *Origin*, and at its
center, dramatizes the issue of Culture *vs.* culture (contact)
and reorients us in respect to the latter, primarily by providing
a new chronology, a larger history, and new (old) goals. Olson
opens, goes back beyond Greco-Roman (humanist) history. He
begins with the end of deglaciation (10,000 B.C.), recovers
Sumer (3387–1200 B.C.), the culture hearth where the city was
coherence (polis), nourishing and advancing all people. He
locates a center from which to measure the falling off that had
occurred long before Homeric Greece, and what is notable here
is that he makes us feel that the past and the falling off of
original impetus is close to us, retrievable, that the first will
to coherence (exemplified in "I, Maximus of Gloucester, to
You") is "back in business." In speaking of the vision quest of
the Indian, he introduces the idea of nakedness, of disposition
to reality, and the idea of polis, for polis depends upon the
fullest common experience; and like Emerson, who had done
similar cultural work, he introduces the hero ("I, Maximus"),
men the size of the old kings because they are able to assim-
ilate energy ("energy is larger than man, but . . . if he taps it
as it is in himself, his uses of himself are extensible in human
directions and degrees not recently granted"). This hero is not
Ahab (howevermuch Melville may have read Ahab out of
Emerson), for he is participant in, not lord of nature, enjoined
to protect the earth and establish an equitable society. He is,
in Olson's brilliantly chosen example of "the whole question
& continuing struggle to remain civilized," Gilgamesh after
he is "corrected" by Enkidu—brilliantly chosen because this is
a primary myth of Culture vs. Nature and because, with all
the insistence on the need for the latter, Olson does not forget
the former, seeks, as the myth does, to adjust or balance their
claims. And to end with myth, with its recognition, is also

brilliant because the effect of making it present liberates our energy and desire.

Having turned our attention to myth, Olson now, in another letter to Ferrini, calls attention to dream. Here the references to Indians and dreams point back to the previous essay and to "Adamo Me," which may employ dream material, and point ahead to an "inner drama" by Katherine Hoskins. The dreams Olson mentions in this letter, itself a field composition, involve Gloucester and connect with "I, Maximus of Gloucester, to You." The letter advises us of an important element in the restoration of human culture and in Olson's work—tells, in fact, what Olson so dramatically presents much later in "The Librarian," that for Maximus and his poem Gloucester is also interior geography, another self, known only in encounter, difficultly, and with distress.

The poems by Katherine Hoskins and Richard Wirtz Emerson that follow offer a brief interval of conventional verse contrasting with Olson's "The Moon is the Number 18," a poem of distress certainly equal to theirs. This poem on his mother's death is notable for the use of tarot (another resource) to both tell and control his grief, to achieve the formal feeling spoken of by Emily Dickinson. It fills out the aspect of Olson's portrait already treated in "The Story of an Olson, and Bad Thing" by showing him using the poem to overcome his helplessness, pressing against the breathlessness of death ("The moon has no air"), using sound itself, the very "human sound" of loneliness and lamentation, to push against "the dirty moon."

Conditions of such extremity, Olson tells Ferrini in the next letter, are the ground of poetry. To surmount the economic difficulties of the writer's vocation will not ease his task, nor will any other action be as politically meaningful as doing it.[69] This is the task Olson faces and resolves (on) in "In Cold Hell, In Thicket" and in the imagery of that poem, perhaps proposed in this letter, sets out:

                    the only object is
a man, carved
out of himself, so wrought he
fills his given space, makes
traceries sufficient to
other's needs

It is the task undertaken in *The Maximus Poems*, as the
closing allusion to Anthony of Padua, from its initial poem,
reminds us.

Of the poems that follow, only Creeley's "Hart Crane" is
important. Constance Hotson's poems are slight, and Richard
Eberhart's is didactic in ways unlike Olson's and to different
ends ("Cannot restore us to the center"). Creeley's poem brings
him forward—he will figure in the next issue—and presents
a poet who, with Williams, is a predecessor (mentioned in
"Projective Verse"). Creeley's Crane, to cite his own later
phrase, is a "saint of exposure," a poet whose task is similar
to the one enjoined by Olson in the letter to Ferrini. Creeley
sympathetically renders the anguish of Crane's life and his
search for ways to move beyond his previous work, and he
understands how much this push, especially when weakened
by the betrayal of his friends (and Waldo Frank's "Culture"),
accounts for his death.[70]

This superb poem of recognition comments on the closing
letter to Ferrini. Here Olson asks Ferrini to let him have
"I, Maximus of Gloucester, to You," a poem originally written
as a letter to him, for *Origin* #1. The function of the letter is
reflexive, closing the field of the magazine even as, with its
reminiscences and dream of Gloucester, it projects other
Maximus poems. Olson also tells his pleasure in the poem,
but what the letter most evokes is the very community of
poets—the polis of *Origin*—that Crane so desperately needed.
It closes: "amo o."

Origin #1 is a collage of voices, many of them Olson's, and

his the most various as well as overpowering. A projective
voice, it both moves us and fills the given space of the magazine. It makes us aware of breath ("man's special qualification
as an animal") and leaves little doubt that in this instance it
comes from the deep resistant center from which "all act
springs." Fenollosa, we remember, said that "our very word
exist means 'to stand forth,' to show oneself by a definite act."
By giving Olson enough space in which to breathe, *Origin*
enabled him to perform this act. Here he stands forth with the
assurance and luster of emergence.[71]

> June 28th, '51, on this horst
> on the Heat Equator, a mediterranean sea
> to the east, and north
> what saves America from desert, waters
> and thus rain-bearing winds,
> by subsidence, salt waters
> > (by which they came,
> > the whelps, looking
> > for youth
> Which they found.
> > And have continuously sought
> > > to kill

So Olson, in Yucatan, gives Rainer Maria Gerhardt his position
and states his American point-of-view.

"To Gerhardt, there, among Europe's things of which he has
written us in his 'Brief an Creeley und Olson'" is the most
important of the several poems of Olson's Mexican experience.
Among his poems it has the place "Human Universe" has
among his essays, and both were published, with Gerhardt's
"Letter," in *Origin* #4. "This," a poem begun at the beginning
of his sojourn, addresses a Mexico more familiar to us, the
Mexico, say, of Lawrence's *The Plumed Serpent* (especially the
chapter on the bullfight) or Lowry's *Under the Volcano*: death-
ridden Mexico. And here, in his encounter with death, Olson

concludes the exceptional reenactment of the bullfight with
"you/ have been/ asked"—that is, makes his own the overwhelming command spoken by Gerhardt's namesake in
"Archaïscher Torso Apollos" ("Du musst dein Leben ändern").
Mexico asked him to change his life—to seek life—and he did,
which is why Mexico is of such moment in his emergence and
why his Mexico (Yucatan, of course, is different) is life-giving,
unlike the Mexico of many writers who preceded him.[72]

Mexico relieved the anxiety of "In Cold Hell, In Thicket" by
enabling Olson to wear his flesh, the instance, in his account
of present-day Mayans, of living fully, in contact with the
environment, in the familiar world, the human universe, and
by proving to him that he could rise up and act. In the words
of "A Discrete Gloss," which in fact glosses "Human Universe," he learned that "what we do with what we are/ is what
ends all distraction." And having also learned that "Man is no
creature of his own discourse"—is not enclosed in (by) a verbal
system of his own making but is himself a center in the field of
forces surrounding him—he declared the new beginning this
radical shift effected: "The day of man returns in your pre-
cisions, kin/ (ahau, katun). . . ." He acknowledged his Mayan
kin, using their way of counting the months and years to begin
history again. (*Ahau, katun* marks the beginning, and *ahau*
has the added significance of great lord or true man, the king
who restores the cycle.)[73]

By going to Yucatan, Olson recovered what Hart Crane had
called the "tribal dawn." He found the "lost home" he said
Melville had been in search of ("He was like a migrant backtrailing to Asia, some Inca trying to find a lost home"); he
found "the lost past of America. . . ." For the archaeologist
of morning, the letters from Yucatan in *Mayan Letters* and
Letters for Origin comprise his *Mornings in Mexico* and bear
comparison with the book by Lawrence that stands behind his
work as well as Crane's. (And when he said of Lawrence that

he was "the only one who . . . stood there [at the watershed of primitive past and industrial present], getting it, as his own" he was speaking also of his own experience.)[74] Mexico was to him what he believed the Pacific had been to Melville (not Ahab), and for him as for Melville it stands against the Mediterranean world—Christendom, Europe. Mexico is space (geography) as against Europe's time (linear history). And like the Pacific, Mexico is source. But it is not, as the Pacific was after the westward movement had conquered the space of the continent, a new field for conquest, exploitation of nature. Instead it is a *place* to inhabit and in which to dig, a direction (down, beneath, back) in which a generation of writers, following Olson, turned to seek renewal. Accordingly, Mexico stands not only against Europe but against the America that had pandered, and not in whispers, to the European dream of America, the America for whom exploiters—ego-maniacs like Ahab—are representative men.[75]

Now to these reasons why Mexico is for Olson a life-renewing place, we must add another which involves the fathers in his concern to recover the way. To say that Mexico, like the Pacific is source, is to introduce what is finally the deepest identification between Olson and Melville—that of the orphaned son in search of the father, the son who discovers the "State-secret" (of the immemorial deposition of the father by the son) and so, as Olson says of Melville, earns "the right of primogeniture." Olson, it seems, earned that right by going to Mexico, and when he addresses Gerhardt from "this horst," he speaks with the authority of a father.[76]

What is especially interesting in "To Gerhardt . . ."—and accounts, I think, for Olson's "belief" in it—is the reversal of roles. A European is now the son and an American the father, and the father, in chastizing the son, does so relentlessly, because he himself is a son deposing a father. Pound stands behind Gerhardt: Pound, "the snob of the West," "the ultimate

image of the end of the West." [77] Gerhardt suffers because he
revives for Olson all his misgivings over Pound. Olson allows
Gerhardt nothing, not even the Poundian prosody to which he
himself is indebted. Even though he thereby admits paternity,
he accuses Gerhardt of being the offending son that he is in
respect to Pound: "so pawed," he begins, "by this long last
Bear-son// with no crockery broken,/ but no smile in my
mouth." The ground of his attack is not Gerhardt's "Brief" but
the "horst" he mentions, the Mayan ground on which he
stands (in which he digs as Pound never did)—this, and the
confirmatory standing forth of *Origin #1*. [78]

In writing his "Brief" Gerhardt did not suspect the extent to
which he was providing Olson an occasion to make, as Olson
said in defending his poem, a "DEMONSTRANDUM" of his
cultural position. Gerhardt was not unsympathetic with
Olson's work. In *Fragmente*, a magazine he edited (for two
issues) after the war, he published Olson's poems along with
those of others, like Pound and Williams, who had not been
heard in war-torn Germany. He had undertaken a work of
recovery, and Olson recognized this by calling his funeral
poem to Gerhardt, who died in 1954, age 28, "The Death of
Europe." But at the time of his reply to Gerhardt's "Brief"
Olson was not moved by loss. *Fragmente*—the title taken from
Eliot's *The Waste Land*: "These fragments I have shored
against my ruins"—was enough to rouse him, especially if he
didn't choose to credit Gerhardt's somewhat different purpose
and interpreted the title in terms of an editorial statement in
Nine ("our position resembles that of a man coming out of a
trance who delightedly perceives the old known world returning to him in unrelated fragments"). [79] If nothing else, the
review of Curtius in which Olson rehearses his response to
Gerhardt's poem tells us that when he received it, he was already alarmed by the conspiracy of Culture.

What is there to object to in Gerhardt's poem? In form it is

indebted to Pound and Williams—chiefly Pound: its montages
are collages, ideographs. And it is chiefly indebted to Pound for
the spirit in which it treats tradition. It lacks the energy Olson
brings to such form, but nevertheless conveys (by its weari-
ness, among other things) a genuine feeling of its own, deeply
European in a way Pound is not. As the form of the poem
indicates, Gerhardt has responded to the liberation of syntax
("the door opened   the dawning"). At the same time, he
finds it painful because, in a motif of the poem, he is "returning home," wants to recover tradition, again be secure in it.
He is aware of civilization—of its beginning, as far back as
Sumer—but also aware of its end, its "rot," the "botch" already
spoken of in *Mauberley*, and would like "a new sign for setting
forth." The new literary method does not enable him, because
he cannot so wholly accept the unbounded as Creeley and
Olson do. Though he would like to take passage via India to
America, the burden of Europe, figured in Dante, won't "let
[him] live. . . ." He feels the weight of "the long departed," and
the work of translating Pound and Williams "in old Europe,"
the "language come home/ in recent poetry," is unavailing.
He is, he finds, too much the European, with "a thirst for
decadence/ an impulse toward destruction," with a dissociated
sensibility, a desire for regular rhythms, and a readiness to yield
to mysticism/death as a way out. The poem turns repeatedly
on this dilemma and warrants Creeley's conclusion about
Gerhardt's life: "There was no way to move in any easy sense
beyond the past, and there never will be."[80] Olson thought
there was. He offered Gerhardt a place at Black Mountain.
Even in his elegy he tells Gerhardt:

> (O, Rainer,
> you should have ridden your bike
> across the Atlantic instead of your mind,
> that bothered itself too much

with how we were hanging on
to the horse's tail, fared, fared

we who had Sam Houston, not
Ulysses[81]

And in his reply ("I am urging you from here") he gives him
advice of the kind he later gave Corman:

Or come here
where we will welcome you
with nothing but what is, with
no useful allusions, with no birds
but those we stone, nothing to eat
but ourselves, no end and no beginning,
                              I assure you, yet
not at all primitive, living as we do in a
                        space we do not need to contrive[82]

He offered Gerhardt space as against time, the totality of
present reality as against "the dead center of the top of time"
he said Gerhardt felt so strongly. He did indeed give him a
present, and he gave him ground and a rod of mountain ash
with which to establish a new vital center.

At the expense of allegiance to Pound and Eliot, and the
tradition from Homer to Goethe. He asked Gerhardt to forget
("forgetting/ is much more your problem/ than you know")
that he might remember his "Grandfather." "You are not/
Telemachus," he told him, but the son of more primal parents,
those for whom the Turko-Siberian "Grandfather" stands. So
in the visible counterpoint of the poem, the usually indented
passages of Turko-Siberian lore answer with their wisdom of
how to live in place what Olson opposes in the Culture called
up by Gerhardt's "Brief." Most of this comes back to Pound,
whose paternity he fiercely rejects, and whose inability to
"come out," to leave tradition for source, results in the fact
that he is "shut . . . in": "A zoo/ is what he's come to. . . ." He

would have Gerhardt learn from this example. "I don't know whether I had said it," Olson wrote in the review of Curtius, "but I meant, to Gerhardt, go out the back door of your inheritance. I did say, plant Odysseus' oar, don't worry about Homer's poetics." In Yucatan, Olson had finally done this. He had learned of the Greeks to be American, and so could tell Gerhardt the way: "On the way to your fathers,/ join them"[83]

Yucatan made the occasion present in a way that it had not been before. The alternative to a generalizing humanism was locked, quite literally, in the people immediately around him, and the conception, that there had been and could be a civilization anterior to that which he had come from, was no longer conjecture, it was fact. He wrote me, then, 'I have no doubt, say, that the American will more and more repossess himself of the Indian past. . . . If you and I see the old deal as dead (including Confucius, say), at the same time that we admit the new is of the making of our own lives & references, yet, there is bound to be a tremendous pick-up from history other than that which has been usable as reference, the moment either that history is restored (Sumer, or, more done, Chichen [Itza] or Uaxactum) or rising people (these Indians, as campesinos ripe for Communist play—as ripe as were the Chinese, date 1921, June 30). . . .' The problem was, to give form, again, to what the Maya had been—to restore the 'history' which they were. For in the Maya was the looked-for content: a reality which is 'wholly formal without loss of intimate spaces, with the ball still snarled, yet, with a light (and not stars) and a heat (not androgyne) which declares, the persistence of both organism and will (human)'[84]

Of Cosmos & History: Essays for *Origin* and Black Mountain College

THREE

DURING THE YEAR that Olson was closing Black Mountain
College and Corman was completing the first run of *Origin*,
Olson proposed for the last issue *The Special View of History*,
a work indebted to the previous essays printed in *Origin* and,
as he said, climaxing them. As always, Olson spoke from immediate enthusiasm, from preoccupation, and, as he had before
in his correspondence with Corman, didn't hesitate to suggest
a book, this time of essays ("so a book, but if not, there in the
file of O the whole . . ."). Corman, it seems, was not as responsive as he had been earlier. At least he did not accept the
manuscript which, as we now have it, is much too long and
unfinished: unsuitable for publication in *Origin*. He did not
encourage Olson to get it ready or, as he had with earlier
essays, act as a necessary editorial agent. Perhaps he wanted
something else from Olson—something less commanding?—
for in a subsequent letter Olson asked forgiveness for not
sending anything ("The thot of having missed Origin 20 is
unbearable. But above all to have you there thinking I fouled
out"). To have missed *Origin* #20! One shares with Olson the
sadness of not seeing the magazine through, of not being there
at the end. Corman's failure to publish *The Special View of
History* is of course regrettable. Had he published it, Olson
would not, in his telling metaphor, have fouled out, and we
would probably have a more manageable essay and, more important, its recognition as an essay for *Origin*.[1]

I stress the last because the essays Olson wrote for *Origin*
are of a piece and comprise a book of almost all his significant
position papers. Four of the essays—"The Gate and the Cen-

ter," "The Escaped Cock," "Human Universe," "Apollonius
of Tyana"—were either written by, rewritten, or published in
1951. They belong to the early days, to the conjunction of
Origin, Yucatan, and Black Mountain College. *The Special
View of History* belongs to the "last days" of Black Mountain
College (and of *Origin*). It is "a schema to cover everything,"
a summary work of all that preceded it and of all Olson had
learned during the subsequent Black Mountain years—all, as
he said, that enabled him to present a fuller account of "the
dynamic first proposed in *Projective Verse*." With the exception of "Equal, That Is, To the Real Itself," which either draws
on or prepares for *The Special View of History*, Olson did not
write anything comparable to these essays for *Origin*. After
them he had only (only!) to provide what they proposed, the
demonstration of *The Maximus Poems*, and the explanations of his ongoing work afforded by these poems in *Causal
Mythology* and *Poetry and Truth*.[2]

The essays for *Origin* are essays for origin, essays in transvaluation and beginning anew. They reorient (a word glossed
in "The Kingfishers") the reader and enjoin him to move—to
move *himself*, as Olson proposes later on in spelling out, in
examples of the middle voice, the imperatives of self-action.
All of the essays, as Olson said of the first, "The Gate and
the Center," are concerned with "where we are, and how we
go ahead."[3] Their metaphysics, as Emerson said of his, is to
the end of use: toward the fundamental change declared by
Olson in the opposition of Old and New discourse, Old and
New humanism. The first essay, at which we have already
glanced, is a gate, an opening to other centers and to the other
essays. It may take its title from Lawrence's *Fantasia of the
Unconscious*: "But not only a triumphant awareness that
There you are. An exultant awareness also that outside this
quiet gate, this navel, lies a whole universe on which you can

lay tribute." Lawrence reminds us that at birth we close this
central gate forever, but that in the sense organs—even, as
Olson points out, at the skin—there are other gates and "marvelous communication between the great centre and the surrounding or contiguous world."⁴ The title, at the outset,
recovers much that Olson would recover: bodily being and
location in the familiar world, that familiar world from which
Heraclitus said man was estranged for the reason Olson
adduces when he begins by attacking Socrates as the progeni-
tor of our system of education, "his methodology still the
RULE: 'I'll stick my logic up, and classify, boy, classify you
right out of existence.'"⁵

Beginning in this way makes education the central preoccupation it is in all of the essays; education, *educere*, to lead
out, is one of Olson's primary tasks, one to which he tried to
commit *Origin*.⁶ And Olson is a pedagogue in all of them, a
"university of knowledges," as Emerson said of the American
Scholar, his show of scholarship as real, as instrumental, as it
is rhetorical because reeducation is reorientation. Is there
another poet so devoted to scholarship, for whom, as in *A
Bibliography on America for Ed Dorn*, bibliography is an art-
form? But then knowledge for Olson is primary engagement:
the fronting of reality and a result of our confrontation with
reality. It is as much as the skin a "meeting edge of man and
the world [and] also his cutting edge."⁷ He insists on scholarship because it is finally the only remedy for our historical
situation he offers us: knowledge and (of) know-how. *How*,
he tells Dorn, derives from the Anglo-Saxon *hū* and relates to
process: how to move, how to proceed. Method, from *meta
hodos*, he defines as "the way after: TAO." So, if "Der Weg
stirbt," as Olson claims in "Human Universe"—if the way is
dead, if we have lost it, then it may be recovered by closely
attending to the field, the process, the world, in which we
find ourselves. *Totality* and *methodology*, nothing more: the

going-reality now and the discipline, the "morality of motion" by which we manage to live in it. Then—this time he is teaching Corman—a way may be found:

> But let's go back to root: to *methodos*, and look!
> with a way,
> with a via, with a path (weg, that which died, and
>   does
> not die, which it is any man's job—and the moreso now,
>   when the old
> way is dead, long live the methodology in other words,
>   the science of
> the path—what could be more exactly what we are in-
>   volved in—it is
> not the path, but it is the way the path is discovered!

In Olson's active sense, scholarship is Tao, the way and the power. *Via* connects this with the historical situation addressed in "La Préface," and the rhythm of the initial phrases asks us to add, "with a will." Olson's program may be reduced to "where there's a will there's a way." And it is not mystical but historiographical, concerned with *'istorin* as finding out for oneself. We succeed by knowledge, the landmarks of Olson's periplus.[8]

So "The Gate and the Center" begins resistantly with the need for reeducation, for inquiries of a kind we usually do not make and our education seldom provides (and that, at first, overwhelm us in Olson's work). We are asked to become familiar with a range of things of fundamental importance to human culture: the invention of the city, the role of geography in it, the requisite foods, the roots of our language. We are introduced to such genuine wandering (far-afield) scholars as Carl Sauer and Vilhjalmur Stefansson and immediately required to think back to Sumer, even to the time of deglaciation, and to consider in Olson's declaration of euhemerism the historical likelihood of mythic time—and see in the current example of Lincoln introduced here that none of this is idle curiosity but intended for use. The two paragraphs that do all this destroy the divisions of learning and Greek classi-fication. In opening up (and out) they reveal our ignorance, enable us to do what Olson says a straight man should: "uneducate himself." In reading them we are not allowed to admit our confusion—the confusing and confounding—because that's what Olson attributes to "Old Stink Sock" and the rest of the academics. Was scholarship ever presented with such razzmatazz? Yet it certifies: here the pedagogue is a poet going for center.[9]

Of all the essays this opener is perhaps the most exhilarating not only for stylistic reasons but because it gives us a new sense of time, the sense of *millennia* in which Olson, later on, when he was pondering Whitehead and preparing for the lec-tures on history, instructed Dorn. Millennia is not, he says, "the same as . . . time as history. . . ." It is not linear history, irreversible time, which Olson recognizes and uses in chronol-ogies to his own ends, but time spatialized, all-history-there-at-once, the fullness of time. Millennia, as the dates he supplies (12,000 B.C.–1955 A.D.) indicate, is the space of all available human history. Such vista of time, perhaps in the way quantity makes for qualitative difference, becomes space, and when time becomes space we are no longer bound to a single, restrictive dimension. Olson knows history (much more than most poets) and requires that we know history, but to the end of liberating outselves from it, and using it. When he tells us of the chronology he takes from L. A. Waddell's *The Makers of Civilization in Race and History*—3378 B.C., the date of the first city in Sumer; 1200 B.C., the end of its bene-ficent coherence ("a city was a coherence," he says, "for the first time since the ice")—and juxtaposes to it recent history, "the 700 years from, say, Dante," he makes the latter, among other things, comparatively insignificant. Not only has he

opened a "backward" beyond our usual beginning in Greece,
he has given us, in an accomplishment of the greatest cultural
importance, an unfamiliar or forgotten measure with which to
try our own. Millennia, to employ an Emersonian term, is
prospect, a way of seeing that we can "exercise," as Olson tells
Dorn, by studying such things as Sauer on deglaciation, books
on migrations, physiographic works, and especially maps (the
"space of the facts and the maps as routes" in Brooks Adams,
"Sauer's space of time"), even astronomy.[10] One virtue of its
vista Olson remarks on, strategically, in his essay: "Suddenly,
by such a smallness of time, seen as back there 3378 to 2500
B.C., the nature of life then is made available, seems suddenly
not at all history." When history becomes space, or "context,"
archeology becomes the requisite "science of inquiry." Considered in respect to the increasing quantity of things that take
place in it, it becomes "field," the totality in which we stand,
to which we actually relate. By such extension it becomes the
material of cosmos and, in respect to "person" (the self in relation to things, not the self as ego), it enables the "poet's technique," the "disposition, to reality," Olson explained to
Creeley in the *Mayan Letters*.[11]

This redefinition of history is a gate, and the center it opens
to in this essay is an actual historical center, Sumer, the city
as coherence. *Coherence* is a pivotal, value-laden term: "until
date 1200 B.C. or thereabouts, civilization had ONE CENTER,
Sumer, in all directions, that this one people held such exact
and superior force that all peoples around them were sustained
by it, nourished, increased, advanced, that a city was a coherence which, for the first time since the ice, gave man the
chance to join knowledge to culture and, with this weapon,
shape dignities of economics and value sufficient to make daily
life itself a dignity and a sufficiency." Note the shift in tone.
To sustain, nourish, increase, advance, make daily life a
dignity—this is *polis*, a word Olson makes his own because

it clusters and proclaims for him the inseparability of such words as politics and citizen, the latter a word he sometimes bandies in addressing us but even so is to be taken seriously, defining as it does in *The Maximus Poems* the relation of Maximus to the reader.

Now the city is a coherence only because man himself has the "will to cohere" and plants himself in space. Accordingly, Olson's concern with polis turns on the hero, whose heroism and human powers are realized in respect to it. "What I am trying to crack down," he says, "is, heroism." He does this— in a double sense—by restoring the hero to the city, by making his tasks the primary ones of civilization (these include the restoration of equality and the protection of the earth—Olson's own democratic and ecological insistences) and by emphasizing the "size of these early HUMAN KINGS. . . ." These heroes belong to the literature antedating the Greek, to epics and myths whose "magnification" may be only apparent to us, but is real enough to him. They become his models ("I am not named Maximus/ for no cause," he admonishes Ferrini in *The Maximus Poems*; he harks "back to an older polis"; he is Maximus of Gloucester, "where polis/ still thrives").[12] And they become the gauge in terms of which he cracks down the modern conception of the hero.

The modern hero (post-Dante) lacks the first will to coherence. His is a "contrary will" to dispersion, to destruction ("this second will of man which we have known, the dead of which we are the witnesses"). Moving outward, horizontally, he cares nothing for polis, and his heroism is not defined in terms of cultural achievement but in terms of the spoliation of nature, "in terms of man's capacity to overthrow or dominate external reality." We know this hero: "the egocentric concept, a man himself as, and only contemporary to himself, the PROOF of anything, himself responsible only to himself by exhibition of his energy, AHAB, end." And this reprise of *Call*

Me Ishmael reminds us that heroism of this kind began with Homer: "Homer was an end of the myth world from which the Mediterranean began."[13]

Ahab's end marks the end of history and Olson's beginning, his repossession of the myth world opened to him by space. That's what Olson declares by asserting that "now, only, once again, and only a second time, is the FIRST WILL back in business." Gilgamesh, whose burdensome behaviour was corrected by Enkidu, and who learned the requisites of civilization, replaces Ahab. The Sumerians are now "this predecessor people of ours," which is to say that we are "the last 'first' people."[14] From them, from the archetypes of behavior in myths and epics (Olson's science of man), we will learn such needed lessons as how to regroup and how to acquire and use energy.

We learn the former, interestingly, from the Amerindians. Olson introduces the vision quest because it is an appropriate model of initiation for a "last 'first' people." Unlike many rituals of initiation, that of the Omaha—of Amerindians, generally—is individual but not egocentric, requires exposure ("nakedness," which in this way enters the essay), and honors dream. It is a second birth especially prized by Olson because its restoration is twofold: to cosmos and community. In this instance Olson says little of cosmos, but "individuation," the Jungian term, tells its importance. Instead he stresses "groupings . . . which create kin," his own hunger for his own kind. But cosmos and the energy it bestows is the central point of the essay, and the gate to that is the example of the "early HUMAN KINGS" whose "size," whose "enlarged dimensions," impress him. They teach the lesson Ahab never learns: that "energy is larger than man, but therefore, if he taps it as it is in himself, his uses of himself are EXTENSIBLE in human directions & degree not recently granted." They teach the lesson of nature Olson finds so instructive in *Gilgamesh*: that

men are not to oppose it but keep in touch with it—keep in
touch "with the primordial & phallic energies & methodologies which . . . make it possible for man, that participant
thing, to take up, straight, nature's, live nature's force."

How urgent this closing sentence is! Olson unquestionably
wishes to be a participant, to acquire energy and force (the
suggestion of phallic aggressiveness, glossed in "The Escaped
Cock," should not be entirely dismissed). Maximus is his
"IMAGE of possibilities implicit in energy, given the METH-
ODOLOGY of its use by men from the man who is capable
precisely of this, and only this kind of intent & attention."
And this sentence, too, is instructive because it indicates what
is noteworthy in an essay on cosmos: the omission of the idea
of sacrality usually associated with it or its assumption in the
ideas of energy and force. The universe Olson recovers in the
brilliant binary casting up of this essay *is* sacred, and (master-
stroke) the sacred is permitted to remain as an essential resonance in spite of Olson's emphasis on the profane. He speaks
of (for) man not gods and seldom brings forward or makes
explicit the religious element of his work. If Olson's concern
with coherence and "multiples" recalls Henry Adams, it does
so only to make us realize that for him an external transcendent spiritual force for unity like the Virgin is absent and that
man himself (not man alone but man sustained by the Great
Mother) possesses the will to cohere. This is the point of his
euhemerism, of the way he uses myth, and of the human use
his backward glance—the feedback of this essay—makes of
history.

Olson Agonistes: the inside title, as it were, of "The Escaped
Cock: Notes on Lawrence & the Real." This essay follows
"The Gate & the Center" in Olson's proposed book—follows
the order of publication in *Origin* even though it was probably
written first, having been completed before he went to Yuca-

tan, about the time of "In Cold Hell, In Thicket." It is immediately interesting because in it Olson amplifies the arrest-
ing phrase of the previous essay, "primordial & phallic
energies." In tracing the last stages of Lawrence's development
from the achievement of place in *Etruscan Places* to the dircct
treatment of "physical or animal" sexuality in *Lady Chatter-
ley's Lover* to the more complex issues of *The Escaped Cock*,
Olson considers the final stage a "step down," that is, a descent
"to the dark or phallic god. . . ." But the dark or phallic god,
he hastens to add, is more dark than phallic: "is not phallic or
penissimus alone but the dark as night the forever dark, the
going-on of you-me-who-ever as conduit of that dark, the well-
spring, whatever it is."

For Olson, as for many early readers of Lawrence, *phallic* is
a charged word—charged by the very need to disclose "the
hiding of sex as force through some phoney Christian concept
of pudor." Unquestionably the phallus has for Olson the "immense resonance" he says it had for all early civilizations. Yet
in the letter to Corman that explains its importance in Mayan
culture, Olson's excitement is chiefly the scholar's excitement
of seeing the original red paint on a Mayan sculpture (red, he
says in the "Notes," is the sturdy sexual thread) and of making
connections between Mediterranean and Mayan, herms and
stelae. As for the phallus, he remarks matter-of-factly that it
was "simply man's most immediate way of knowing nature's
power—and the handiest image of that power." [15]

Now "nature's power" resides in the dark well-spring, and
the dark, as Olson reveals in his remarkable statement, has
even greater—deeper, more disturbing—resonance for him.
Descent is "out of the light, into the painted tomb" and is a
way of recovering bodily being, one's "WHOLE SENSES" not
merely the "FIRST SENSE, sex." But this salutary result, he
says of Lawrence's descent in *Etruscan Places*, involves an
"extraordinary contest" with place. Olson's presentation is

oblique and difficult, and all that is certain here is that the dark (the uroboros) is not easy to enter and that sexuality is terrible encounter (Olson even maintains that love is guerrilla war-fare); that the requisite thing ("what happens between," what the encounter, likened to crucifixion, enables) is the awaken-ing from it: to hear the cock's crow and to "stay OPEN," which is to say, rise from the darkness to stand forth, free and single, in the world of light.

The story by Lawrence that gives these notes their title is more familiarly, and less shockingly, known as "The Man Who Died." In it Lawrence treats Jesus' death—the paradigm of Christian initiation: dying to the flesh in order to be reborn in the spirit—as a dying to the spirit that makes possible the resurrection of the body. In terms less reverential than Lawrence's treatment Olson puts the theme of the story: "Is an X-fiction worth a cock's crow?" (*X-fiction*: Christian fiction, crucifixion, sex-fiction.) His not wholly rhetorical answer is "yes." For he himself seeks deliverance not from the flesh but from the puritan (and puritan Catholic) attitudes that cause the flesh, in his powerful image, to "choke." "Who puts this on, this damning of his flesh?" he asks in "In Cold Hell, In Thicket," where he also seems to give the reason for his criticism of Lawrence's "goddessissing" woman when he writes of his own "selva oscura":

> Who
> can endure it where it is, where beasts are met,
> where yourself is, your beloved is, where she
> who is separate from you, is not separate, is not
> goddess, is, as your core is,
> the making of one hell[16]

One of Olson's injunctions is "Live in your body," for only by doing so can we recover a human universe and realize the teaching of his work: "Paradise is a person come into this world." Not a partisan of Wallace Stevens, Olson nevertheless would endorse Stevens' belief that "the greatest poverty is not to live in a physical world."[17]

But how difficult it is to live there! So difficult that for Olson the chief interest in (and of) writing is not "what they call story, plot," but "the writer's contesting with reality, to see it, to SEE." Writing, too, is contest. As O'Ryan says, in Olson's sequence of poems on the difficulties of sex:

> Don't fool yourself
> Underneath all them poems
>
> it's night
>
> you got a hard on
>
> and it's
>
> to be made[18]

And the point of these contests is that the writer, as Olson noted later in distinguishing "men's acts of form" from the complete(d) systems of philosophers, is an "*agonistes*, contester," like "the actor in a Greek tragedy."[19] The drama this conception of writing restores belongs to the "struggle" of the man in the field, the poet in his occasion. Olson asks us to attend "the issue of this contest, the ISSUE of the man who writes," and in amending the notion of form as the extension of content to "content (contest leading to issue arriving at change equals) form," visually shows us how much for him this *agon* has become the heart of the matter.

It is, of course, the heart of *The Maximus Poems*, and in the sexual sense, as O'Ryan, the counterpart of Olson's holy men (Maximus, Apollonius), tells us, the *agon* is sublimated—treated mythically, cosmogonically. The weave of *The Maximus Poems* is not without its sexual thread, but it is not especially personal (in the way, say, Olson's account of his friendship with Ferrini is) nor very red. The drama is very little sexual but rather, as we find it in the insistence of these "Notes," the drama of the contester's attempt to become

naked, to know place sensuously, immediately, originally.[20]
Lawrence may have had an "extraordinary contest" in finding
place, but not Olson, who did not have to search for it because,
as we see in "Apollonius of Tyana" and *The Maximus Poems*,
it is natally given. His drama, accordingly, is to "stay OPEN"—
to be a poet in terms of the advice he gives Corman and Gerhardt—to stay open in order that he may search it out, come
"IN," as he says, to every aspect of it—history, geography,
geology—and so, finally, come to know it vertically in the
dimensions of the self and the cosmological dimensions of
heaven, earth, and hell. And if the drama of staying open is
very little sexual, it is evident that the mythic world to which
it introduces him is SEXUAL (to adapt his way of emphasis),
and that what he *recognizes*, thereby acknowledging correla-
tives in himself, is Creation, *archetropos* and contest of
cosmic magnitude. Where Lawrence is sexual, Olson is tropic.

Of the three maxims from Lawrence's story with which
Olson concludes the "Notes"—

1: the day of my interference is done
2: compulsion, no good; the recoil kills the advance
3: nothing is so marvellous as to be done alone in the
   phenomenal world which is raging and yet apart

—the last, often repeated by Olson, declares the value of
nakedness. (The others, of ethical import, are taken up in
"Apollonius of Tyana.") To be naked is to be exposed, to risk
contact with *the* universe outside the universe of discourse.
To be naked is to become "primitive" in the sense of primary,
"as how one finds anything, pick it up as one does new—
fresh/first."[21] Creeley stresses the importance of this motive
in Olson's work by choosing the following verses from *The
Maximus Poems* for the epigraph of *Selected Writings*:

He left him naked,
the man said, and

nakedness
is what one means

that all start up
to the eye and soul
as though it had never
happened before

And when Creeley cites these verses in a testamentary lecture,
he provides the best gloss. He speaks of "primary situations,
primary terms of experience," and then goes on to say that
" 'Nakedness' is to stand manifestly in one's own condition, in
that necessary *freshness*, however exposed, because all things
are particular and reality itself is the specific content of an
instant's possibility."[22]

This hard-won privilege of divestment is the heroism of
"Negative Capability," and to conclude the "Notes" with it is
to be reminded that it is a measure of achievement, a lifelong
task, the thing still (always) to be achieved. Lawrence said that
a glimpse of chaos was our birthright and that we had the right
to be naked. Olson tells us that it is also a rite of birth and,
in keeping with the resurrectional theme of "The Man Who
Died," may come only at the end of time. In a passage from
The Maximus Poems complementing the previous verses,
Olson says:

            And one desire
that the soul
be naked
at the end

of time (the screech
of the tunnel
says
it better be, or
what's all this

for[23]

Nakedness defines the human universe, and "Human Universe," the third of the *Origin* essays, names Olson's project.
As he told Creeley in the *Mayan Letters* from which so much
of the essay derives, it is "*another* humanism," the "precise
contrary to, what we have had, as 'humanism'"; it is, he says
in the essay, an "alternative to the whole Greek system."
Already in his thought and pressing him to position papers
(in verse and prose), he may nevertheless be said to have discovered it in Yucatan ("I come on . . . what seems to me the
real live clue"). Yucatan was to Olson what he believed Etruria
was to Lawrence, one of the few places, Lawrence observed in
Fantasia of the Unconscious, where the old (human) wisdom
survived. So the essay celebrates the rewarding Mayan researches—reading an early version of it at Black Mountain
College on his return was Olson's "first act"—and passes over
to us the Mayan just as "The Gate & the Center" the Sumerian.
Indeed, as he told Creeley in their correspondence, here was
"the gate to the center." [24]

The essay has the confident force of this discovery and is one
of Olson's best—brilliant, clear, well-spoken, and, notably,
learned but free of scholarly display. Compact and solid, without the usual broken texture of presentation prose, it is easy to
see why he wanted Corman "to make it a sort of huge & simple
piece of Mosaic stone"—Mosaic, of course, because in it he
announces the laws ("There are laws," the essay begins) but
laws in the anti-Mosaic sense of Tao or Way that nevertheless
supports the effective biblical resonance that the human universe to which he leads us is the promised land. The essay,
Olson claimed, was "the body, the substance, of my faith," and
there is no question that it gives us a new dispensation. It
works, chiefly, by opposing Old to New (Old Humanism *vs*
New Humanism, Old Discourse *vs* New Discourse), by showing us what, and how much, the Old has denied us, and,

finally and masterfully, by letting us enter the New, the human universe, in the revelation of myth (what is said), the lovely myth of sun and moon that showed how "hot" the Maya were for the world in which they lived.[25]

"Human Universe" treats more thoroughly the problems of man's "dynamic" first presented in "Projective Verse" and most fully developed in *The Special View of History*, and this may be the reason Olson did not choose to follow the order of publication but suggested it be placed next to *The Special View*. We are familiar with its essential ideas, having already considered them, but it is useful to look at them again, especially in the light of Olson's concern with the particular. What moves Olson most in this essay, and historical chronology stresses, is our present condition: the fact that we "have lived long in a generalizing time" and do not inhabit "the close world," which Olson at the outset tells us is "human . . . because it is ourselves and nothing outside us," and that now we must fight for "particularism." Why is it we are divided from the universe, outside not inside it, observers not participants, and burdened by the necessity of finding ways to "bear in" and "stay in" it?

The answer is a matter of history; and 450 B.C., the only date in the essay, provides it because it locates the advent of the Greek system, the crucial moment when logos displaced "live speech," and discourse itself became an arbitrary, closed universe. *Logos*: generalization, logic, classification; Idealism, dualism—the work of Socrates, Plato, and Aristotle, here accorded respect ("the great Greeks"), has shut us out, "intermit[ted] our participation in experience, and so prevent[ed] discovery." We are no longer organisms in an environment (to use the terms of pragmatism and gestalt psychology Olson may have adopted), and language is no longer an instrument (to use another term inherited perhaps from Dewey), an instrument enabling us "to hew to experience," language itself an

"act of the instant," of discovery, and not an "act of thought
about the instant," a distanced, after-the-fact action stopping
and diminishing the fullness of the "going-on" (on-going
process). We need only cite such touchstones of the revolt
against formalism as Justice Holmes's "The life of the law
hasn't been logic but experience" to remind ourselves that
Olson's argument belongs to a central philosophical tradition—
one, moreover, contemporary with a poetics that opposes, as
his does, image to symbol and enactment to description and
representation.

Olson rehearses these distinctions between the closed world
of discourse and the "close world" because he wishes to make
us realize the inheritance of nakedness, how much nakedness
is discovery and the first will a will to contact as well as coherence. The difference between the Old and New Humanism
that especially concerns him is what, as he told Creeley, each
involves in the "whole disposition of self." It is essentially a
matter of center. In the Old Humanism, "man, out of proportion of, relations, thus, so mis-centered, becomes, dependent
on, only, a whole series of 'human' references which, so made,
make only anthropomorphism, and thus, make mush of, *any*
reality, conspicuously, his own, not to speak of, how all other
forces (ticks, water-lilies, or snails) become only descriptive
objects in what used to go with antimacassars, those, plante-
tariums (ancestors of gold-fish bowls) etc."[26] The domestic
interior of this passage in the *Mayan Letters* translates into
the cultural critique—and critique of commodity capitalism—
of the essay. The Greek system begets another in which the
"virtue" of things, including human beings, is lost, and value
perishes. Fun and spectatorism, Olson says, in his despair of
choking, replace work and participation, and man, bought off,
conquered by passivity, "reverts to only two of his compo-
nents, inertia and gas."

And when man is not mis-centered but centered as he is in

the other humanism? Then, as Creeley said of nakedness, he stands in his "primary" situation—occupies his own space-time, stands at the center of his portion of the field, face-to-face with particular things that petition him by their particularity. The descriptive and referential functions of discourse do not keep him outside. Instead, as Olson declares in a key passage that speaks for his sense of the world, things impinge on him: "What really matters: that a thing, any thing, impinges on us by . . . its self-existence, without reference to any other thing, in short, the very character of it which calls our attention to it, which wants us to know more about it, its particularity." In a lecture at Black Mountain College, Olson acknowledged his love of particulars but did not mention what the essay tells us—that the love of the particular is a love of the intimate. The human universe is a universe of energies: "man as object in field of force declaring self as force because is force in exactly such relation." But it is also an intimate universe because every thing has force and stands forth, makes its presence known by impinging on us. "What continues to hold me," Olson says of the Maya in the earlier part of the letter just cited, "is, the tremendous levy on all objects as they present themselves to human sense, in this glyph-world. And the proportion, the distribution of weight given same parts of all, seems, exceptionally, distributed & accurate, that is, that

```
    sun
          moon
              venus
                        other constellations & zodiac
        snakes
            ticks
                vultures
        jaguar
            owl
                  frog
```

```
feathers
        peyote
                water-lily
not to speak of
fish
        caracol
                tortoise
&, above all,
human eyes
        hands
                limbs (PLUS EXCEEDINGLY
                CAREFUL OBSERVA-
                TION OF ALL POS-
                SIBLE INTERVALS OF
                SAME, as well as ALL
                ABOVE (to precise di-
                mensions of eclipses,
                say, & time of, same
                etc. etc.)
```

And the weights of same, each to the other, is, immaculate
(as well as, full). . . ."[27] Every thing in this Mayan world is
intimate, particular. Did Olson, perhaps unconsciously, use
Williams' triadic line in appreciation of Williams' dictum on
things? In his little poem each word is an image/thing. As he
said of the signs on glyphs, they "retain the power of the
objects of which they are the images." So here: the poem Olson
incloses is a poem of the human universe to be compared with
"A Discrete Gloss," a meditative poem arguing its existence.

   The correlative of the particular is "human sense" ("objects
as they present themselves to human sense"), and Olson also
found the impressive clue to this in the Maya, specifically in
the way, to use his striking metaphor, they wore their flesh.
In the letter to Creeley in which he relates his excitement
over being jostled in the bus—that the passage was taken over
in the essay indicates its importance—he says that "the flesh

is worn as a daily thing, like the sun, is—& only in this sense,
a common, carried as the other things are, for use." The human
universe is intimate because it belongs to those, like the Maya,
who "naturally" possess their bodies, inhabit the "human
house," and have learned how to "touch." It belongs to those
who appreciate the "identity of definition and discovery,"
knowing that the senses themselves, not the soul, "make
decisions!"—that "the skin itself, the meeting edge of man
and external reality, is where all that matters does happen
[and] that man and external reality are so involved with one
another that, for man's purposes, they had better be taken as
one." And it belongs to those who have learned to attend (are
"acute at the door") and, following the method of transfering
energy proposed in "Projective Verse," have learned to stay
"fresh" and properly use the energies of the world.[28]

For the close human universe enjoins responsibility. Not
only have we lived too long in a generalizing time, we have,
because of this, for too long, Olson says, misused nature: used
her for "arbitrary and willful purposes," even against herself,
with deplorable waste of energy. With the Maya it was otherwise. Their glyphs, he finds, "disclose a placement of themselves toward nature of enormous contradiction to ourselves."
They define a centrality fitting the human universe, distinguishing the New from the Old Humanism. Man is central
in both humanisms, but in the New Humanism he has no
dominion, is not "the center of phenomenon by fiat or of god
as the center as god's chief reflection." The glyphs, Olson reported excitedly to both Creeley and Corman, were built
around "ONE central HUMAN figure!/ (no god, or abstract
concept, no 'ideas,' but/ ONE MAN!" The "human figure [is]
part of [the] universe of things"—that is, individuated, as he
says in the essay, by "his own special selection from the phenomenal field." The glyphs simply (wonderfully!) depict a man
with the requisite attention to things, that "ego," he told

Creeley, "which you, me, Mayan X were (are), he who is interested enough to, seeing it all, get something down."²⁹

Maximus is such an attention-centered man, neither Emerson's spheral man nor Stevens' central man. So it is not inci-
dental that during his stay in Yucatan, when Olson was preoccupied with the Maya, he also carefully considered the ways
in which Pound and Williams organized their long poems. In
The Cantos Olson approved Pound's creation of a space-field
abolishing historical time but not the way Pound dominated
the material—"EGO AS BEAK," not the small ego [self] of "ego
which you, me, Mayan X were (are)." In *Paterson* he appreciated Williams' "emotional system," which permitted a freer,
more responsive movement and recognition of things, but not
the use of history, the way Williams "lets time roll him
under." Of the two, Pound offered the greater challenge, and
at this time Olson was especially interested in finding an
"ALTERNATIVE TO THE EGO-POSITION."³⁰ "Human Universe," with its Mayan alternative to the Greek system, provides much of the argument that enabled him to find it.

If we had no other evidence of Olson's residence at Black   II
Mountain College, "Apollonius of Tyana" and *The Special
View of History* would probably be enough to convey the
artistic and intellectual (I hesitate to say academic) style of the
place. It is unlikely that Olson would have found anywhere
else the incentive or talent necessary to the writing and production of his "Dance, with Some Words" or, in the case of
his lectures, an audience so willing to confirm him in intellectual adventure and accept the measure of achievement he
suggests by referring in the title to Einstein's *Special Theory*.
With "Human Universe," which he worked on concurrently in
the summer of 1951, "Apollonius of Tyana" marks the beginning of Olson's permanent connection with the college;

The Special View of History marks the end. Both are Black
Mountain College pieces.

Seen in the context of Black Mountain College, "Apollonius
of Tyana" is a demonstration of the "Theatre Exercises" Olson
initiated there in the summer of 1949. Art had always been
important in the curriculum of the college, and at this time, as
Olson explained in a letter, dance, because of the presence of
Katherine Litz and Merce Cunningham, was "the most forward of the disciplines" and hence the core of the performing
arts.[31] Olson himself was acquainted with dance, as anyone
who professed to teach posture, as he did, may be expected
to be. As a young man he had had some training at the Gloucester School of the Little Theatre and had even danced—
motionless—in a Massine production of *Bacchanale* in Boston.
John Finch, Olson's classmate, who delightfully relates this
high theatrical moment, tells of Olson's infatuation with
ballet.[32] But that was in the 1930s. By the time he prepared
"Apollonius of Tyana," Cunningham and Litz, in what might
be called the vernacular tradition of Isadora Duncan as against
the classic tradition of ballet, had begun to introduce the
innovations—the advances—that restored the impetus of
modern dance. Their work was to contemporary dance what
action painting was to painting and "projective verse" to
poetry, and Olson was quick to appreciate it, all the more so
because of all the arts this supremely kinetic art most fully
accorded with his own.[33]

The dance and the dancer were—as he knew from studying
Yeats—conspicuous in the Symbolist imagination as an
"emblem of true poetry."[34] But true poetry for Olson is not
symbolist, and he invokes the dance not in the service of the
transcendent but of the immanent, as a practical discipline of
body-consciousness—of proprioception, posture, movement.
He invokes dance because for the dancer—he speaks always
as a participant and not as an observer—it is a projective art,

the paradigm of stance and movement-in-space and of the
truth he so highly prizes, that "we use ourselves."[35] It might
well be a central discipline in a college that from its inception
proposed, in the words of John Rice, to teach "life's own free,
dynamic method" so that students would "learn to move [in
the world] . . . without fear." Such fearless movement and self-
possession impressed Olson in the Greek dancers of "Name-
Day Night," and, with the expressive tropic character of dance,
contributed to his belief that "to dance is enough to make a
whole day have glory."[36]

Of course there were other reasons for Olson's predilection:
dance is the art of the gods, of creation, the primal-mythic
work, as his reference to Tiamat in "A Syllabary for a Dancer"
indicates, by which chaos is subdued; dance, Confucius says,
is the Tao of heaven. Dancing, then, is a way of sharing the
rhythms ("of rhythm is image") and controlling the cosmos
("'He who controls rhythm/ controls'"; "he who has rhythm
has the universe"). And as Susanne Langer says in explaining
the fact that of all the arts only dance becomes a high art in
prehistory, "In a world perceived as a realm of mystic Powers,
the first created image is the dynamic image, the first objectifi-
cation of human nature, the first true art, is Dance." Dance is
an image of process ("interacting forces") and moves us because its syntax, to recall Fenollosa whose assumption Langer
shares, follows or accords with the tensions, balances, and
rhythms of the natural process. Always intent on beginnings,
Olson recovered for his model the first true art. Is it fanciful
to think that his polis, like the prehistorical tribes, would be
composed of dancers?[37]

The prospect of a summer with Ben Shahn and Katherine
Litz was one of the reasons that Olson decided to return
directly to Black Mountain from Yucatan. Writing to Corman
about this he suggested that he devote an issue of *Origin* to
the present state of the dance; and caught up in his own en-

thusiasm—in recollections of previous summers with Litz and Cunningham and of a dance production during the winter session of his "Pacific Lament"—he set out for Corman some ideas on the dance. These included glyphs ("what movements, gestures, investigations of nature these glyphs, contain!") and the fact that the body was to be considered as an "instrument" and dance as a "problem of space" (at this time he was much concerned with problems of space and time, and space-time). And, perhaps most applicable to "Apollonius of Tyana," he spoke of dance as "motion *around* language" and insisted that "any player is (has to be) 1st dancer," meaning, it seems, that any member of a company is equal to the others and performs as a single, solo dancer.[38]

During the summer of 1951, Katherine Litz, whose art was notably solo, performed "Glyph," a new dance, undoubtedly inspired, as the title tells us, by Olson's enthusiasm for the Maya. This, too, was a "Theatre Exercise," utilizing the graphic, musical, and literary skills of Ben Shahn, Lou Harrison, and Olson, the other resident artists. I mention this as an example of the "happy business"—the unusual excitement and concurrence of the summer session—which was so much the occasion of "Apollonius of Tyana." But it is to be mentioned also because, though "Apollonius of Tyana" is characterized as "A Dance, with Some Words, for Two Actors," it is a solo dance, in its own way a "glyph." Olson specifies: "The dancer, Apollonius/ The voice, Tyana, or place." This is not prescriptive, since both dance and speak, but it is generally true, and Olson himself, not merely for the sake of the pun, called his dance "Apple Loner."[39]

"Apollonius of Tyana," which Olson was under such pressure to complete, was not performed. It is difficult to imagine it as an enthralling dance, but it might be used as a scenario, that is, danced without the accompaniment and intrusion of words. But of course the "Theatre Exercise" was intended to

use not dispense with words, and "Some Words" in the subtitle means what it says, even though it understates con-
siderably and "motion *around* language" is more exact. The
words are very important; without them "Apollonius of
Tyana" would lose its force. There is more speech than
dance—more *muthos* than *dromenon*. The speech is formal,
clear, didactic, serious, and for the most part justifies the statement of Tyana, who speaks for Olson (who himself was to play
Tyana), that "I shall not let issue from myself . . . the slightest
ambiguity, any double talk." This statement belongs to the
occasion. It is directed to criticism ("Mr. Sprague said that he
doesn't know how to pin Mr. Olson down") and intended to
prepare an audience already intimate with Olson for what is
after all patent self-disclosure.[40] The stern seriousness of the
piece not only comports with its serious theme but helps
Olson maintain a necessary distance—which he sometimes
imperils, as for example when he says that "surely Apollonius
was no monk . . . no thin fellow without a roar in his chest . . .
he was loaded with an appetite for the real world. . . . He
craved to talk . . . to get at things by talking about them. . . .
He was one of those who talked to live."[41]

As he does here, and without ambiguity. For the dance, his
unbound thinking, enables him, a "dancing thinker," to express the ambiguous, the unmentionable. Olson calls the
dance episodes of "Apollonius of Tyana" "moves" in keeping
with the recognition he discussed with Nataraj Vashi in "A
Syllabary for a Dancer"—that "the kinetic [is] the act of life:
literally, to move."[42] So there are five moves, traditionally,
in terms of drama, five acts: acts of life, and all, conspicuously,
self-acts.[43] These are not equivocal, but rather the dances in
the Introduction, a Dance of Passage (before Move four), and
the Disappearance, all of which enact—what the *Life of
Apollonius* altogether omits—Apollonius' relation to Tyana,
or *place*. In terms of a "life," the initial and concluding epi-

sodes provide the completeness of the trajectory from birth to death. Formally, they enclose the work in *place*, or, since the movement is one of going from and returning to place, provide the circular movement that transforms time into space. And "Apollonius of Tyana" is notably a dance of place *and* space, relation to the former securing the passage to the latter, which for Apollonius, "Man of Tyana," as he liked to be called, and preeminent wandering scholar, constituted the then known world, or all the world. And this space also becomes place because Apollonius may be said to inhabit it—for a dancer not only moves in (through) space but "celebrates his union with space."[44] "The whole earth is mine," Apollonius exclaims, "to journey through it—as is my life." But, as we will see, it is the tension with place, with Tyana, that empowers him.

Poems, Kenneth Burke says, dance attitudes. Here the dance dances Olson's fable. Apollonius is Olson's model, as Olson is ours. Olson's humorous remark to Dorn, when instructing him in "how to," that he refer to "how to live, by Charles Olson," is earnest.[45] Apollonius, the holy man and teacher, appealed to him, and he used his life as an example of the Way. For the most part Olson respects the text, Philostratus' *Life of Apollonius*. There are telling omissions, like Apollonius' vow of chastity, and liberties, such as the treatment of the Nakeds, even errors such as the misquoting of Apollonius' advice to Vespasian.[46] But the *Life of Apollonius* served him well because it was so little known, and could become the scenario of his scenario.

The dance fables a *life* and is especially fitting as a means because it is itself preeminentally the self-act. Much of the dance concerns self-making, "how men, once born, seek to be born another way," and framed (limited) by birth and death, it is quickened by the urgency conveyed in Tyana's account of Buddha's life ("they, too, had work to do to shape themselves before they . . . died"). Even though—or because—Olson dis-

counts the spiritual or religious aspects of second birth, the
awful importance, the centrality of this work, remains. It is
life's work, a lifelong task, what must be done before undertaking other tasks, for example, teaching others. Olson's educational policy prescribes it: "there is only one definition of
work, the pursuit of one's own soul. There is no other. There
can't be. It is what work is. And there is a vow, a secular vow
at Black Mountain: that kind of work."[47] Perhaps the completion of this primary work constitutes the genius of Buddha,
Confucius, Lao-Tze, and Christ, the holy men with whom he
places Apollonius. It is work Olson has not completed, and the
fact that he is now involved in it (age: forty) enlivens the
dance-drama and accounts for its emphases. "Let me remind
you," Tyana says, "that men, first, deal with their lives, their
discoveries therein—in their own and other lives—and that
they seek by their actions, if they are serious men, to concentrate their own and others' attentions to the closer intervals,
not of any removed place but of the intervals which surround
us here, here in the distraction of the present and the obvious,
in short, that which surrounds us, what we make, what we
live in and by and (not so often) for." The percussive phrases
register Olson's insistence, and we not only think of Maximus
(of whom Olson is probably thinking), but recall "An Ode on
Nativity," written later in the year. Here he tells us,

> Man's splendor
> is a question of which
> birth

observes

>   . . . the cries of men to be born
> in ways afresh, aside from all old narratives, away
> from intervals too wide to mark the grasses
> [and the] unborn form, you are the content of, which you
> alone can make to shine . . .

and concludes

>   . . . is there any birth
>   any other splendor than
>   the brilliance of the going on, the loneliness
>   whence all our cries arise?

These verses tally with what is spoken at the end of Move two, where Tyana says that the "telesma [Apollonius] had his eye on" was "how/ consecrated a man can make/ himself," and Apollonius says, in response to her comment on the inadequacy of any symbol to represent the "going on" (the process), "because I am going on." And these verses help us see something we might altogether miss in the fable of the wandering scholar. Fielding Dawson says of Olson that "all his life he kept departing toward himself, each time leaving in his wake the scores of men and women that loved him. Charley is his personal image of his moving man, culminating in Maximus."[48]

Almost everything in Olson's scenario becomes a fable. Most important, clearly, is the fable of this vocation, of the disciplines involved in second birth, and then of the commitment to a public task, heroism that accords with the Way ("the path which doesn't die, the path which is no more than yourself"). This involves other insistences, such as migration and discovery, and enables Olson to both consolidate and elaborate the ideas of previous essays. In this dance Olson returns to a center that includes a still older center, to the Mediterranean world of the early years of the Christian era, a world still in touch with Sumerian culture; he returns to cities, and to the problem of coherence and dispersion treated in "The Gate & the Center." The form of the work enacts the "contest" of the notes on Lawrence, and the chief Lawrentian statements of that essay are assimilated to Apollonius' teaching. We learn here, as in "Human Universe," about nakedness: the treatment of the Nakeds has little basis in the *Life of Apollonius*, and tells of Olson's present happiness at Black Mountain College which is in fact the polis, the local, or decentralized community, that underwrites what he says in "A Dance Of Passage, before *Move* five," even the statement that is only true for him and only promissory, that "he stayed ten years." It is from this vantage that he speaks to the issue of generalization, striking up for the particular and the local. For Apollonius did not in any explicit way war against Caesarism and Christism. These are the universals Olson abhors: they attack "the roots of life" and jeopardize his humanism. And although it is true that Apollonius instructed rulers (first mentioned by Olson in "The Gate & the Center") and denounced tyrants, these dramatic episodes of his life are important to Olson especially because they define heroism in terms applicable to himself and to Pound's failure to achieve it. Apollonius says that "tyranny is the surest test of philosophers"—and Olson, appropriating Apollonius' life, would add, of poets.[49]

This figures centrally in Move three and the subsequent Dance of Passage, dances of commitment eloquently expressing what most concerns Olson now. The previous moves are preparatory: they involve disciplines of body and mind. The first, "the dance of the body," addresses Olson's interest in the body, "the physical thing," his Pythagoreanism (though, unlike Apollonius, he was not a vegetarian), and his belief in resistance.[50] The second, "the dance of the mind as a mute," similarly transforms Apollonius' life, in this instance his five years' silence, to Olson's ends. Silence, here, becomes the bit by which one restrains easy generalization, and, less clearly, because allusively, a "descent" (Olson uses Williams' term) into one's own darkness, that "blind place . . . wholly related to light . . . the light of the mind." This dark place, the place of dreams and interior life, Olson explains later in *Poetry and Truth*, is the tropic center, *the* center, where a sun within the self radiates the darkness ("my feeling is a sun of being . . . sits in this mass of blackness"). This is as much as Olson ever says about his sentiment of being and the source of his own self-acts.[51] But the passage records a profound awareness of self; and now with heart and mind united by these disciplines, his "warm mind" secure, Apollonius turns to his public task, the necessary work, Olson insists, for which one undergoes the disciplines of second birth.

This move is called the "dance of the world." It depicts Olson's huge curiosity and enacts stages of his emergence as well as his present commitment. In fact, the dance-drama itself is an act—a declaration and celebration—of commitment. It proposes Olson's great undertaking: the repossession of man's dynamic, the work of "Human Universe" ("to inform all people how best they can stick to the instant"). And it acknowledges the chief poetic work in which he demonstrates this—speaks for the present occasion and the difficulties he is having with *The Maximus Poems*. "He is troubled," he says, "to cause objects to stay in place, to see clearly his place. . . . The problem is, how to extricate what he wants from the mess he is surrounded by, how to locate what he himself feels: that life as spirit is in the thing, in the instant, in this man. And then to fix it, in such a way that no one can see him act or hear him talk without, from that illumination, knowing how rich their own life is." No demonstration is more important, for what is demonstrated is the life of a particular man in his immediate occasions, the very thing that he means by the "roots of life" and that, historically, Caesarism and Christism threaten. The historical condition fostering this is the qualitative change worked by the increase in quantity, the "second chaos," Olson says in "A Syllabary for a Dancer," that demands of us work of creation equal to the first.[52] This condition of increase in the Mediterranean world is of course a present condition also, as Olson learned from Ortega's *The Revolt of the Masses*, and what he says of cities, of coherence and disper-

sion, has its analogue in his poem: "Form (which, from the
first cities, had stuck by the glue of content to particulars) was
suddenly swollen, was being taken as a thing larger a thing
outside a thing above any particular, even any given man."
In *The Maximus Poems* Olson would like to give us a first city
and a man in proper relation to it, and it may give us, as he says
of Apollonius in a significant passage on his own relation to
Gloucester, a sense that "that binding [of Apollonius and
Tyana] was an image of health in the world."

This binding is of crucial importance because it recovers
the roots of life, the organic condition of original nurture: "He
had earlier found that his body and his mind could not be con-
ceived as separable from each other. Now he took it that man
and his world too were a sheaf at the harvest, just as seed and
the earth were blackly joined in the growing." This resonant
passage speaks for Olson, who rightly says that this time "his
return to Tyana" (read: Olson's return to Gloucester) "is the
major one." There is no such passage in the *Life of Apollonius*:
Apollonius' relation to place is only nominal; Tyana is of no
vital importance to him. But for Olson the relation to place
treated here is (with the sun that sits in his darkness) all-
empowering. For him Gloucester, as he says of Tyana, is a
"first fact . . . in some way intimately connected with the
job"—the task that, "now 40 years old" (Olson's age), he is at
last aware of, the task to which the binding of this dance of
verticality, of rooting and centering the self, commits him.[53]
For Olson, if not for Apollonius, this is the relation that gives
him "new confidence."

Olson might have called this passage a dance of *topos*—the
earlier dances of the Way, of shaping the self, are dances of
tropos and those of his task, of shaping others, dances of *typos*.
The longest of the three dances involving Tyana, it both contributes to and takes resonance from the others. It is central,
standing midway between the darkness of seed and earth at the

beginning and the darkness of harvest at the end—powerful images that move us, as does the reference to "touching . . . for the last time." The dances of *topos* address the unmentionable, a profound relation to the mother, a birth from place, from earth itself, with which Olson, having an overwhelming sense of the presence (present) of myth, feels organic connection. These are dances in which he may be said "to take up, straight, nature's, live nature's force."[54] At the close, in the Disappearance, a dance of death that in terms of Olson's career is prefigurative and wish-fulfilling, the full erotic nature of his relation becomes clear. "They [Apollonius and Tyana] shape together an ambiguous, double backed thing as darkness returns and is final."[55] Olson welcomes the finality of this death, the fulfillment of fulfillments ("He had done his work. He was near home. And with pride and ease, let the dancer go back to Tyana, let him come in slow to her as she sits as she sat at the beginning of the play, and let him come down to her, go forward into her arms"). Here, indeed, to use *lusimeles*, a word from Hesiod's *Theogony* noted by Olson, he "loosen[s] the limbs of love."[56] And we think of Merry in "MAXIMUS, FROM DOGTOWN—I," as Olson does in explaining his relation to earth in *Poetry and Truth*—we think of that remarkable poem, prefaced by the Hesiodic lines on "lusimeles," in which Merry, the braggart, meets the Great Mother in death and how

> . . . only
> after the grubs
> had done him
> did the earth
> let her robe
> uncover and her part
> take him in[57]

Only the dances of *topos* require two dancers, and the transit in them, as Martin Pops says, is "from the mother to the

mother, [from] individualism to individuation," the latter the
fulfillment of psychic wholeness spoken of by Jung. Pops's discussion of the eroticizing nature of the dance ("dance as the
stance of process sexualizes the world in perpetual enactment") and of the recovery in our time of the Great Mother
("a powerful re-expression of maternal primitivist imagery") is
of central importance to an understanding of Olson's work.[58]
But this dance, as we have seen, is accompanied by others,
those of *tropos*, which entail those of *typos*, and in "Apollonius of Tyana" we learn as much as we do in *The Maximus
Poems* about the statement, "tell you/ what is a lance, who
obeys the figures of/ the present dance."[59] Olson is not wholly
opposed to Ahab, whose lance, evoked in this passage, is
directed at nature, because, like Ahab, he opposes tyrants—
fathers. That, too, is something unmentionable the dance expresses. Apollonius, Olson tells us, relinquishes his patrimony
and slights "the Olympian gods in favor of the older and more
local heroes and divinities." This is not merely an example, in
the context of Caesarism and Christism, of preferring the local
to the universal and rejecting the tyranny of unity occasioned
by multiplicity. It is, like Olson's own treatment of Hesiod's
Theogony, a rejection of the usurping gods, of tyrannical
patriarchy. Apollonius restores the worship of Aphrodite
(*"ancient phallic worship intact"*) and the Eleusinian mysteries of Demeter and Kore (*"ancient chthonic, & mother-
daughter rites"*). His *resistance* is wholly to tyrants, and of
all the words he speaks among the most agreeable to Olson are
those he utters when Domitian is murdered: "Strike the
tyrant, strike."

Violets: an image, not obsessive but not infrequent in Olson's
early work, is telling here. Tyana says of the advent of holy
men that we should note "how men spring up, when they are
needed, like violets, on all sides, in the spring, when winter

has been too long." This image and explanation first appear
in "The Story of an Olson, and Bad Thing" where Olson associates the fragrance of violets with blood and the smell of
life—with birth.[60] The birth so difficultly and imploringly
spoken in this early poem—

all, all

must be born out of

(God knows you know,
Old Goddess, &
tremendous Mother)

—may be said to be achieved in "Apollonius of Tyana."
Olson's dance announces the birth of another holy man or, if
this is too arrogant, of a needed man, one whose task is necessary to the times.

Violets appear in Olson's work whenever he recognizes this,
and thus it is not fortuitous that he mentions them again—
even rehearses their entire cluster of meaning—in a lecture he
prepared at Black Mountain College in 1956. This lecture
begins with praise of Whitehead, whose *Process and Reality*
he had "discovered" a year before. Whitehead's thought is a
violet, and in what follows so is Creeley, who had given Olson
the notion of form first stated in "Projective Verse," and Olson
himself, who connects violets with "men's acts of form" and
with his own essential principle of "The Bunch" ("like violets
we are a bunch"; he gathers his thought in a basket; *conjecture*:
to throw together). Whitehead, of course, is occasion enough
for speaking of violets but Olson recalls them here because the
lecture already projects *The Special View of History*.[61] And
here the circuitous connection is a poem Olson undoubtedly
knew: Williams' "St. Francis Einstein of the Daffodils," in
which Einstein is a violet. In celebrating Einstein's visit to
America, Williams celebrates "the seasons of man" Olson
noted in his lecture. In conjunction with Einstein's revolu-

tionary thought, Williams celebrates the equally revolutionary forces for change—and springtime—of poetry.

Robert Creeley acknowledged Olson's achievement in "Apollonius of Tyana" by placing it, in a section of its own, at the center of *Selected Writings*. Writing to Williams on September 27, 1951, within a few weeks of its completion, Creeley said: "I think he [Olson] has damn well rung the bell again. Very exciting thing, and prose,—really he hasn't handled it this firmly since *Call Me Ishmael*." Yes: one agrees with the judgment and the comparison. "Apollonius of Tyana" and *Call Me Ishmael* are unusual works. Works of prose, they are acts of poetry; and, both, as Martin Pops reminds us, are dances.[62]

Perhaps *The Special View of History*, the lectures Olson gave at Black Mountain College, were known, as an earlier series had been, as "Olson's thing." There is no mistaking his lecture style: a certain tidiness in organization, the kind begotten by his predilection for schema, and the circular way of proceeding ("I do go in circles," he explains midway in the lectures, "in fact believe that only if one does does one finally suck up the virtu in anything"). And there is no mistaking his push, his way of advancing ideas—ideas important to him not so much because they are his as because he believes they are needed at this juncture in history. It is easy to imagine the excitement at the announcement of these lectures, the summons to the tidings. An Olson performance was an event, and this one, as the reader discovers, must have continued in excitement from week to week as Olson transformed the idea of history in keeping with his belief that the individual is equal to events (events here, in the Whiteheadian sense).[63]

Everything in Olson's thought proposes these lectures. From the start he had been concerned with history: with the crisis

of his time, with the past and its records, with the idea of
history, with using and writing history. His work begins in the
necessity of changing history (the disaster course of temporal
events) and eventuates in a redefinition of "history," in what
Emerson calls a silent revolution of thought. He might have
taken as the text of the lectures the statement in the essay on
Curtius: "I ought to . . . elucidate what history is, in the face
of the historism now plaguing all Europeans, and so the world,
by proselytizing from that center."[64] This reminds us of the
cultural and political context in terms of which Olson considers history, of the association for Americans (Emerson,
again, for example) of history with Europe and the past, and of
their desire to free themselves from bondage to it. But in
elucidating what history is, Olson rises above such exigencies.
The lectures are notable for intellectual purity and for the intellectual feat of taking a term, in this instance preeminently
modern, whose centrality is proved by how much of significance is treated in elucidating it. Though the lectures as we
have them are sketchy, their logic is complete. Olson recognized their climactic character and so perhaps appreciated the
ripeness of their achievement.[65]

The Special View of History is Olson's major work of transvaluation, and Old *vs* New Humanism, Old *vs* New Discourse
are subsumed in it. Olson says at the outset: "The assumption
is that everything's been turned about." The transvaluation
is of the largest kind, involving reassessments of *man* and
nature, and for this reason, and others as well, it is fitting to
think of the lectures in relation to Emerson's *Nature* (1836).
Olson, of course, is not outrightly Emersonian; his work is a
reaction to elements of transcendentalism and romanticism,
and yet more than he realized, or admitted at this time, it is
continuous with them.[66] By virtue of what it proposes, *The
Special View of History* is Olson's most Emersonian work,

and at one point even rises to utterance as challenging as Emerson's at the beginning of *Nature*:

for we live now and have all the problems, and what do we care for those who have done it previously? What is equal to our own inventions? Are we not also estranged? What did they do to lessen that? Who are they, other human beings, to have been more or less incompetent? None are at fault, says Lear, but if what turns out to be interesting is not the extent of the powers of human imagination but the limits of those powers, what are we to do but break the egg of history, and get outside?

Like Emerson, Olson would renew our experience, quicken our sense of life here and now, in the present world, and by repossessing of us of our dynamic—"Man is, He acts"—enable us to cope with the occasions the world presents us.[67] Unlike Emerson, he does this not so much in terms of "nature" as in terms of "history"—and by breaking the egg of history, the mythic metaphor evoking the shock of primal creation. This characteristic force involves a series of redefinitions of history that bring the argument to a turning where history (now his-story) becomes cosmos and inner and outer (man and nature, psychology and physics, mythology and cosmology) join in the creative act, an act, initiated by "actual willful man," a self-act, insistently tropic, that orders process and brings cosmos out of chaos. "Actual willful man" is indeed the subject of *The Special View of History*, and in creating cosmos is closer to Emerson's "creator in the finite" than earlier versions of Olson's hero. That Olson makes willfulness acceptable and in treating man as equal to events avoids the aggrandizement of Emerson's hydrostatic paradox is part of the excitement of these lectures.

The redefinitions of history resume much of Olson's thought. The fundamental transvaluation makes history, as he may have learned from Ortega, a function of man rather than an agency of the external universe—history as Fate or Destiny or Spirit working its will. In a remarkable reduction, history becomes simply his-story, the story of our acts, of what we as individuals do with our (limited) energy or force. His-story is life-story, the story of a particular life, a quantum of energy.[68] (*Special* in the title of the lectures may refer to particular since there is a distinction in respect to general in *Relativity: The General and Special Theory*.) To say that history is the story of our acts is to say that we must act, that only then do we have our *life*, live intensely in an occasion. Only when existence rises to act, when we use our "determining power," can we be said to have a his-story. Only as the record (measure) of *tropos* can his-story be said to be an "allegory."

Both history and his-story involve acts and are represented by versions of the "great man." Creeley reports that shortly before giving the lectures Olson taught a course on history in which he considered the nineteenth-century idea of the great man (a concern he shares with Emerson) as a foil for the great man of the twentieth century. By treating each in his respective moment in history—and undoubtedly in terms of respective ideas of history—Olson derived a "vocabulary for acts and perceptions."[69] By now we are able to supply that vocabulary ourselves, or at least evoke such representative men as Ahab and Maximus, and so fill out Olson's prefatory summary of the lectures. Transcendental-mad, Ahab is Emerson's great man gone amok, a Carlylean "hero" more than the "representative man" by means of which Emerson sought to ameliorate his force. He is the man of genius, the man of power, in Keats's phrase, intent on shaping History, on adding *his* event to its linear, progressive course. Maximus, a man of methodology, is Keats's man of achievement who does not (try to) make History but enacts his-story—a his-story that involves using the past (history) spatially, as the necessary material of present event. For all of the heroic grandeur of Ahab's effort, he is still bound by the determined, irreversible course of History and willy-nilly functions in its behalf. Maximus, whose heroism also involves resistance but lacks such arrogance, is freer because he accepts limits and by using the past as feed-back both alters and energizes a course (or better: a composition) of events that has possibility, or a future. His heroism requires—to cite again the Emersonian phrase characterizing the scholar—a "university of knowledges," and, as Olson goes on to show, historiography must be included among them.

For the first act in this new disposition to reality is finding out how we stand. "By history," Olson says, "I mean to know, to really know"—and to really know is to know reality, the "mystery," to "run up against the wall." We think of Ahab and the whale and also of "First Fact" in *Call Me Ishmael* and of "The Resistance." But Olson neglects "mystery" here, treating it later in terms of Negative Capability—"the condition itself is the penetralium (the innermost secret)"—and so pointing out a way of avoiding Ahab's furious response to inscrutability. Instead his concern is with "the restoration of the principle of fact," with "fact as the place of the cluster of belief," and the stance spoken of in the chapter heading is that of the histori-ographer, man intent on finding out "what happened." To this end Olson drives "history" back to '*istorin* ("finding out for oneself") and proposes Herodotus, who actively looked for evi-dence, as the exemplary historian. Olson himself wished to follow this practice, as he tells us in Letter 23 of *The Maximus Poems* (written in 1953), where he first treats the issues elucidated here:

> . . . *muthologos* has lost such ground since Pindar
>
>> The odish man sd: "Poesy
>> steals away men's judgment
>> by her *muthoi*" (taking this crack
>> at Homer's sweet-versing)
>
>> "and a blind heart
>> is most men's portions." Plato

> allowed this divisive
> thought to stand, agreeing

> that *muthos*
> is false. *Logos*
> isn't—was facts. Thus
> Thucydides

> I would be an historian as Herodotus was, looking
> for oneself for the evidence of
> what is said . . . .[70]

The historian who practices '*istorin* is also a *muthologos*. For *muthos* and *logos*, Olson learned from J. A. K. Thomson's *The Art of the Logos*, originally meant the same thing: "what is said," story. This etymological move demythologizes myth. Myth is merely story, or, as Olson finds in Jane Harrison's *Themis*, "'the spoken correlative of the acted rite.'" Myth (*muthos*), accordingly, isn't false, as Plato claimed, and as story may be easily appropriated in his-*story*, an equation of terms that introduces into "the practice of life as story" the natural, supernatural and psychic dimensions of experience omitted by the discourse logos has come to be.[71] For at the same time as Olson cleanses "myth" of all that has made it suspect, he restores, in examples from *Themis* and remarks on demonism and Hopi space-time (and later, as he circles, in references to Jung), the full range of its meaning. So his-story in *The Maximus Poems*—for it is here that Olson is most devoted to the practice of life as story—is his history and his myth.

The next definition links history and place: "History is the new localism, a polis to replace the one which was lost." This may be restated in the following way: his-story, the story of the self-acts or tropic acts of a particular individual, inevitably involves, as the Hopi language teaches us, a particular place, here not there, and by creating a place (re-placing us, to adopt the verb in Olson's statement, in a world of particulars) gives us a polis.[72] "polis is/ eyes"—and polis, Olson says in "Letter

6" of *The Maximus Poems*, where he continues the instruction of Ferrini in the previous letter, requires attention and care, the citizenly equivalents of *'istorin*.

By associating his-story and place Olson is able to address the theme of estrangement set forth in the epigraph from Heraclitus: "Man is estranged from that with which he is most familiar." But the estrangement that especially troubles him here is not the "permanent" one of man's relation to nature, for which he finds a remedy in the Keatsian notion of Negative Capability set forth in the second epigraph of the lectures. He is moved instead by another estrangement, that of "the contingent, of touch on all sides—of the company of the living, that they are distracted and dispersed." And Heraclitus speaks for this estrangement, too, his anger at "the loosening of the old place" very much Olson's, who cites Heraclitus' remark that his own people were "too filthy as citizens to pay attention." Olson's anger is instructive because it tells us how much human community means to him. "Man is not ideal," he asserts, "and life is not an isolation, and the falsest estrangement of all . . . is contemplation." He does not opt for nature and solitude as Emerson did but for society: "Man has the content of his own species for his self or he is a pseudo-creature." Nor does he opt for contemplation—knowing it too well—but for action. The his-story of acts of attention which, in *The Maximus Poems*, constitutes his weaving, is the very act by which he restores the fabric, and familiarity, of place.

Historian, then, is citizen, or becomes citizen, as Olson charmingly tells us in the last volume of *The Maximus Poems*:

> Said Mrs. Tarantino,
> occupying the yellow house
> on fort constructed like
> a blockhouse house said
> You have a long nose, meaning
> you stick it into every other person's

business, do you not? And I couldn't
say anything
but that I
do[73]

In this volume, where Olson is truly at home in place, his
his-story involves what he speaks of too succinctly in the lecture: how "history . . . restores God as well as locality," or,
perhaps, how knowing the local restores God. "In the end," he
says, "when all the estrangement is over, when the familiar is
known, who isn't up against the face of God like a wall?" But
not like Ahab because Olson has learned that "history is the
confidence of limit as a man is caught in the assumption and
power of change."

Perhaps this definition, again put too succinctly, is explained in the following section, which begins with another
definition: "History is the practice of space in time." For history, Olson insists, is not nature. History relates to man, to
what he calls "man-time"; it is "the continuum which man
is," and it ends with him. To practice space in time is to live
in the awareness of this limit, but it is also to live without
estrangement because one's lifetime has the universe, all time
and space, for its context. "The man-line [personal time, the
time of the vertical of self] occurs," he says, "in a universe
which is the context of his events"; we live out our lives, we
create our own space-time, in "the common field of reality."
And this is so, as the Whiteheadian language indicates, because we no longer live in the universe given us by the Greeks.
Whitehead, Olson says in the preface, "has written the metaphysic of the reality we have acquired." We do not live apart
from space-time, and we "inform it." Our occasions belong to
the process.

For all of Olson's dependence on Whitehead's metaphysics,
he provides little enough explanation of it. At this point, where
the lectures turn to considerations of history and cosmos, he

should have enjoined us, as he did with Whorf's article, to read *Process and Reality*. Failing that he might have cited the Hopi in behalf of the new metaphysics, which is what Whorf, a critic of Western metaphysics, does: in distinguishing the metaphysics of classical physics from "the recent and quite different relativity metaphysics of modern science," he aligns the Hopi metaphysics, which does not recognize "static three-dimensional infinite space, and kinetic one-dimensional uniformly and perpetually flowing time," with the latter.[74] For the common ground of Hopi and Whiteheadian metaphysics is the very thing Olson values in the New Humanism—that it "re-set[s] man in his field," places him in the process, gives him an actual particular familiar world, a space-time of which he is the center. The only absolute, Olson remarks in reference to Whitehead, is the actual particular occasion, the event in which man himself creatively participates. This is why Olson says that our condition is history and that our curiosity (*his* curiosity: see *The Maximus Poems*) "is only satisfied by the creation of the history of one's self." To be in the field is to be compelled to find out for ourselves. History, then, is "motive," the necessary human act, and in the figure of the circle, of center and circumference usually associated with deity, it becomes the space-time—the "reality," the human universe—we create for ourselves by our acts.

We create it, we give it form. That is what it means to act in the field—or now means to Olson, who rehearses much of what he has said elsewhere about negative capability, attention, risk, knowing, selecting and using the materials of the field, but is chiefly concerned with the will: with making good the connection between negative capability and man of achievement (the latter a significant addition to his citation from Keats), with recovering a positive sense of the will and defining "actual willful man" in terms of the union of will and beauty. (When separated, will and beauty, according to

Olson, yield "death and culture," which may serve as a touch-stone of his critique of the civilization produced by willful men like Ahab.) This concern with the will—with power and *tropos*—prompts a discussion of Hegelian dialectic, which is useful to Olson in defining *tropos* and in distinguishing the man of achievement from the man of power. *Tropos* is the moving force of dialectic: "'it is the dynamic which lies at the root of every natural process, and, as it were, *forces nature out of itself.*'" It is, as Hegel says of reason, "'the unconditioned, thus self-contained and self-determining,'" and is connected by Olson with the will ("the innate voluntarism of to live") in a summary definition: "the act of will of the self [that] assert[s] the unconditional, thus the self-contained and self-determining powers of same." But the will, Olson notes, is of two kinds, "a will of power or a will of achievement." In the first "the will collapses back to the subjective understanding— tries to make it by asserting the self as character." The second, however, "makes it by non-asserting the self as self," which leads Olson to conclude that "the true self is not the asserting function but an obeying one." Like Louis Sullivan who spoke of the beneficent and baleful uses of our powers, what counts for Olson is choice: "the use of positive and negative is not as of reason so much as it is of will: one can choose to use the implicit powers either negatively or positively." And this, finally, makes all the difference, for one is power and the other achievement: "One is the self as ego and sublime [Keats's Egotistical Sublime]. The other is the self as center and circumference."[75]

This figure, clearly, is an important one, and it stands, variously, for what Olson has learned from Keats about the penetralium, from Whitehead about process and reality, and from Jung about individuation. Olson says that "the self (that which a man might achieve) Jung has put once and for all in his dictum, 'The self is at once center and circumference.'"

But in context, this citation means that at any moment, in an event-happening, the self embraces the totality of the actual. Self is both agency of act and its end; it is complete, attains fulness of being, only in the instant of experience, in the actualization of its occasion, or when by its acts, it creates cosmos.[76]

Cosmos is form, the issue of events, and like history is a function of man. "*Order,*" Olson insists in the underscoring, "*is man*"; and art, which he said in "Human Universe" is the only valid metaphysic, is now of further importance because it not only enacts but orders life. Art is "the order of man, specifically man, and not nature, not history, not a creator God but simply man's own powers of imposing form on content"—though man's powers of order, Olson soon tells us in treating Whitehead's cosmology, "are no longer separable from either those of nature or of God." Chaos, moreover, is not the fearful condition of the old cosmology but a kind of cosmic sea, a condition of unselectedness that in itself gives physical pleasure (we recall: "nothing is so marvellous as to be done alone in the phenomenal world."). It is Whitehead's process, Keats's condition of things, and order is not imposed on it from outside but emerges within it in "the chance success of a play creative accidents." Olson explains this in terms of Whitehead's three stages of feeling and, in what is perhaps the most brilliant passage in the lectures, translates them into mythic terms. He says that Whitehead "only refines and corrects the most ancient myth-cosmos [of the Phoenicians and Hesiod]," and then goes on to explain: "In the first stage of feeling, the chaos of physical enjoyment is both the reality and the process, but as process (in other words, as in motion) already Spirit (which is pneuma and means breath—wind, air) is operative. In the second stage, when the individual impresses his or her sense of order on the multiples, already Desire or Eros has begun to leaven the matter; already the vision of form (Kosmos, order

harmony the world) is operative. And in the last stage, satisfaction, when both the enjoyment and the desire are one (the
desire for form is the creative force, or what has been usually
called God), the process of feeling becomes the reality and man
is 'satisfied.'" These stages have equivalents in Whitehead's
account of an emergent event, or actual entity, and so we are
reminded that the order achieved in this way is aleatory, im-
permanent, and relative to its creator, who must continue in
the endless work of creation. But he must do this not only
because this is the way of the new cosmology. He must do this,
Olson adds, because "the very motive powers, enjoyment and
desire, require it."

And so at the end of the lectures we come to the beginning,
to first things. We come to myth, the cosmos within, the center and source of order—and reach back again to the tropic
darkness and *know* why Olson preferred to call himself a
mythologist. Myth, he says in his all-too-brief account, is "the
science of human being." It concerns the cosmos of our interior life, "roots," *tropos*—the vertical of the self, for which
his image is the "shaft," or better, as he realizes, a growing
thing, a tree or plant. The myth to which his discussion refers
is cosmogonal, the Hesiodic myth we noted in speaking of
"Apollonius of Tyana," reduced here to a sentence: "out of
Chaos (which he says was mist and darkness) was begotten
Erbos and Night as well as Eros or Desire." This now serves
him well because it tells of motive power. Eros, he says in
respect to the self, is "most like kin"; and "it is with EROS,"
he insists, "that mythology is concerned," concluding, in consequence, "that as a psyche man is only an order comparable
to kosmos when he . . . is in love—that only love is order in
the vertical of the self." This glosses "love is form," the declaration of the first *Maximus* poem, and tells us that the tropic
energy is beneficent and follows a law (a Way) that is not
imposed but "supple."

Olson's treatment of myth as interior cosmos brings together Jung and Whitehead and underscores the fact that as
a mythologist Olson is also a psychologist. Once the new
cosmology is established, his primary concern is with the
"kosmos inside" ("reality is busy inside any one of us"), with
all that sits in darkness and enables creation, and with the
creative act itself. His schema, he said at the start, would cover
everything "as it presents itself inside and out," and both
Whitehead and Jung contribute to this, the one by implicating
us in the creation of events, the other by treating, in the law
of enantiodromia (which Olson mentions at the end) the
dynamic of the psyche, the double movement forward into
consciousness (and "outer" world) and backward into uncon-
sciousness (and "inner" world). Olson calls our attention to the
latter because the distinction between man of power and man
of achievement also depends upon it. "In and out . . . the passage of acts is a two-way circuit, in and out"—in saying this
he refers us to "Human Universe," and here we find, in his
discussion of the unity of self-and-world, the injunction to
stand responsibly at the open door of experience. "If man
chooses to treat external reality any differently than as part of
his own process, in other words as anything other than relevant to his own inner life"—if the unity is not acknowledged
and the balance kept, then nature herself is at the mercy of
"little willful modern man." [77] To remember this is to realize
how much is at stake in Olson's redefinition of history and
conception of actual willful man.

Man is, He acts. In *The Special View of History* Olson defines
man "so that his present energy sits in a concept of himself."
History is cosmos because history is his-story and "creation is
man's *work*"—and the creation as well of self and poem. [78] The
lectures may be said to be Olson's emendation of Lawrence's
remark on "the human potentiality to evolve something mag-

nificent out of a renewed chaos." Although their mood, like Emerson's in *Nature*, is optative, Olson more readily acknowledges difficulties and failure. He puts his difference—the "view" of the lectures—in the following: "[the] universe is not there for our appropriation but for us to be part of [,] to make it happen." (Or as Whitehead puts it: "For Kant, the world emerges from the subject; for the philosophy of organism, the subject emerges from the world.") And Olson admits that the system he has (so ingeniously) devised is dogmatic, perhaps, as Yeats said of *A Vision*, only "metaphors for poetry."[79]

As for Olson's work, the lectures remove the difficulty of being both poet and historian, and revise Pound's dictum about the epic.[80] The epic is no longer a poem that contains history, it is his-story, the story of creation, of actual willful man.

FOUR

The Maximus Poems   FOUR

I–III
Gloucester,
and myself
as here-
a-bouts

AND SO, already well into the first volume of *The Maximus Poems*, Olson answered in the lectures on history the question his poetic undertaking had raised for him: "After all the 'thought,' what act? what shall we do with Papa's shovel? what shall we do?"[1]

The Maximus Poems are Olson's his-story, the demonstration with which he hoped to justify his declarations. The adequacy of the poem-as-act had been an issue from the start, and the early poems of *The Maximus Poems*, like some of the concurrent poems of emergence, rehearse it. They begin with their own uncertainty and difficulty, the very declarative force of the initial poem, "I, Maximus of Gloucester, to You," telling the need Olson still feels to be the "tumescent I" (of "The K") and to rise up and act (as summoned by "The Kingfishers"). In 1948 he had been, we remember, a "mere son."[2] But in the following year he had been reborn as Maximus:

> Maximus, Hero, a metal hot from boiling
> water, born in the winter, 1949–50, age 38–39.
> Sprang easily into anything, including buses;
> and in the spring, year 1952, succeeded
> easily in walking through New York City, in
> one day, to the tune of $2500. A day.

The ebullience with which Olson assimilates this birth to that of American folk-heroes is notable, but even more is the fact that Maximus belongs to Olson's biography, and his emergence recalls the similarly late emergence of Whitman, whose simmering genius Emerson had brought to a boil.

This recollection is not adventitious. Olson might well have

said of Maximus of Gloucester what Whitman says of himself
in "Song of Myself" (his his-story), "Walt Whitman, a kosmos,
of Manhattan the son," for he not only shares with Whitman a
concern for place but a concern for the "'cosmos of the individual'—cosmos of being."[3] He might have offered us (the
you to whom, in Whitman's fashion, he speaks—yes, and out
of loneliness and want of touch)—he might have offered Maximus as a stock personality, for that is what he is, a new onto-
logical possibility, a new model of the self, a "root person" as
radical as Whitman's. And as outsetting bard he might have
told us what the poems tell us—that he too would not cease
until death, that he had begun the poem, as Louis Zukofsky
says, a man writes all of his life, the poem he both lives for
and with; that as he himself said of *The Cantos*, his poems
would be "a walker" ("something," Creeley explains, "you
could take a walk with daily, and have as experience of daily
possibility") and he intended to keep them open.[4]

Did he go back to Whitman, of whom he says so little in his
work, because this birth was at the expense of more immediate
fathers?[5] In what follows the announcement of the advent of
Maximus, he says:

> Ok. That took care of Ma. The Hero though has
> also to be the king's Son. This is very difficult in
> a democratic society. In a democratic society
> all men are fathers, like all women are mothers.
> This is not the same as being the King. By no
> means. The old man has to die, you have to
> succeed and not that one, here, of success;
> it has to be rule. You *are* omnipotent. Thus
> you do be what you were which you were
> born for. . . .[6]

In order to be reborn (to the tropic end of achieving that which
"you were born for") the old man has to die. This rebirth is as
troubled as the syntax of the concluding sentence. It suggests

the motive, partly Oedipal, of Olson's work—the fact, as he acknowledged in an autobiographical statement, that he was still "hugely engaged with [his] parents" and that his "work of the days," like Hesiod's in the *Theogony*, was genealogical, to find the true lineaments of himself by "facing up to the primal features of these founders who lie buried in us." The *agon* of Olson's his-story is not only the contest with reality treated in "The Escaped Cock." In the autobiographical statement Olson draws on Lawrence and Melville to put the double contest, his double concern with outer and inner cosmos, with Whitehead and Jung: "What I mean is that foundling which lies as surely in the phenomenological 'raging apart' as these queer parents rage in us."[7] The hero, we see, is a foundling (like the archetypal divine child) concerned with founders, and in "I, Maximus of Gloucester, to You," where he takes on the fathers (his father, who had had an historical interest in Gloucester, and such literary fathers as Pound, Williams, Crane, and Eliot) he plants the oar, as Olson subsequently tells Gerhardt to. He plants the vertical of the self, establishes in his own "root person" a new cosmic center, the "root city."

The birth of Maximus is a second birth. Maximus is not a persona, a mask, but a model in terms of which to shape the self. "Maximus" names Olson's desire to be born another way, to follow Buddha's instructions, to shape himself before he dies, to shape a shape out of himself. He names the "unborn form, you are the content of, which you/ alone can make to shine," and as his name in calling up Maximus of Tyre suggests, the self to which he aspires has taken for its model a teacher devoted to polis and so adds a public burden to the private burden of self-making. "The only object is," Olson told Ferrini, in explaining a poet's social action, "a man, carved/ out of himself, so wrought he/ fills his given space, makes/ traceries sufficient to/ other's needs." Much of the difficulty expressed in the early poems of *The Maximus Poems*—the question of private or public task, and the movement within some single poems and in sequences of poems from elation to despair—is due to the double task, especially the assumption of social action, a necessary aspect of Olson's conception of the self. With this in mind what he says of Buddha applies to his work in *The Maximus Poems*: "he was no more than a man who . . . spent his time doing his fashioning, that was all."[8]

The drama of *The Maximus Poems* is of this being and becoming. Maximus is an aspect of Olson ("I, as Maximus," he says), the naming of what by means of the poem he would become; Maximus is *homo maximus*, Jung's individuated man, the man who has realized the self, who, having reconciled the opposites of his nature, is whole. In Kenneth Burke's term, Maximus is Olson's entelechical motive; in Whitehead's, the subjective aim (the ideal of what the subject of an actual entity could become which shapes the very becoming and, if achieved, brings "satisfaction," the maximum all-rewarding feeling). The one thing to insist on, as Olson did, is that Maximus is not a persona. To assume a mask, as he does in "This is Yeats Speaking" and "O'Ryan," is to assume a voice other than your own and to measure from another center, and this is contrary to Olson's poetics, which as much as anything accounts for the recent programmatic scuttling, noted by Lionel Trilling, of "the sacred doctrine of the *persona*." Olson told Corman that "the revolution I am responsible for is this one, of the identity of a person and his expression," and later, at Vancouver, he said of *The Maximus Poems*, "no persona & no personality—VOICE." Fielding Dawson says that "Charley was possessed by his voice" and that "if you want to understand Charley's poems, he's talking." Voice (and breath) is at the heart and root of Olson's poetics, and, as Gary Snyder's etymological gloss on vāk (vox) reminds us, voice, granted by the goddess Vāk, is the inspiriting cosmic agency of the deepest self. Olson himself says that Maximus is "the figure of speech, the figure of the speech"—that is, the figure who enables him to stand forth.[9]

Self, not ego. Not the "EGO AS BEAK." The self in its own space-time is the essential formal element of the poems, and its story, the sequence of its occasions, is the essential narrative, as Williams recognized on reading an early installment: "This is a story of . . . the particular events [occasions] of a man's experience."[10] *The Maximus Poems* comprise a mono-drama of the self in quest, discovering, founding, mapping itself, doing the measuring of "Letter 9." And as the title tells us, this unceasing adventure of inner and outer cosmos, is maximal. This as well as the breath of life gives the poems the "projective size" Olson speaks of in "Projective Verse," makes them the epos he said the new poetics might encourage. The quest in *The Maximus Poems* is archetypal, and Olson considered his poems an *archetext*.[11]

Fielding Dawson, who observed it, says that the key move for Olson in the momentous period of change from 1949 to 1951 was "his withdrawal from his outer ego structure to enter the long sequence of his Maximus Letters, and his personal emotional past for the first time in his life."[12] Certainly Olson is a man in crisis, of vocation and middle life, in search of his soul. But this Jungian motive is only a single dimension of his work, and not a sufficient one, or only became sufficient when he realized, at the time of the lectures on history, that all along he had also been demonstrating in his poems the very thing that for him made them especially significant *acts*, acts worthy of a supplanting son. "I am not aware," he said in a lecture at Black Mountain College, "that many men's acts of form yet tap the total change of stance or posture . . . of which Whitehead's 'philosophy of organism' is one completed exemplification."[13] His do, and Whitehead justified them. His acts of form are the occasions of an event—and at the same time they are the means of achieving individuation, the completed event comporting with it and bringing satisfaction.[14] This distinguishes *The Maximus Poems* from most of the precedent poems.

To begin to begin again, as Williams says in *Paterson*, is incredibly difficult. It requires an act of creation such as the one with which *The Maximus Poems* begins. "I, Maximus of Gloucester, to You" opens for us as well as Maximus the possibilities of the field. Here beginning, emerging, getting underway are everything: Maximus rises up and acts, even challenges his predecessors. We feel the immense effort of doing this in its push, its tropic force; and the achievement is so great and so exhilarating that much of what follows seems subdued and diminished, Maximus having now to make good the bold beginning of planting himself in the many excursions of the long journey of the poems. It is not that he retreats from his task in this first installment of ten poems published in 1953, but that he works through to the point of being better prepared to do it, and finally only by beginning his historiographical work. After all, the new, as Olson says in the *Mayan Letters*, "is of the making of our own lives & references," and the self-act of the initial poem only enables Maximus to undertake this arduous work.[15]

"I, Maximus of Gloucester, to You" is a self-act because every act of form is such an act and also because, in this instance, it is "the act of birth" Olson spoke of to Corman, not perhaps the ideal self-begetting he had in mind but nevertheless an "actual begetting, the physical fact."[16] Epigraphs are conspicuous in Olson's poems. His poems are often meditations on them; to a considerable extent he dances sitting still. But none is as important as the epigraph of the initial poem:

> Off-shore, by islands hidden in the blood
> jewels & miracles, I, Maximus

a metal hot from boiling water, tell you
what is a lance, who obeys the figures of
the present dance

Maximus is "of Gloucester," yet his birth—his emergence in
the poem—is at sea, out of the unconscious, out of the inseparable waters, the sea-blood of self-and-world, the very
process that is the reality of the poem. Throughout the poems
he is identified with the sea: he talks familiarly of the sea, of
ships and fishermen, and is linked with the seafarer Odysseus;
he harkens back to an "older polis," the earlier flourishing port
of Gloucester. With him, as with the fishermen he listens to
in "Letter 2," the sea is restored to Gloucester ("as fresh as it's
always been/ to hear him talk of the sea"); and because his
position offshore is privileged, he "can still hear" the bells of
the Church of Our Lady of Good Voyage and, like the guardian
of the Portuguese fishing community and the tutelary presence, the Great Goddess, of the place and the poems, remind us
that "it is elements men stand in the midst of." He himself
has this exemplary disposition to reality and would, if he
could, teach us "the swimming"—how to accept as conditions
of being and creation, as he does, the unfixity and the risk, the
unselectedness and the accidents of the sea.

He emerges as a teacher, still hot from the boiling water, as
urgent in his purpose as Ahab (evoked by tempering and
"lance") but to tell us to front reality in another way, not
demonically, out of hate and revenge, but out of love, in obedience not in opposition to the "present dance" of reality, rhyth-
mically, and in harmony with it, as the rhyme of "lance" and
"dance" indicates. For "Maximus, Hero" is not a man of power
but a man of achievement (more Bulkington than Ahab) and in
spite of his assertiveness exemplifies Olson's belief that "the
true self is not the asserting function but an obeying one"
because "the actionable is *larger* than the individual and so

can be obeyed to."[17] "Lance" is qualified syntactically by
obedience, and his lance is not Ahab's but that of common
fishermen ("how shall you strike,/ o swordsman, the blue-red
back") and the poet (for the lance is also a pen and the figures
of the dance are syllables). Both fishermen and poet are active
men of skill ("hands"), of attention and care ("eyes"), and
Maximus assimilates them to each other throughout the
poems, explicitly in "Letter 6." Their stance is exemplary:
they have the readiness, the responsiveness to the field, the
quick attentiveness to change, to the moment, the possibility
that summons one and defines "that which you can do!" And it
is creative because in this participant action one is himself
the mover of the instant, compelled by the tropic force of love,
which, Maximus states in "love is form," is the agency of creation, of order, cosmos. Love is a verb, an action, Olson told
Fielding Dawson.[18] Love is form because, as Maximus says of
William Stevens, the colonial carpenter, the "first Maximus,"
it doesn't exploit nature but adds to it, makes things, necessary
things, nests, houses, poems.[19]

The position of Maximus in this poem is similar to his position in "The Librarian":

> The landscape (the landscape!) again: Gloucester,
> the shore one of me is (duplicates), and from
> (from offshore, I, Maximus) am removed, observe.

Maximus is offshore and so observes Gloucester in overview
and as Olson's private landscape. His position evokes a discoverer (public task) and a voyager returning home (private
need) as well as the fisherman, the heroes of Gloucester he
most often celebrates. It is a necessary initial position because
it establishes one of the values of landscape for Olson—that
landscape is the field defined by the limits of a single view
(single self)—and it is necessary because it enables Maximus
to discover Gloucester, "to bring the land into the eye's view,"

which, in turn, Olson considers an action, a verb, the creation of cosmos.[20]

Sea and land provide the primary polarity of the poem, perhaps deriving immediately from Melville but of course from cosmogonal myth, and they convey, as in Melville and his contemporary writers, the basic division of the self, that between the real and the empirical self or, in Jungian terms, Self and Ego. In "The Librarian" we learn how disorienting and disquieting this relationship of selves can be, how distressed Olson often must have been by psychic discovery, the search for "materials . . . for Maximus. . . ." If this is not admitted in the early installments of *The Maximus Poems*, it may be because Maximus stands so clearly in opposition to the shore—not to the harbor but to the city—and in spite of his concern with love (and because of it) exhibits a considerable anger, the "violent prejudices" of which Williams complained. Olson's poem, no more than the *Cantos*, recalled here by reference to Pound and "pejorocracy," lacks in melodramatic, even conspiratorial oppositions—in scapegoats who may merit his revulsion but also earn it because they bear his burdens. It is not the moralizing of the scene that is particularly noteworthy but how extremely Maximus does it.

The initial verses introduce us to Gloucester, place us in space, in what Williams calls a "culture of immediate references."[21] We are in the harbor-section, the old, preferred, still virtuous part of Maximus' city, itself bowllike, a nest, dominated in this poem, as in no other, by the gulls, tutelary birds, immemorial presences of place, exemplary, too, nest-builders, form creators, weaving from miscellaneous materials, as Maximus himself is doing and will continue to do, and, what is more, of all creatures, for him, most wonderfully equilibrated in the field, paragons of stance and attention. (We remember Olson's excitement over the chii-mi in the *Mayan Letters* and his admiration, in "A Round & A Canon," for a bird in "his

own world, his own careful context.") The opening verse, so
evocative and kinetic, is marked by modulation of voice,
exquisite vowel-leading, careful phrasing, and visual scoring:

> the thing you're after
> may lie around the bend
> of the nest (second, time slain, the bird! the bird!
> And there! (strong) thrust, the mast! flight
> > (of the bird
> > o kylix, o
> > Antony of Padua
> > sweep low, o bless
>
> the roofs, the old ones, the gentle steep ones
> on whose ridge-poles the gulls sit, from which they depart,
>
> > And the flake-racks
> of my city!

These lines poise us: excite us, call us to attention and call to
our attention, as in some still undisclosed way connected with
our search and our need to act, the nest and the mast, related
images of building and birthplace, of *omphalos* and cosmic
center. After the prosaic opening lines, the words quicken
almost beyond the power of notation, a quickening in which,
with the thrust of the mast, the vertical of self, time is slain
and the bird, epiphanically, set into flight, released into space.
With remarkable economy the subsequent lines depict the
port, the roofs mounting from waterside as the lengthening
phrases mount, asking us, as we would, to attend more particularly to their condition, and then, in the next line, to
observe (more sharply defined by "ridgepoles") the gulls, whose
sitting and departing are also enacted in the balanced phrases.
And then, after a visual pause or lingering, the flake-racks (of
Stage Head, geographically the very center of the poem), reminders of the city's origin and continuous economic life, of
the fishing and the present Portuguese fishing community, to
whose patron Maximus appeals, his supplication ("sweep low,

o bless") both guiding us to the subsequent lines and filling
the visual space with the quiet present-yet-reminiscent tender-
ness of the last lines ("And the flake-racks/ of my city!").
Space, here, is full not empty, eroticized by the verbal dance,
more sacred than profane; we enter a universe of rhythm;
feelings-things (those "gentle" roofs!), inner-outer, are one;
with Maximus, we bring the landscape into the eye lovingly.

This description is not exhaustive—for example, there are
recollections of Eliot and Pound and Olson's "The Kingfishers"—but is sufficient to suggest Olson's art and a poetics
of man-in-space, whose metric, as Maximus later explains, is
mapping. This verse already exhibits the weaving attributed to
the bird and supports the proposition ("love is form") enter-
tained in the next section and subsequently developed fugally,
section 2 resumed by section 4, and the answering section 3
resumed by section 5. (Section 6 both closes and forwards the
poem by bringing together all the threads—themes, or better,
insistences since they are not imposed, but issue from the
field—at the same time as it more percussively enjoins the
creative act of section 1.)

Love is form. The proposition addresses the work of the
poem and the act to which it summons us: the gathering and
weaving to the end of creating haven (nest-house-polis-poem).
Eros creates cosmos. Eliade says that "nothing better expresses
the idea of creation, of making, building, constructing, than
the cosmogony"—to which Olson would assent, turning it
about, so that nothing better expresses cosmology than the
act of making, building, constructing, in this instance, the
nest, which is related to the founding act of self, of the
"tender" mast, and of the city (whose founding has always
reenacted cosmic creation).[22] The reference to alchemy alerts
us to the Jungian aspect of this making, and the bird gathering
materials for the nest reminds us of the fundamental unit of
Whitehead's cosmology, the actual entity which becomes

itself by prehending other objects. In the end, Maximus says, what is gathered makes "the sum," an allusion to the preface of *Paterson* ("To make a start,/ out of particulars/ . . . rolling/ up the sum. . . .") and to the fact that form is the extension of content but, more important, a way of saying that in this making the self stands forth, becomes "I am." To use the nest as exemplum is bold, when we remember its use in "The King-fishers," and more so in the light of Havelock Ellis' note on the relation of the primary arts of dancing and building—that "the nest . . . is the chief early form of building, and . . . may have arisen as an accidental result of the ecstatic sexual dance of birds."[23]

There are two variations on "love is form": "one loves only form" and "love is not easy." Love is not easy in either, in the first because of the travail of birth, when "the thing is . . .// born of yourself" (here the verse paragraphs have the forward thrust of Williams' triadic line), and in the second because the imme-diate environment from which one gathers the materials of creation is no longer attractive. Olson had already considered the latter difficulty in "ABCs (3—for Rimbaud)" and Maximus resumes the argument, adding to "mu-sick," the sick music and muse, and the muzak, the equally revulsive worse rule and false language of "pejorocracy." But now Maximus accepts them as a cosmologist accepts chaos, as a necessary condition—

> the underpart is . . .
> is, as sex is, as moneys are, facts!
> facts, to be dwelt with, as the sea is . . .

—and so identifies the act of the poem with renewing, the redemption of Gloucester (New England, America), the resto-ration of polis.

> (o Gloucester-man,
> weave
> your birds and fingers

> new, your roof-tops,
> clean shit upon racks
> sunned on
> American
>
> braid
> with others like you, such
> extricable surface
> as faun and oral,
> satyr lesbos vase
>
> o kill kill kill kill kill
> those
> who advertise you
> out)

Lear's cry of outrage in the last verse is the extreme expression of revulsion and identifies both an object of hate and a
moral direction. The juxtaposition of verse paragraphs puts an
issue Olson had considered with equanimity during his visits
to Pound: "I think of the presence in his [Pound's] work of the
worship for [of?] past accomplishments and a kind of blind-
ness to the underground vigor of a [the?] present. Yesterday
we batted around the radio, the movies, the magazines, and
national advertising, the 4 Plagues of our time."[24] They are
plagues to Maximus, too, because, like muzak, they distract
us, keep us from hearing what we have just heard ("when even
our bird, my roofs/ cannot be heard"), and in his poem they
name a late stage of capitalism—the consumer he opposes to
the early productive capitalism of the fishery—and an action
("advertise . . ./ out") which relates our estrangement from the
familiar world to the misuse of language. Against these be-
trayers, in the equally vigorous, percussive expression of the
subsequent verse, he enjoins the opposing action, the "in! in!"
of (poetic) creation:

> in! in! the bow-sprit, bird, the beak
> in, the bend is, in, goes in, the form

> that which you make, what holds, which is
> the law of object, strut after strut, what you are,
>   what you must be, what
> the force can throw up, can, right now, hereinafter erect,
> the mast, the mast, the tender
> mast!

Here the argument may indeed be said to be phallic, like
Whitman's, and Williams' too, who links going-in with discovery.[25] It has unusual physical force, and, as in the introductory verse, bespeaks a determinate will. Complementing
the female nest, it completes the image of wholeness.

In opening the world and themes of *The Maximus Poems*,
this poem reminds one of "Proem: to Brooklyn Bridge." Like
Crane's poem, for all that is dismaying in what it surveys, it
is optative, a call to do the high work that subdues chaos.
Maximus is not overcome by mu-sick. He can, as he says, "still
hear," and having the power of listening Olson treated in
"Projective Verse," he know how to play (it) by ear, both attend
the syllables and play the things in the field as they come. For
him the commonplace is wonderful, and "life as spirit," as
Olson says in "Apollonius of Tyana," "is in the thing, in the
instant, in this man." The universe is still open—prospective,
according to Whitehead—and in meeting the instant he may be
equal to its occasions.

The Maximus Poems 1–10 is a better book than Williams
thought it to be. There is no need to be defeated by it, as
Williams admitted he had been by the omission of the essential and the inclusion of the inessential. This is not the case
in any acceptable sense of "essential" because there is no
spurious information in the poems—spurious information
being, Williams says, that "which is unrelated to the contacts
of experience"—and because now, thanks to George Butterick,
there is annotation enough to make the poems readily acces-

sible.[26] The poems vary in immediate difficulty—it is helpful
to read "A Syllabary for a Dancer" along with "Tyrian Businesses"—but, as with *Paterson*, they may be quickly read
through with pleasure. The poems, singly and together, are
coherent, having the intrinsic order-tension demanded by field
composition. If the way in which the themes are woven together suggests that the poems follow a track and Maximus'
practice of gathering themes together in concluding sections
(at the end of "I, Maximus of Gloucester, to You," for example)
seems artful rather than spontaneous, consider Olson's skill
in minding spontaneity, how in his letters and lectures he
follows/guides the threads of thought through digressive
movement. Maximus, like Homer and Whitman, is a rhap-
sodist (from "Rhapsodia," *Greek*, songs stitched together), and
more than the weaving we should notice in this volume of
poems the tightness of the texture.[27] This may accord with the
intense concentration of beginning. Later volumes are of looser
weave, their energy diffused throughout a wider and deeper
field. They comprise a serial poem, where volume one, perhaps
constrained by the challenge of Olson's predecessors, is a
long poem.

   Though this his-story tells a story, there is no narrative line.
The poems do not advance, have no particular forward direction. Instead their motion is circular and multidimensional,
to the end of exploring/filling the cosmic space represented in
The Special View of History by the double cone of myth whose
axis is the vertical of the self. The first installments get this
large work underway, chiefly on the lateral plane, and now
Maximus begins the moving in place by which he takes possession. He follows Olson's advice to Ed Dorn to dig (in) one
place, though he has not yet consulted in the poems any docu-
ments, and the colonial and precolonial history, prominent in
the later poems, becomes foreground only, and only briefly,
in "Letter 10."[28] These initial poems involve present-day

Gloucester and Maximus' need to undertake morning work: to move, to work in, and to set out the terms that chart the field and enable him to tell "the Fables and the Wills of man."[29]

The terms have thematic importance and are binary, composed of opposing elements, each pair clustering with others to develop the range of values. As we have seen, the geographical pair, sea *vs* land, is of primary importance. To it, one adds the directions, outward *vs* inward (outward, here, connected with the sea and Our Lady of Good Voyage, belongs with discovery, and thus with the "in! in!" of the first poem);[30] the occupations, fishing (and poetry) *vs* capitalism (slaving, advertising, etc.); the polities, polis *vs* pejorocracy; the economies, local *vs* absentee; the stances, the "old measure of care" (of eyes, of ears) *vs* carelessness (abstraction); the applications, work *vs* sloth; and the goals, eudaemonia *vs* euphoria. These values, moreover, are told by the senses, by the immediacy of Maximus' contact with the environment, and so, with him, have location in the world, the field of the poem. They are told by sight (white *vs* black, as in "Letter 2"), by smell (tansy *vs* gurry, the slime of ownership), by hearing (bells *vs* mu-sick), by touch (contact *vs* withholding). In charting the field, they dramatize the morality of stance, what Olson called "the binary problem"—"that at any moment of essential experience you are making a choice."[31]

The most prominent concern of these poems—it is prominent also in subsequent installments—is "the practice of the self." As in his early poems and the writing that culminates in *The Special View of History*, Olson is preoccupied with a question of public and private urgency: how to act? In "The Songs of Maximus" ("Letter 3") Maximus says:

> And I am asked—ask myself (I, too, covered
> with the gurry of it) where
> shall we go from here, what can we do

> when even the public conveyances
>   sing?

Gloucester now, and the city he enters in "Letter 2," its
"underpart" exposed, the city itself fixed by its inheritance,
its foundation in moral failure, and thus difficult to change—
this overwhelms Maximus, who takes heart only by recalling
the sea and the fact that the fishing still continues and
counts, that

> While she [Our Lady of Good Voyage] stares,
>   out of her painted face,
> no matter the deathly mu-sick, the demand
> will arouse
> some of these men and women

But fishermen are not the only saving remnant he has in mind.
His question relates specifically to art as an action and finds
an answer in "Letter 5," the longest, most reproving and
scornful poem of this installment.

In this letter, Maximus addresses Vincent Ferrini of Gloucester, a poet and the editor of *Four Winds* (a little magazine
in which Olson published three of the *Maximus* poems!).
Ferrini, he feels, has misconceived his task, has bungled it
as badly as the skipper who in a storm abandoned two men at
sea. Unlike *Origin*, his magazine is not a polis, a "place we
can meet." Ferrini has betrayed that possibility by seeking
guidance everywhere except in the "context of/ now," the very
Gloucester Maximus knows intimately and, in recollecting,
immodestly claims as his own. In terms of the issue of language set forth in pejorocracy and mu-sick (song, poetry,
muthos, are alternatives), Ferrini belongs with the other word-
mongers who alienate the only polis there is, who, with the
absentee owners, advertise us out.[32] He has failed at "men's
business," that which confronts the elements and requires the
"old measure of care." Not only has he failed to see out of his

own eyes, which is the privilege of stance Maximus announces in "Letter 6" ("There are no hierarchies, no infinite, no such many as mass, there are only/ eyes in all heads,/ to be looked out of"), he has not had "the polis/ in [his] eye. . . ." And Maximus has, as Ferrini should know, having published "Letter 3," in which Maximus complains of the loss of polis as localism.

In respect to Ferrini, Maximus considers himself a model, but he is overbearing because he has not yet proved himself in terms of the competence by which he tests his friend. In respect to Marsden Hartley, another artist treated in these poems, he yields to the exemplary figure of his father. The issue in this letter (#7), which continues the consideration of eyes, attention, and care in terms of hands ("hands are put to the eyes' commands"), is unmediated contact with things and is directed to Maximus' own marriage with place. Hartley, a painter connected with Gloucester only because in the 1930s he painted her landscape and chiefly that of Dogtown, the uninhabited moraine north of town, is not contemned. Maximus acknowledges his "many courages." What he disapproves of is his "transubstantiations," the way in which he transformed all things to cloth, made the Whale's Jaw, the particular instance related to his father, a "canvas glove." This is as much as to say that Hartley engaged reality with his gloves on, that he did not follow the way of objectism but that of the egotistical sublime:

> Such transubstantiations
>
>> as I am not permitted,
>> nor my father,
>> who'd never have turned the Whale Jaw back
>> to such humanness neither he nor I, as workers,
>> are infatuated with

This passage is also of interest because Maximus identifies with his father and defines the artist—the carpenter prefigures

this—as a worker. His father, he says, took the Whale's Jaw
"as he took nature, took himself." A man of attention and care,
he dealt directly with things, and Olson, in "Stocking Cap,"
depicts him with an admiration that measures his own in-
capacity. Here, he is Jehovah!

> . . . Jehovah, he looks that strong
> he could have split the rock
> as it is split, and not
> as Marsden Hartley painted it
> so it's a canvas glove

But why did Hartley do this? Why transubstantiate? Because
he refused "woman's flesh," a disclosure that may be justified
because its truth was already public and because contact with
the body of the world is a requisite of stance.

   Much in these early poems involves stance and preparatory
enabling acts. We learn, for example, that Maximus has
adopted voluntary poverty. "The Songs of Maximus" ("Letter
4"), in which he tells of the "blessings" of the leaky faucet and
the faulty toilet—this particular song recalls Williams' "Le
Médicin Malgré Lui"—are themselves repudiations of the
wanting encouraged by advertising. He sings because he
"wants" something else, because "wondership," as in the
account of recognizing Nike in a girl crossing the square,
moves him more than "ownership"—wondership is the reward
of the nakedness he desires ("he [the "lovely pedant"] looked,/
the first human eyes to look again"). As in "The Green Man"
called up by these songs—Maximus is the "fool" who there
had turned from politics to poetry—he "furiously sing[s]!"
because he is both isolated in and outraged by contemporary
culture. We also learn in "Letter 6" what he confesses later
in "Letter 12": that the sea is not his trade, that he lacks the
skills of professionals, wastes his eyes. He admits that "I have
suffered since,/ from that enthusiasm," but it's competitive-

ness as much as enthusiasm, as the anecdote of climbing the Bright Angel trail tells us. He acknowledges the folly but is proud of the fact that his sharpness comes of "pushing . . . limits." In the context of "Letter 5"—"Limits/ are what any of us/ are inside of"—the implied injunction is to move outward beyond them. Maximus here reminds himself that the adventurer risks himself.

But Maximus' proper work, which he meditates on in "Tyrian Businesses" ("Letter 8") and "Letter 9," involves movement of a different kind. In "Tyrian Businesses," the poem under hand is his "exercise for this morning," an example of "how to dance/ sitting down"; in "Letter 9," which develops the idea of *tropos* in the previous letter, the concern is "self-acts" and "self-things," intrinsic growth and the making of poems.

Olson tells us in "A Syllabary for a Dancer," the essential gloss on "Tyrian Businesses," that man is "a thing which simultaneously thinks and dances"; man is a dancing thinker, to think is to dance, to move, in place. Olson is concerned with using himself, with self-originating action, with "the kinetic as the act of life," the movement that engages things and makes them yield "that life which matter is so astoundingly capable of anew each day in each new human hand." For Olson, movement is the basis of renewal: only get under way, begin the work by which one attacks chaos. But it must be movement of the kind exemplified here, vertical movement, having its *tropos* in the chaos within oneself, in what is "implicit in himself, inside himself, what he is and what he is impelled to do, that is, how to move." The distinction between vertical and horizontal movement, as we have seen, is crucial. The horizontal belongs to the conquest of space, here to the discovery of America and the subsequent westward movement—activities represented perhaps by Olson's own turn at sea and rambling in the West. The "frontierism" of American history—we will remember it later when Maximus treats Gloucester as a cowtown—follows the course of post-Sumerian history traced in "The Gate & the Center": dispersion, loss of center and coherence. Horizontal movement, accordingly, no longer serves "the last first people," Olson's characterization of the Americans in *Call Me Ishmael* ("We are the last 'first' people. We forget that. We act big, misuse our land, ourselves"). The business of "Tyrian Businesses" is indeed Tyrian, that of a Maximus concerned with, prescribing for, his country, "my countree," he says in "Letter 10," the true, still to be truly planted, America. In these poems, as in the "Syllabary," one may still be hopeful for America ("It is still/ morning"). With dispersion behind them, the Americans, Olson believes, are "green again"; at last they have discovered "physicality" and "know what the earth is. . . ." Now they need only learn to sit.[33]

Section one of "Tyrian Businesses" transposes the "Syllabary," and section two continues the poet's morning work, much of it his seemingly casual consulting of the dictionary—an exercise also in creative accident. Naming is proper morning work, and it answers to Olson's affirmation of himself as an "archaeologist of morning," to the concern with beginnings doubly stressed in this stirring phrase. "Beginner—and interested in beginnings," he says of Melville in a passage that speaks for himself, and in his declaration he says: "This is the morning after the dispersion, and the work of the morning is methodology: how to use oneself, and on what. That is my profession, I am an archaeologist of morning."[34] And he is such an archeologist because he would overcome darkness and death, his and history's. Motion signals *tropos*: "The seedling/ of morning: to move, the problems (after the night's presences) the first hours of . . . ." Maximus' problem is still that of emergence, of rising (in the morning) and acting, of moving himself, when so much around him is unfavorable to "growth." His scholarly morning work dramatizes this. *Heart, metacenter, tropaeolum, eudaemonia*—the definitions of these words, among others, provide the substance of a meditation on *tropos*, the inward-arising motion, the twisting and turning common to organic growth and verse. *Tropos* is self-action and its linguistic complement is the middle voice, mentioned here and in the "Syllabary" and defined later in *Proprioception* as the voice of "*proprious*-ception/ 'one's own' -ception." In the middle voice, Olson explains, the subject is represented as acting on himself, for himself, and on something belonging to oneself—actions, incidentally, that yield him articles of faith: will, believe, be graceful, obey, accept self-responsibility.

Here, too, beginning proprioceptively with the contractions of the heart, Maximus ponders the courage needed to live in the process world. And having associated heart and flower, he considers *his* flower, the nasturtium, "my nose twist, my beloved, my/ trophy"—a flower of the genus *Tropaeolum*, a kind of cress, pungent like tansy, connected by him with "Tansy from Cressy's/ I rolled in as a boy" ("Letter 3") and so calling up childhood and the wondership of a pristine past. Flowers and flowering, as the subsequent poem bears out, are primary images of *tropos*, as important to Olson as they are to Williams. When he speaks in the "Syllabary" of vertical kinetics, his example is "growing, and waving from the spine, like flowers are, or branches, on a tree"; in *The Special View of History* the image of the vertical of the self is a "tree, or any plant, in any case so the presence of a ground (or begrunden), roots, stem, and photosynthetic growth out in the air among the leaves (or acts) are seen."[35] Moreover, since growth is dancing sitting still and such motion is a "gravity question," he is properly concerned with the relation of M to G, metacenter to gravity. A ship, after all, must be self-righting in all weathers; and a ship, as he shows from his own experience at sea in defining "felicity," must move in accord with reason and nature, and must trust in more than its sturdy construction ("futtocks" cover this), in the favor of the Goddess, of Lady Luck ("fylfot,/ she look like,/ who calls herself// (luck").[36] By the logic of these definitions Maximus concludes that felicity results from a life of activity in accordance with his own tropic necessities.

Or, as he declares in "Letter 9," the splendid poem of spring following on this poem of morning, felicity comes of obeying what Emerson called the soul's emphasis. The analogue of the self is the flower; the "likeness," he says, "is to nature's"; and "there are these necessities [the process]/ are bigger than we are." *Tropos* is the motion within the self that answers to these necessities. It is not willful. As Olson wrote in "Concerning Exaggeration, or How, Properly, to Heap Up" (1951),

> And I twist,
> in the early morning, asking
> where
> does it stop

"Letter 9" celebrates a double flowering, that of "the flowering plum" and of his book of poems, *In Cold Hell, In Thicket*, just published in Mallorca by Robert Creeley. And since the latter reminds him of the fate of *Call Me Ishmael* ("as, in another spring,/ I learned/ the world does not stop/ for flowers"), it raises for him the disturbing question of contemplation *vs* action, of the way of art *vs* the more acceptable, usual way of public usefulness. Maximus' ends are public, though not acknowledged by the public. He says here that he wishes his book of poems "might stop/ the workings of my city," and that it doesn't troubles him:

> it puts a man back
> to find out how much
> he is busy, this way,

> not as his fellows are
> but as flowering trees

And it makes him extremely defensive, quite as much as in "Knowing All Ways, Including the Transposition of Continents": "I have had all I intend/ of cause or man: the unselected/ (my own) is enough/ to be bothered with." The intrinsic success of flowering becomes, as it had for Thoreau in "Wild Apples," his chief argument, rehearsed here to earn again and reaffirm his choice. Flowering, whether in the growth of the self or in the publication of books, is, he claims, an end in itself ("these things/ which don't carry their end any further than/ their reality in/ themselves"). And what interests him now is not extrinsic success but rather his own emergence, his spring-like condition:

> It's the condition in men
> (we know what spring is)
> brings such self-things about
> which interests me
> as I loll today
> where I used to
> atop Bond's Hill

His posture recalls Whitman's in "Song of Myself" and his survey of Cape Ann recalls Thoreau, in *Walden*, the monarch of all he surveys—the only monarch Maximus chooses to be. And one element of the condition in men that accounts for such self-things as this poem is resistance, the *versus* the poem insists on as Maximus opposes himself ("myself") to King Alfred, to history ("tempestuous/ events"), to the tasks of the nation ("men's affairs"). He would obey only the imperatives of his own being:

> versus
> my own wrists and all my joints, versus speech's
>   connectives, versus the tasks
> I obey to

He obeys his own turnings and twistings, and verse, itself a turning, is his opposing force. He is defiant, in what is, according to Olson's poetics, his fitting task:

> I measure my song,
> measure the sources of my song,
> measure me, measure
> my forces

The bee to which he likens himself already buzzes here—the bee who has failed its object, the flowering plum, "and gone and got himself caught/ in my window," the bee whose buzzing comes of blockage, as Maximus' comes of impasse, from the closed window, yet teaches him to persist, to overcome what the concluding lines tell us has been an extreme and not altogether fruitful response to the invitation of spring:

> And the whirring of whose wings
> blots out the rattle of
> my machine)[37]

And so, in "Letter 10," which concludes this installment but opens into subsequent poems, he turns outward, to his public task:

> on founding: was it puritanism,
> or was it fish?
> And how, now, to found, with the sacred & the profane—
>   both of them—
> wore out
>   The beak's
> there. And the pectoral.
> The fins,
> for forwarding. [These images resume "Letter 1"]
>   But to do it anew, now that even fishing . . .

Past and present juxtapose. Founding *and* refounding. The past begets the present, and the way its possibilities were dispossessed is repeated, the destructive agents, like Endecott

Fitz Hugh Lane, *The Old Fort and Ten Pound Island, Gloucester*
(Courtesy Cape Ann Historical Association)

(later associated with J. B. Conant of Harvard), destroying the beneficent founders, like Roger Conant, whose Tudor house, the first house built in Gloucester, "sat [at Stage Fort]/ where [Maximus says] my own house has been/ where I am/ founded." The history to which this poem is prologue is of battle and destruction, of fierce oppositions, and it is still alive for Maximus because historical dispossession is also personal dispossession. Maximus' concern with origins—with the founding—is prompted by the present need to refound. "The green republic now renewed": this entry in early notes on "Man is Prospective" states his public theme. The correlative private theme involves what is often a reverie toward childhood—an imaginative repossession of place, as the true place, the "my countree" of being and well-being with which he closes.[38]

II   Yes, as Paul Blackburn complained, he twists:
         He sd, "You go all around the subject."
         And I sd, "I didn't know it was a sub-
         ject." He sd, "You twist" and I sd, "I do."

In what follows in "Letter 15," Maximus tells us that his poem will not make us comfortable because it does not follow a linear track to a foreseen destination. In addressing his method, he reminds us of his weaving and of the indivisibility of his concerns—and of his materials, since everything, as with the bird, everything (immediate observation, document, recollection, dream, myth) is the common real material of his poem. In the field there are no boundaries—artificial divisions, categories, classifications: *hierarchies* is his word—and the field he enters is not a subject but the reality he fronts, the place of his attentions. His subject, if he may be said to have one, is man-within-the-field; that, and the twisting and turning, the tropic insistence to which he has told us he obeys.

This explains both the small amount of early American history and the way in which Maximus presents it. "Letter 10" and the transition to Captain John Smith seem to promise historical treatment; Maximus has, among (with) others, a historiographical task. But *The Maximus Poems* is not a historical poem and history of that kind is ancillary to the his-story, the present acts, of the poet, who, in taking up history, is diverted from it by more immediate concerns. His concerns in this installment, all of it written in the spring of 1953, are continuous with those of the previous volume: origins (Gloucester's and his own), the difficulties of his stance (compounded as they are by the divorce of economics and poetry and his revulsion from present-day America), *tropos* and the honor that accords with it. More historical material of the period of discovery and colonization enters this installment than the earlier one, and also more personal material of childhood. There is a much stronger erotic current, and, most conspicuous, the incorporation of dreams. Which is to say that in living in and extending the field of the poem, Maximus finds himself fronting hitherto neglected aspects of his experience: the *tropos* of his childhood and youth, and the public, historical reasons for its faltering, for the pain of his twisting and turning.

Maximus, in "Letters 19 and 20," puts the case in terms of his baby daughter—in terms of clarity and confusion, waking and sleeping. "She wears [he says] her own face/ as we do not,/ until we cease to wear/ the clouds/ of all confusion. . . ." The Wordsworthian echo is significant: the glory he seeks is of new birth, the splendor that accompanies honorable acts.[39] And: "how your own child awakes/ how you have slumbered)," where the ambiguity of *your own child* tells us that the central fact of these poems is the awakening (recovery) of the child in him, a liberation of tropic force that would enable him to emulate his daughter's resistance—

And my daughter, naked
on the porch, sings
as best she can, and loudly,
back

—and that, in "Letter 22," restores the confidence, the assertiveness with which, he says, he moves "among my foes. . . ."

How to act is a central motive binding the historical past to
his own present concern with *tropos* and honor. The epigraphic
verse of "Letter 14" states it: ". . . on the puzzle/ of the nature
of desire [desire is later defined in tropic terms: "to tend to
move/ as though drawn"]"; ". . . on how men do use/ their
lives. . . ." John Hawkins, notable in this instance, is an
example of misusing one's life—is one of several historical
figures in this installment, John Smith, Columbus, Nathaniel
Bowditch, Stephen Higginson. Hawkins "broke open/ the
Spanish main" to slave trading, with consequences in war
comparable to those of Cortes in Mexico and with consequences later in Gloucester "for some of those who built/
white houses"; he did not plant a civilization but the feral
Roman present of American empire. Bowditch, founder of
insurance companies, "represents . . . that movement of NE
monies/ away from primary production & trade"; with him
finance capitalism may be said to begin. And Higginson, a
member of Congress in the early Republic, trafficked in arms
and disparaged the fishermen of Gloucester who, for Maximus,
engage in primary production, the true source of wealth. These
figures serve as nodes for Maximus' profound sense of the
betrayal of the New World and for his outrage with the present
begotten by it—the present in which "the true troubadours/ are
CBS" and poets, as he tells Creeley, are reduced to bartering
their wares among themselves. And because such men are also
"confusers" whose betrayal has profoundly tropic as well as
economic consequences—"was it puritanism,/ or was it fish?"

Lynn Swigart, "Ten Pound Island from State Fort, Gloucester"
(Courtesy Lynn Swigart)

puts these consequences too—outrage is now variously and openly expressed: in the contrapuntal response to Sir Richard Hawkins' statement of intent, in the punning on pejorocracy in "Letter 16" on Bowditch and Higginson, and in the oath provoked by Higginson's letter to Vice-President Adams.

The great exemplary figure is Captain John Smith. Mentioned in the earlier installment, he now enters the poem, significantly in Maximus' recollection of childhood in "Letter 11." This remarkable poem is a turning that provides a new departure because in it Maximus sets out the idea of his-story later developed in *The Special View of History* and finds that in childhood he was already intimate with the major elements of the his-story he is now enacting so hesitantly and with such difficulty. Like the previous poem, "Letter 11" addresses the founding of Gloucester and involves Maximus' founding, his childhood play in Stage Fort Park where "Historie [the romance of it is in the archaic spelling]/ come bang [as it is visually presented here] into the midst of/ our game!" The poem begins with Tablet Rock, commemorating Roger Conant's arbitration of incipient conflict between Captain Hewes of the fishermen settled at Gloucester by the Dorchester Company and Captain Miles Standish of the Plymouth Colony. The episode is focal, and Maximus returns to it in later installments, because "was it puritanism,/ or was it fish?" is the historical question he wishes to answer. But it is also focal because it took place where Maximus tells us he is founded, and that is the deeper concern (of the indented verses) to which his historical inquiry immediately yields. That, too, he finds, is what "The rock reads. . . ." For implicit in his recollection of scaling the rock—the verse manifests it—is the fact that he *still* knows the rock "by my belly and torn nails," and what is of unusual interest is how this "triumph" works with the central historical episode of opposition to lead on to Maximus' recollection of his father's death and his wish that his burial had established his nativity. By this route his father's life becomes the chief instance of the idea of his-story, and the extent to which it is a family matter is told later in the story of William, John, and Richard Hawkins—a story in which the sons are not as worthy as the father. But another relationship of father and son figures here: the child is the father of the man, and, in realizing this, Maximus is also telling us "how I got to/ what I say. . . ."[40]

The John Smith of Maximus' childhood is the romantic figure who had adventured in Hungary and Transylvania and had named Cape Ann "Tragabigzanda" after a Turkish princess. He is a figure of pageant, of "Historie," and Maximus vividly recollects the wonder of his appearance in his childhood game even as he tells from his adult perspective Smith's unusual achievement as a discoverer. This account of childhood has erotic color and echoes Williams' passage on the lovers in the park in *Paterson II* and Crane's evocation of Captain Smith in an episode of childhood in *The Bridge*. This shows Olson's close familiarity with precedent poems and reminds us of another aspect of the occasion of this poem—his review of Bradford Smith's *Captain John Smith: His Life & Legend*.[41] Though Smith's book was published in 1953, internal evidence suggests that Olson did not have it during the period of the poem's composition and that his review, along with the reply to Grover Smith mentioned in it, was a defense against the inhospitable reception of his work. The review is a valuable gloss because in it Olson upholds his choice of Smith as a central figure ("The name is Smith, John Smith. And that's what I'm bucking"), mentions other figures in the poems (Pytheus, Columbus, La Cosa, Stendhal, Elbert Hubbard), and vehemently rehearses the theme of advertising ("Why I sing Smith is this, that the *geographic*, the sudden *land* of the place is in there, not described, not local, not represented—like all advertisements, all the shit now pours out, the American Road, the

filthiness, of graphic words, Mo-dess . . ."). And just as valuable
is his defense of Smith's prose style—his own also convincing
us that "style is, the man"—and, as in the reply to Grover
Smith, his championing of the then deprecated work of Pound,
Williams, Crane, and "some others." *The Maximus Poems*, we
remember, were not written in an auspicious time and were
necessarily adversary.

Maximus doesn't so much buck the Smith of his childhood
recollection—for what he remembers is Smith with the swoon-
ing princess in his arms—as summon with it the equally
cherished Smith who "sounded/ her [New England's] bays, ran
her coast, and wrote down/ Algonquin so scrupulously Massachusetts . . ."—the Smith whose virtue of discovering is one
with writing, who, Olson says in the review, put New England
down "in prose I can feel now the way his boat bent along the
same coasts I know." ("Mind you," he adds, "he was doing it
for one of the very first times, it's a different thing, to feel a
coast, an ancient thing this Smith had, what men had to have
before Pytheas, to move.") Yet this Smith is an underdog. He
"got shoved aside" and was not fully credited with the founding he made possible nor appreciated by the theocracy for
recognizing the wealth of fish, "the eye he had/ for what New
England offered. . . ."

Smith is another model of the self with whom Maximus
identifies. He is a discoverer, namer, map-maker, who has the
distinction of so faithfully charting things we recognize them.
And he is a lover of the princess—the Goddess. The boys who
witness his "Historie" already know the lay of the land and
have parted the bushes; they, too, know the Goddess. And
what they see in play is the scenario of Maximus' present task.
"Actors," Maximus says, "where I have learned another sort of/
play"—where he has learned to be *act-er* in the field. The contrast here is also one of the wholeness and wondership of child-

hood and the incompleteness and ownership of adulthood. It is true that Smith got shoved aside but in the context of the verse thus introduced—in the context of theocracy—his discomfiture is Maximus' and points to the lack in himself of the "femininities" he says Smith had. Smith speaks of himself as a "'sowe'" and so provides Maximus a needed model of completeness, the androgyne, as he says later on.[42] Discovery and mapping for Maximus have this psychic goal.

He identifies with Smith in both his successes and failures. In the deservedly praised confession of "Letter 12," Smith is a measure of "agilities," a man, unlike Maximus, at home at sea and in the world, not, as he says, "estranged/ from that which was most familiar." Smith's growth, we know, was not delayed like Maximus', nor was he, himself a poet and writer, divorced from the "world's/ businesses." This self-deprecatory confession turns back to the exercises for the morning of "Tyrian Businesses" and to the self-vindication of "Letter 9," and points ahead to the consideration of poetry and economics in "Letter 15," where Smith's "The Sea Marke," the only poem incorporated in *The Maximus Poems*, serves as a landmark of English verse and as a warning to Maximus ("If in or outward you be bound,/ do not forget to sound").

Maximus' soundings here are inward: he is troubled by his passive, contemplative, secondhand scholar's life. He has not, he feels, been equal to his notion of stance; his capabilities are negative and he has "had to be given/ a life, love, and from one man/ the world." Even his *tropos*, he feels, was dependent, not freely moving but moved by others and by resistance: "But the stem of me,/ this I took from their welcome,/ or their rejection, of me. . . ."[43] Thus his dismay is owing not only to lack of agility, of competent activity in the world, but to the tropic faltering that causes it, the argument for which he raises but does not gladly accept:

> ... not content with the man's argument
> that such postponement
> is now the nature of
> obedience,
>> that we are all late
>> in a slow time,
>> that we grow up many
>> And the single
>> is not easily
>> known

And yet he has negative capability. As he says in taking more positive stock of himself, he is "a wind/ and water man," who, unlike Ferrini, knows where weather comes from. Even "sitting here," in the dancing-sitting-down that constitutes the poem, his stance is of the right kind.

> But sitting here
> I look out as a wind
> and water man, testing

He misses confirmation but he knows that the business he is necessarily about concerns the "single," is much more involved with his psychological readiness for self-action than with the "world's/ businesses. . . ." The singular in "undone business" insists on this as does the sea, the unconscious that he has already been moved to explore:

> It is undone business
> I speak of, this morning
> with the sea
> stretching out
> from my feet

From his feet: everywhere, for everyone, there is a world to discover, to map, to found, and, as Smith said, he can only learn to tell it "by the conttinuall hazard of my life."

To some extent Maximus' revulsion with pejorocracy is a

gauge of these difficulties. The inadequacy expressed in "Letter 12" probably accounts for the disdain in "The Song and Dance of" (Letter 13). Here indeed is a "dreamless present" of "merchandise men" in which it is impossible to move, in which the truth and promise of the New World has been betrayed by lies, and the Goddess, embalmed, is merely Jean Harlow (the sex symbol of Olson's youth), "As she lies, all/ white." The title, with its reference to vaudeville, recalls Crane's poem on the National Winter Garden and its comparable burlesque of Pocahontas (the Goddess of *The Bridge*) and Williams' treatment of this eminent American theme in "The Desert Music" —it was published in 1952, and Olson's poem in 1954—and reminds us that Maximus treats the betrayal from an American point of view. In the contexts of lies, Columbus, "the Mediterranean/ man," seems to be another betrayer, a foil to Smith, not a discoverer so much as the bearer of an idea of America formed in Europe, "where all the previous celebrating/ comes from." To some extent he is, though the ambivalence with which Maximus treats him and the unusual reversal of values—in no other poem does Maximus consider the promoters of North Atlantic fishing and exploration "conquistadors"—suggest that his contempt arises from the betrayal of the idea of America he himself cherishes.

The juxtaposition of sections I and II proposes several possible readings, among them a favorable one. The new departure of the section may not initially confirm the lies but call up the Goddess who has been betrayed. "'Always the land,'" it begins, a famous passage from Columbus' journal used by Williams in *In the American Grain*,

> "Always the land
> was of the same beauty,
> and the fields
> very green"

And in the meditation that follows—

> The Isles
> of the Very Green. Meneptha,
> then. The previous Caribbean,
> when the sea first
> awoke to men's minds. Cyprus.
> Or which True Verte?

—Maximus, his mind filled with references to the early Mediterranean world treated by Bérard, is himself a Mediterranean man, in this instance concerned with the birth of consciousness that was also the birth of Venus. His own comparable experience in Yucatan is already at work here and emerges at the end of the section in a passage recalling the poem to Gerhardt and his concurrence in Pound's view of favoring climate:

> And the nerve ends
> stay open on this horst
> of the heat Equator
> as surely as it is evident they did
> —an American sd they did,
> the last one to celebrate
> the old axis. . . .

Maximus' feeling in this poem is for the South, for the warm, erotic, and pagan; for the world where Olson said that he could wear his flesh. The North, though serving interests usually valued by him, interests however that now produce "the meretricious," is as barren as it once seemed to treasure-seekers. He tells us this in the emptiness of the following widely-spaced lines:

> Venus
> does not arise from
> these waters. Fish
> do.

And he tells us that he would have her rise—as much as Crane and Williams he seeks this end—and that chiefly because she doesn't the Mediterranean view does not hold.

"Letter 14" treats the Hawkinses ("the family/ span America from the finding/ to the settling of those fishermen") and fulfills the intent of the epigraph, to show us "how men do use// their lives." But its deeper interest, and continuity with the previous poems, is in Maximus' meditation on "the puzzle/ of the nature of desire." This is his morning work, and again he consults the dictionary, finding under *constellate*, "to unite in one lustre/ as stars," a definition he feels applies to *dreams* and to his lack of singleness. His own dream of explosive sexuality-come-to-nothing is evidence of this, of inability to contact the Goddess who has (masterfully) created an appropriate situation by backing "a station-wagon/ underneath a porch"! Even in his dream he finds his reluctance silly, and in the subsequent meditation names "the sense of vulgarity as separating me" and sees himself as Prufrock ("after the passage-way of the toilets/ and the whores . . ."). Here the recollection of the movie-house, merging possibly with the Old Howard, where John Finch says that he and Olson were "enchanted by burlesque" and witnessed the rape of Leda by the swan, once more summons Crane, his ambivalence in "National Winter Garden," even his use of the second person.[44] And in its way the recollection achieves a reversal comparable to his:

> [the] ceiling
> as they used to have, glowing
> as of stars, by god, pricked out
> so that, in the bad grotto of the bad scripts,
> you had the firmament
> over your head

By god, indeed! The stars pricked out uniting in one lustre so that in that "bad" grotto he is Geb happily arched by Nut!

The vulgarity admitted here ("fundament" plays off "firma-

ment," itself a "bad" pun) is salutary, in the spirit of the recollection, like "plugged" in his recollection of Conant and
Standish in "Letter 11." It calls him back to the dictionary
where he notes the definition of *tropism*, and it prompts
another recollection, this one of the young man at the Gloucester School of Little Theatre standing "in shorts, in front of
her [the teacher, a Goddess more puritan than pagan],/ doing,/
her bidding: 'Buttocks/ in & under, buttocks. . . .'" This lesson
in posture—"It was in our minds/ what she put there"—had its
utility but was more repressive than liberating and did not
promote the growth of the "ripe sun-flower" nor enable the
"annunciative man" (of "Apollonius of Tyana") "as he was
shown, arms out, legs out, leaping," but, as he says, punning,
"another Adam, a nether/ man. . . ." And so the meditation on
his own tropic difficulties "stems," to use his own powerful
polysemous verbal, reaching the point where he realizes that
the sense of the sash-weight, the "ape's line" she called for, is
also that of explosive sexuality released, which is possible, he
tells us,

> if you are drawn, [answer *tropos* and move toward the
>   Goddess]
> if you do unite, [in *one* lustre]
> if you do be
> pithecanthropus

The last line asks us to supply "erectus" and to see in the comparable open spacing of the verse an answer to the previous
verse on the absence of Venus.

Which takes us back to the historical argument of that
poem, the argument now resumed here. The history of the
Hawkinses is one of treasure, of Negro slave-trading, not of
fish, and constitutes for Maximus one of the two elements in
the "moral struggle" of America. Yes, economics is a moral
science and in *The Maximus Poems* must always be con-

sidered as one term in the "interlocking trio" that Olson treats
in the discussion of *tropos* in *The Special View of History*.
The "inclusive factors in the single life," he says, are *Eros,
Economos, Ethos*.[45] This trio of terms, none of which, he
believes, makes sense without the others, has both private and
public bearing and provides a convenient way into the poems.
The moral struggle of the founding is as divisive as Maximus',
and if he prefers fish to treasure, which is of course the sound
choice, it is not because of the outcome of the fishing—"the
hat-makers of La Rochelle, the fish-eaters of Bristol" under-
write the "merchandise men"—but because the discovery of
the fishing banks anticipates the discovery of the New World
and is associated by him with the primordial unity of Pytheus'
sludge. The most important passage in the Hawkins' chronicle
concerns Pytheus, the first explorer to describe the Atlantic,
whose appearance in subsequent poems is always significant:

> it was two things, first: the Banks
> which the Basques, maybe,
> first found, though Pytheus
> had he sounded the sludge
> he took the water and the air and the sky
> all to be one of
>   Ultima Thule

Ultima Thule, so conspicuously set out, may be glossed by
Olson's letter to Creeley, in which he comments on its relation to *Tule*, the Mayan word for "place of origin," the place
where "'the great father-priest' . . . [gives] the first captain . . . a
present . . . ," a place, clearly, of unity and cosmological
creation.[46]

The historical inquiry begun in this poem carries over into
the historiographical treatment of Bowditch's reputed naviga-
tional skill in "Letter 15." Here it founders on "lies," and
because the historiographical task of recovering fact is heavy,
Maximus yields, by way of comment on his own poems and

Smith's, to his own "ruine," to the miserable economic state of
poets and the usurpation of poetry by advertising. Parody here,
and the Poundishness of "Letter 16," in which historical
investigation explains pejorocracy, show him at impasse. He
has traced a history of decline and even as it supplies the
causes it tallies with his own difficulties and dismay.

The historical sequence within the poems is not chronological
but imaginative—history, as Emerson said, may be an apologue
of our being and becoming—and in the subsequent poems Maximus recovers his confidence by rediscovering the New World.
He does this in two ways and from two directions: by moving
from the East with the discoverers in the outer (and inner)
sea to the New World and by moving from the West, from
Worcester, his "inland waters," to Gloucester. Like "Letters 15
and 16," "On first Looking out through Juan de la Cosa's Eyes"
(Letter 17) and "The Twist" (Letter 18) are companion poems,
and nothing shows better the incredible liberation in the
resumption of this installment than the juxtaposition of these
sets.

   "On first Looking out through Juan de la Cosa's Eyes" is as
brilliant as its title and marks an occasion—a discovery in history—as momentous for Maximus as Keats's discovery of Chap-
man's Homer. (And for Maximus, his Homer, in evidence in
this installment, is Victor Bérard's, the Homer of *Did Homer
Live?* and *Les Pheniciens et l'Odyssee.*) By looking out through
La Cosa's eyes, Maximus sees (and sees how to see) the New
World new, for the first time; sees it as sailors in the long history of discovery saw it, emerging from the nothingness of
Martin Behaim's globe, "out of the mists// (out of Pytheus'
sludge. . . .// out of// waters. . . ." La Cosa helps him recapture
the enthusiasm he had for Smith and for the methodological
work of his poems, the mapping in terms of which he associates Smith and La Cosa ("Smith got it into words, didn't, as

Juan de la Cosa did it so handsomely, by a map").[47] Before La
Cosa, he says, "nobody/ could have/ a mappemunde" and
perhaps before Columbus, who figures here more as a representative of treasure-seeking than as a discoverer, nobody
could have the *imago mundi*, the sense of the earth as *orb*, the
"Earth," as Olson explains in *Causal Mythology*, "as a *One* . . .
[as] conceivably a knowable, a seizable, a single, and *your*
thing."[48] Columbus' image of the world as a round ball with a
prominence like a nipple is as significant as La Cosa's map, for
it gives Maximus the World as woman—in terms of "love and
woman," which Olson later said, is the poet's subject, in terms
of Our Lady of Good Voyage ("Virgin Mundi")—and provides
an important link with the "The Twist," the "flower" Olson
planned to offer next, the poem, he noted, that "Ed Dorn said
was where I really started to get on."[49]

The passage in "On first Looking out . . ." on the cost of life
at sea and the memorial ceremony of throwing flowers into the
Annisquam River anticipates this "flower." "The Twist," a
wonderful (-filled) poem, much of it recollection and dream,
tells of Maximus' twisted (intertwined) discoveries of Gloucester, sexuality, and poetry. The poem enacts its tropic
theme, uniting its elements in one lustre. It locates the tropic
core of childhood, and twists with the flowing/flowering (from
neap to full tide) of his experience, an essentially outward and
thrusting possession of the New England landscape that comprises his world.

Maximus recalls how, as a child, in the company of his
father, he discovered space (always feminine) in gathering
May-flowers and walnuts, and in riding the trolley to "the
outer-land/ (where it is Sunday," a landscape, the "promised
land," whose eros, troubling him as a child, he now brings
forward in the recognition that "my wife has a new baby/ in a
house at the end of/ such a [trolley] line. . . ." The poem
presents an idyllic boyhood in Worcester, tells of the journey

to Gloucester—in a lovely line, "I go up-dilly, elevated, tene-
ment/ down"—and recovers the rainy day when, five or six
years old, he first saw the sea, and the St. Valentine's Day
storm fifteen years later that prompted his first poem (about
the Annisquam, its full tide now associated with the Goddess)
and, he now recognizes, makes the sea his unitary source as
much as the acknowledgment of it in Pytheus' sludge:

> The harbor the same
> the night of the St. Valentine
> storm: the air
> sea   ground   the same, tossed
> ice   wind   snow   (Pytheus) one

The poem merges the boy of five, the young man of twenty, and
the present self, and it is true to dream-work because, though
the material of dreams concerns discovery, the country in
them is familiar: "I recognize/ the country not discovera. . . ."
   What he recognizes is the conjunction of sea and Goddess,
how his coming to consciousness, in terms of both inner and
outer seas, is an erotic/tropic awakening. The childhood-
fairytale dreams of cake houses and toy houses, like all that
concerns his "waters," involve a nameless female presence (the
"She" we also find in Williams' *In the American Grain*): "She
was staying,/ after she left me/ in an apartment house/ was like
a cake. . . ." Abandoned, he searches for her in his childhood as
well as in later dream landscapes, recalling another explosive
sexual episode of his Harvard years and even an explicit wish
to sleep with Schwartz' mother-in-law (an actual woman
Olson had gone boating with on the rushing Annisquam River
and who was very much present to him, he says, when he first
wrote about myth).[50] The recollection of the night of the St.
Valentine's storm occurs in this sequence, and the storm,
linked with "cakes falling," enacts sexual possession, the
"whiteness," Maximus says in the subsequent section about
waking in a toy house, that "sent me. . . ." The child in the

dream is not entirely comfortable with this stunning waking,
whose evident meaning Maximus recognizes in connection
with the Cut:

>   I am seized
> —not so many nights ago
> by the sight of the river
> exactly there at the Bridge
>
> where it goes out & in

Maximus recognizes the relation of eros and tropos, and the
necessity of singleness, wholeness, unity of self—the need he
has to contact what Williams called the "supplying female."
He recognizes, particularly in the rushing waters of the river,
the full force of creative power, power at once sexual and
poetic, and makes us realize that his need in poetry, like
Williams', is a need to discover (enter) and marry the world.
The twisting of the concluding lines expresses in flowering an
immense energy, a release and overflow of being:

> the tide roars over
>
>   some curves off,
> when it's the river's turn, shoots
> calyx and corolla by the dog
>
>   (August,
> the flowers break off
>
>   but the anther,
> the filament of now, the mass
> drives on,
>
>   the whole of it
> coming,
> to this pin-point
> to turn
>
>   in this day's sun,
> in this veracity
> there, the waters the several of them the roads
> here, a blackberry blossom

"Veracity" ties back to "la verité" in the preceding poem, and the passage itself recalls the annual floral tribute mentioned there. Even in this moment of unparalleled fullness of life, Maximus remembers the risks of living and the apprehension of death that moved him to resistance and poetry.

Tropos is resistant, and tropos discovered doubly so. "Homo maximus," Duncan remarked, "wrests his life from the under-world as the Gloucester fisherman wrests his from the sea."[51] This is the conspicuous work of the previous poems, and we now find Maximus in "Letter 19" not only standing up to the importuning minister but claiming resistance to God: "And turned away,/ turned. . . ." Such twisting prompts his concern with honor in the concluding poems. Maximus knows that the language of honor, like that of heraldry, may be considered "Professor stuff," but he employs it for several reasons: be-cause as we already know from "Tyrian Businesses," the "nasturtium/ is [his] shield"; because honor accords with his notion of stance, of a universe in which we are no longer clothed in the garments of hierarchical thought but, standing naked in the face of reality, must, by our own acts, the deci-sions we make each instant, clothe ourselves in honor; and because honor is also Lady Luck, the Goddess whose favor is necessary:

> and just at the moment that the heat's on,
> when it's your dice or mine, all
> or nothing, that she be there
> in all her splendor

And he honors Honor because he believes She favors the tropic (veracious) action of the self, acts that reveal us to ourselves (". . . we are only/ as we find out we are"), and those acts in which we trouble to lift the real to clarity.

These qualifications are important. As we learn in the dream with which "Letter 22" begins, the discovery of the uncon-

scious may easily yield to the "relaxation" Maximus opposes
in "Tyrian Businesses" when he speaks of "children,/ who
want to go back, who want to lie down/ in Tiamat." Chaos, he
now insists, "is not our condition" and "All,/ has no honor as
quantity." It is true, as his dream of eating the polishing cloth
shows—its colors are alchemical black and gold and it is indistinguishable from "the billowing dress/ the big girl wears/
every so often"—it is true that man is an "omnivore" and "eats
anything/ every so often. . . ." But chaos is attacked by work, as
Olson says in "A Syllabary for a Dancer," or, as Maximus says,
by man-the-"amorvore," the man for whom, we learned at the
outset, "love is form."[52] And this form, realized everywhere in
the activity of these poems, is merely the imperfect form we
manage at risk; it is not perfect, responsive to neither the
hierarchical perfection of God, or Beauty, but only to the atten-
tive (selecting) self:

> And the attention
> in each of us
> is that one, not the other
> not the perfect one. Beauty,
> is too quick
> for time

Maximus readily admits that dreams, opening the way to
Tiamat, are his facts as much as any others. But the dreams of
these poems, turning on tropos, turn him forward not back.
Though the poems confirm the want of the kind of action
Maximus misses, they themselves comprise honorable action.
In them Maximus risks descent—to use Williams' term—in
order to ascend, to lift the real, to make it clear. He enters the
sea and begins to make his mappemunde. He pushes against
limits, with the happy result of achievement he acknowledges
in the dream of maneuvering the car. For now he is the driver.
And though this dream proposes the dream material at the
beginning of the poem, he concludes with it because, as in the

case of the car in the dreams of "As the Dead Prey Upon Us," to drive as he now does is proof of adult responsibility, of taking up the world's business. Even more, such poetic activity is heroic, worthy of celebration as much as other courageous deeds poets tell, worth "stopping the, battle,// to get down. . . ."

III   So much now for movement of the vertical of the self. There are, in this installment, other turnings and twistings, those of history on a horizontal plane. "Letter 23" is a new beginning, or a resumption of the historical inquiry begun in "Letter 10." The format is new, and in respect to method and basic theme this letter, the only letter of the installment written at Black Mountain College, is prefatory. It begins after the fashion of *Call Me Ishmael* with facts ("The facts are") and enacts Maximus' practice of *'istorin*, Herodotus' "finding out for oneself." Maximus is not concerned with general or abstract truth but with particular evidence ("Altham says/ Winslow/ was at Cape Ann in April,/ 1624"). He works in behalf of the "restoration of the principle of fact. . . ."[53]

Maximus fulfills this purpose in the subsequent poems, notably those on the rush and decline of fishing at Gloucester during the years 1623–1627, where his practice supports Olson's contention that "if you have ever cut behind any American event or any presentation, you will know the diminishment [in the usual academic practice of history] I am . . . asserting."[54] "Letters 23–32" give this installment its marked historical character not only because they provide the historical center of *The Maximus Poems*, the fullest, extended treatment of the founding of Gloucester, but because the poet's activity in these poems (as in another sequence, "West") is conspicuously that of a historian finding out for himself, discovering and pondering the evidence, and restoring the fullness of a crucial event ("the littlest is the same as the very big, if you look at it").[55]

Maximus practices the new history demanded by the new humanism. Call it "careful localism," to borrow a phrase from Olson's comment on Pausanias; or consider it a history of "men and things, not of societies and commodities," as he said of Herodotus. Referring to the pure localism of Hopi space-time, he told Elaine Feinstein that "such localism can now be called: what you find out for yrself (*'istorin*) keeps all accompanying circumstance"; and he told Dorn that one also gets "the space-time thing" by "the imagining of men," that is, as Maximus does with Winthrop, Osmund Dutch, and others, by imaginatively entering another's space-time, space reminding us not to neglect the particular geography ("You want geography: the *locus* is now both place & time [topology]").[56] The process of historical imagination that Olson commends and Maximus follows is exemplified by Victor Bérard's work on the *Odyssey*. The historian moves "from 1) a place person thing event—to—2) the naming of it—to—3) the reenactment or representation of it, in other words/ object name image or story. . . ." In this way he avoids traditional written history—dependence on "literary antecedence," "fiction to fiction"—and finds himself in the field, continuous with millennia, intimately connected with the past by "acts-of-imagination . . . -arising-directly-from-fierce-penetration-of-all-past-persons, places, things and actions-as-data (objects)."[57] For Maximus, centered in Gloucester, historical time becomes space in which with this fierce penetration he freely moves.

Maximus' historical and historiographical concerns account for much of the excitement of these poems. Sometimes he directly presents the documentary evidence, as in "The Record" (Letter 29); sometimes he meditates on the evidence or the search, speaking to himself ("Letter 23": "The facts are"; "But here is the first surprise"; "What we have here—and literally in my own front yard, as I sd to Merk"; "What we have in this field is the scraps among these fishermen"); sometimes he speaks directly to us, as in "Maximus, to Gloucester" (Letter 25): "I don't mean, just like that, to put down/ the Widow Babson. . . ." There is the excitement of search rewarded in "The Record" ("Here we have it": the Weymouth Port Book, page 873), for what we have *is* the record, immediate contact with essential particular evidence, which is charged for us both by the fact that it is present testimony, the past restored to our present, and by the place of this poem in the sequence. We should not overlook Maximus' excitement and the tribute of this transposition, for one of the discoveries of great moment to him is Frances Rose-Troup's *John White: The Patriarch of Dorchester and the Founder of Massachusetts*. Rose-Troup, as the evidence she supplies tells us ("fox/ racons/ martyns/ otter/ muskuatche/ beaver": I cite what Maximus himself cites again in "Letter, May 2, 1959"), is a historian of the kind Maximus values, like Frederick Merk, his teacher at Harvard; and her careful localism may be measured by comparison with Samuel Eliot Morison's *Builders of the Bay Colony*, a book, she complained, levying on her work without sufficient acknowledgment—a graceful but less evidential and authoritative study that Maximus had relied on in earlier installments for information about the founding and the career of John Smith.

As important as the evidence is the accompanying effort of the poet-historian to imaginatively verify it—to see it new—and to see its representative historical value. Here, Maximus' practice follows that of Carl Sauer, a geographer who troubled to find out for himself, who tested the received historical record against his own personal experience of the human landscape. Sauer belongs to the "company," Maximus says, that "throw[s] down hierarchy" and insists that "the history of weeds/ is a history of man"; he has not followed historical canon but entered space to read the history of man in terms of his use of place.[58] And Maximus' practice, unacknowledged by him, also follows that of Thoreau, who recovered history by means of his own experience, his own original relation to nature. In "a Plantation a beginning" (Letter 24), for example, Maximus lives into his realization of the hardship and cost of planting by way of his own present awareness of the weather:

> I sit here on a Sunday
> with grey water, the winter
> staring me in the face[59]

This immediately calls up and verifies the words of John White's *The Planters' Plea*, the archaic spelling vividly recovering rather than distancing historical reality, which in any case for Maximus belongs to the same space:

> "the Snow lyes indeed
> about a foot thicke
> for ten weekes" John White
>
> warns any prospective
> planter

Maximus also realizes—and evokes—the rocky shore from his own experience: "where I as a young man berthed/ a skiff and scarfed/ my legs to get up rocks. . . ." And difference as well as similarity of experience enables him to reconstitute the past and, as in the contrast of present "leisure" and past "worke" in the recollection of Stage Fort Park, to judge the present, as in fact his entire historical inquiry does, by making us realize the heavy human and financial cost of beginning ("don't mistake there wasn't/ money"; "It cost $30,000//to get/ Gloucester/ started").

Stage Head is the geographical center of *The Maximus Poems* and the historical center of the letters that treat the planting. It is also the personal center: as Maximus says, in "Letter 25," "all the hill and hollow/ I know best in all the

world"—his *place*, as Olson indicates in a letter to Joyce
Benson ("I was raised in a house which is the ear on the g of
Stage (Fort) on the back cover [of *The Maximus Poems*]").⁶⁰
"Letter 25," part of the sequence on the planting, provides this
perspective. Again, the "beginning" is deeply linked with his
own, and Maximus is explicitly concerned with imagining the
beginning and acquiring for himself what the men who first
planted had—the "nakedness" that enables them to see it new.
Now his memory—and much of our memory of all that precedes this poem—gathers at this geographical center:

> But just there lies the thing, that "fisherman's Field"
> (Stage Head, Stage Fort, and now and all my childhood
> a down-dilly park for cops and robbers, baseball, firemen's
> hose, North End Italian Sunday spreads, night-time
>   Gloucester
> monkey-business) stays the first place Englishmen
> first felt the light and winds, the turning, from that view,
> of what is now the City—gulls the same but otherwise
>   the sounds
> were different for those fourteen men, probably the ocean
> ate deeper at the shore, crashed further up at Cressy's (why
> they took their shelter either side of softer Stage Head
>   and let
> Tablet Rock buff for them the weather side: on the lee,
> below the ridge which runs from my house straight to
>   Tablet Rock
> these Dorset Somerset men built the Company house
>   which Endicott
> thought grand enough to pull it down and haul it all the
>   way
> to Salem for his Governor's abode . . .

Maximus is aware that his present position in a rented house
on Fort Point, like that of the house of his childhood, is a vantage of historiographical utility because it permits him "to
view/ those men/ who saw her [Gloucester]/ first" as nakedly,
as freshly/ firstly, as they viewed Cape Ann in 1623.

That he can do this, and that "Gloucester can view/ those men," is a reversal, a turning outward to beginnings, an imaginative newing by becoming aware of what newness was, cost, meant. This turning is an essential act of the poem, and the passage is important because it defines nakedness, Maximus' preferred condition:

> He left him naked,
> the man said, and
> nakedness
> is what one means
>
> that all start up
> to the eye and soul
> as though it had never
> happened before

Historical inquiry, of the kind exemplified in these poems, has made this possible; and for the time being, "The point is not," as Maximus says, "that Beverly/ turned out to be their home,/ that Conant Norman Allen Knight/ Balch Palfrey Woodbury Tilly Gray . . ."—the point is not what followed the beginning, what the possessors (nicely echoing Emerson's "Hamatreya") made of it, but that he has recovered it:

> A year that year
> was new to men
> the place had bred
> in the mind of another
>
> John White had seen it
> in his eye
> but fourteen men
> of whom we know eleven
>
> twenty-two eyes
> and the snow flew
> where gulls now paper
> the skies
>
> where fishing continues
> and my heart lies

Imperatives psychic and historical meet in Maximus' desire
to repossess the beginning, the origin. Like the mythmaker,
in C. Kerényi's account, Maximus-the-historian is concerned
with what "originally was," with the grounding and founding
(both from *begründen*) of Gloucester. For him, a *Begründer*
("Beginner—and interested in beginnings," as Olson said of
Melville), the historical refounding is concurrent with—a
condition of—psychological (mythical) refounding. He himself
observes that the founding of Gloucester is a historical rhyme
—and in later volumes supports Kerényi's view that foundings
of this kind are "hallowed by a mythologem of origination." [61]
Yet simply as history Maximus is concerned with genesis.
Like Sauer, he knows the importance of small beginnings
("culture hearths") and men unheralded by history. He appreciates and practices what Sauer calls "genetic human geography"; and Sauer's account of his discipline—his field work—
helps us understand Maximus' activity in the field of the
poem. "It is real discovery," Sauer says, ". . . to take old docu-
ments into the field and relocate forgotten places, to see where
the wilderness [or the city, for that matter] has repossessed
scenes of active life, to note what internal migrations of inhabitants and of their productive bases have occurred. There
comes a time in such study when the picture begins to fit together ["Letter 28" is fittingly called "The Picture"], and one
comes to that high moment when the past is clear, and the
contrasts with the present are understood." [62]
Maximus also treats the founding of Gloucester as atten-
tively as he does because it is a representative event of the
larger historical conflict of the time ("Letter 22" concludes
with remarks on the significance of the fight for Stage Head in
respect to "mercantilism" and "nascent capitalism"); because
it is an event in the still longer history of human migration
("the motion/ (the Westward motion)/ comes here,/ to land");
and because it is a frontier situation that anticipates the sub-

sequent stages—the dispersion—of the movement westward. Our greater familiarity with the later stages—fur-trapping, the Mormon trek, the gold rush—helps us evoke conditions appropriate to the fourteen men who first planted on the rocky shore. Their adventure, Maximus says, was "the adventure// of the new frontier/ (not boom, or gold,/ the lucky strike,// but work, a fishing. . . ." And "1622 to 1626 was the fish rush," Gloucester was a "cowtown," and Stage Fight, which he re-enacts in these terms, was "a Western." The jumble of the large block paragraph opening "So Sassafras" (Letter 26) is the most evocative presentation of these themes, a verbal event recapturing the energies and multiple purposes of the historical event.[63]

Within the sequence on the planting, "Letters 30, 31, and 32," which conclude it, form a smaller sequence or set, as Olson called them, of especially significant poems.[64] In "Some Good News" (Letter 30), Maximus again brings forward John Smith, now as one who in the long chronicle of discovery "changed/ everything"—named Cape Ann "so it's stuck,/ and Englishmen . . .// sat down, planted/ fisheries/ so they've stayed put. . . ." Smith—"old mother Smith"—is now the central figure of a meditation on the creative accidents of history. With Columbus, General Grant, Melville, and Maximus himself, he is an exemplar of an acceptable kind of hero, the neglected and passive man who meets the occasion in history that calls him into action. Maximus takes his theme from Melville's *Moby-Dick*: "the hustings of the Divine Inert" (treated by Olson in "Equal, That Is, to the Real Itself"), and addresses his own difficulties: the Oedipal ("a man's/ struggle// with Caesar's/ dream/ that he'd been intimate/ with his mother"); the related concern with being a man of power or a man of achievement; and the turning with which he is still involved, the emergence of the proper hero from "the collapse/ of the previous// soul. . . ."[65] In this letter, with its angry awareness of current history and apprehension over the future, Maximus tells the occasion that calls him forth and, himself no bearer of "good news," summons us to a newing that may provide it. This is the public intent of *The Maximus Poems*. Maximus' work is comparable to Smith's in *A Description of New England* (1616). "It wasn't new," he writes, "what happened,/ at Cape Ann. It's where,/ and when it// did. Smith,/ at Monhegan/, 1614, and telling/ about it, in a book,/ 1616. . . ."

Where "Letter 30" tells of the importance of the "small" news of the planting, "Letters 31 and 32" tell of the subsequent Commonwealth and the betrayal of the newing. "Stiffening, in the Master Founders' Wills" (Letter 31) treats the "faulting" or fracture of the Puritan establishment and the stiffening in doctrine, the inward turning or refusal to meet the conditions of "American space," occasioned by this. The "Moses men," according to Maximus, who at the outset names the agency of change by relating Descartes to Boston's settling, "tried/ to twist back to Covenantal/ truth" the new truths of individualism and secularism. But backward twistings are never efficacious, and the consequence, as Williams had already observed in *In the American Grain*, was "sweet ["dry"] souls to whom/ outward was inward/ act when inward-outward/ was, by being here, being// turned. . . ." Also, as a refusal of the Corinth-movement, the creative accident-occasion of history so much the concern of the previous poem, it followed that the welcome bronze of that destructive fire was here only a "cooling into mettle-/ someness. . . ." Winthrop, the prominent figure of this letter, tried to forestall change and secure the Commonwealth (a polity he likens to a family), when he himself had experienced the change in environment on a winter's walk in the woods and had acted on economic changes in the arrangements he made with his son for the apple crop ("The pertinence/ of yellow sweetings"!). The occasion missed, the change that inevitably came was hardly salutary, in our time,

the failure to recognize and the refusal to serve any mystery
("dead ceremonies/ of white bulls, or surplices/ of whiteness of
the soul's/ desire to be blind")[66] and the loss of polis, of genuine
commonwealth ("We pick/ a private way/ among debris/ of
common/ wealths"). The private way, however, is also a new
way, in which "dimensions stay personal," and the "we" who
follow it are those in the subsequent letter who take up a different "housekeeping" than Winthrop's or even Anne Hutchin-
son's, going back perhaps to the housekeeping "old mother
Smith/ started," or to Christopher Levett's. For the private way
is not the isolated individual way of Descartes, who did so
much to create the modern epistemological problem and em-
power rational consciousness and more than any modern
thinker contributed to our estrangement from the familiar.
Maximus observes that "Proportion's [relationship]/ not the
easiest thing/ to bring if character's [ego]/ (Cartesian monads)/
desperate densenesses// be not washed out in natural [process]/
or bubble bath."[67] And he concludes by reminding us that for
him the preferred way of being is to be in the process: "And one
desire,/ that the soul [not ego, but self]/ be naked/ at the end//
of time. . . ."

What is important to Maximus in "Capt Christopher Levett
(of York)" (Letter 32) is *Economos*: not that the settlement at
Cape Ann "led on/ to Commonwealth" but that Levett, like
Roger Conant, built a house. Levett, he says, is a "measure"
(the word includes the idea of proportion). A measure of attention because he respected the newness and speaks of his house
"as he does of each/ new thing he saw and did/ in these new
parts. . . ." And a measure of the cashing-in on the New World,
the spoliation of the new, that outrages Maximus. Unlike
Levett, we, at this "poor end" of time, he says, find nothing
tolerable, not to say wonderful, for our "eyes" to "strike." And
since in the course of these poems Maximus has recovered the
wonder of newness, he now despairs of "the dirtiness of good-

ness// cheapness shit [that] is/ upon the world." His polis,
his housekeeping, accordingly, will be a defense against a despoiled America, not, as with Levett, " 'those savage people' ":

> We'll turn
> to keep our house, turn to
> houses where our kind
> and hungry after them,
>
> not willing to bear one short walk
> more out into even what they've done
> to earth itself, find
> company.

Thinking of all that has happened since "these two men [Levett
and Conant]/ put down two houses," and wonderfully evoking
again the landscape of beginning, "by fish flakes and stages/ on
rocks near water with trees/ against sea," Maximus comes to
the "single truth" about America:

> the newness
>
> the first men knew was almost
> from the start dirtied
> by second comers. About seven years
> and you can carry cinders
> in your hand for what
>
> America was worth. . . .

His denunciation measures the enormity of his sense of loss:

> May she be damned
> for what she did so soon
> to what was such a newing

Juxtaposition makes the break between the two sections
into which this installment divides, and tries to purge despair
by turning once more to examples of attention and care. In
"1st Letter on Georges" (Letter 33), Maximus considers the
hazards—and by implication, heroism—of fishing. Themati-

cally, this letter on the storms and disasters of 1862 and 1905, goes back to "Letter 2," where fishermen, one an informant in the later poem, are celebrated; it carries all the resonances of fishing in *The Maximus Poems* and, since fishing is both the past and present *work* of Gloucester, may be considered continuous with the letters on the fish rush. It is also continuous in another way, as an example of Maximus' historiographical *work*. (He attacks chaos by work.) Yet there is a break, answering to the rhythm of his despair and hope, a turning which prefigures that enacted in "Letter 36" on the annual flower ceremony for fishermen lost at sea, the letter, with "Letter 33," that provides the frame of this section.

The intervening letters tell of current city politics, of "the greased ways/ of the city now," but also of resistant John Burke who still has the polis in his eye, and of Maximus' own careful excursion as cultural geographer. The latter, "Letter, May 2, 1959" (Letter 35), begins and ends with the visually presented mappings of Maximus and Champlain, and in between it answers the question Maximus ponders as he stakes out old sites on Meetinghouse Green: "What did Bruen want?" Bruen, he finds, wanted what everyone since has wanted: "From// then to now nothing/ new, in the meaning/ that that wall walked/ today"—*nothing new*, despoilers all, come to possess and exploit. The past, to adopt Sauer's words, is now clear enough to Maximus, and the contrasts and continuities with the present are understood.

Hence the almost overwhelming despair of Maximus' meditation on beginnings-and-ends. Several elements darkly thread it, among them Stefansson's notion of the progressive northwest movement of civilization, which Maximus considers a "dead end . . . in the ice," and a uroboric sense of forces and events returning on themselves, the circular movement exemplified by the poem, which ends not only with the sea that antedates discovery but with Maximus' return to the landscape of childhood and to Kent Circle (Kunt Circle) where he wrote his first poems and essays.[68] The stable, cherished landmarks of his excursion are natural, the body of the Great Mother: marsh, river, rocks, dunes, sea. But his knowledge of the cashing-in and ecological negligence ("dogs of the present don't even throw anything back") distresses him. A profound desire, related to his boyhood, prompts his wish to live in the Gloucester that he, like Rose-Troup, has worked so hard to repossess. Both historically and psychologically, *The Maximus Poems* concerns repossession, and among its most moving lines are Maximus' childlike remonstrance, "Go 'way and leave/ Rose-Troup and myself."

Not only has the natural landscape been despoiled by noise and smell and "rubbish/ of white man"—Maximus, with Crane, suffers the rape of Pocahontas—but the sea has been forgotten. The dogs of the present neither remember, in the words of anniversary sermons recollected by Maximus, "the great sea the influences/ of it the salt breath of it/ . . . the sadness of it [prefiguring the following poem on death at sea]," nor the time when "Gloster" was difficult to approach by land and so was not heavily populated. This is not the case now, with Route 128 and the A. Piatt Andrew Bridge connecting Gloucester to the "nation"—the bridge, the roar of the overhead traffic, reminding Maximus of fission and the fact that he is "interfused" not with the sea, the generative chaos, but with another kind of chaos, man-made, the very "rubbish// of creation. . . ."

Because the sea had admitted these invaders to this end, Maximus finds the sea's breath bad and the river "unmellowed" and yields to apocalyptic feeling. Stefansson's theory, which he again entertains, is one of doom, the end of all the dreams, of the migrations of peoples, that began when Pytheas discovered the fishing grounds ("Stefansson's ice, what trade

replaced Pytheas's sludge with"). Gloucester is not a new beginning but, as the old railroad joke has it, the end of the line,
and Maximus' poem, to borrow Kenneth Burke's idea of termi-
nistic development, has reached the end of its line. Because
historiography, the active search for evidence, has been an
exploration of space, Maximus has recovered beginnings; but
history, as temporal sequence, as "the memory of time,"
negates this, and brings Maximus to an impasse. Now, already
impelled toward death, he would have the sea and ice repossess
the Cape, that we might "start all over":

> step off
> onto the nation   The sea
> will rush over   The ice
> will drag boulders   Commerce
> was changed the fathometer
> was invented here the present
> is worse give nothing now your credence
> start all over step off the
> Orontes onto land no Typhon
> no understanding of a cave

Starting all over, which in a way is what Maximus is compelled to do in the next volume, is comparable to stepping off
the Orontes onto land; it brings us back to the violence of
geological and mythic origins, to the continental rift of Mesozoic times and to the cosmological battle of Zeus and Typhon.
But now we lack mythic understanding and, as before, at the
time of the planting, are hindered in building (rebuilding) by
"'times of combustion.'" This is the context in which Maximus reminds Gloucester of Rose-Troup—Mother-Clio, we
might call her, a Mother as much as Smith—who "solely gave
you place in the genetic world" and whose work is of such
fidelity that he "connects [it] back to Champlain." By way of
both he works back to the historical concerns with which he

began and to the harbor charted at the end of the poem. The
final turning of his thought is to the genesis of Gloucester, to
the beginning, to the sea from which the newcomers quickly
turned and to which he returns because, in consequence of
their (and "Our") turning, "its earth which/ now is strange. . . ."

Turnings of thought and feeling answer to other turnings,
and by returning to the sea, whose motions for Maximus as for
Whitman are cosmic and mysterious and of ultimate rhythmic
importance, he brings the poems, in "Maximus, to Gloucester,
Sunday, July 19" (Letter 36), to the all-gathering depth of
source, of beginning-and-end. "Letter 36" is one of the great
achievements of *The Maximus Poems* because it answers the
deathward movement of the previous poem with its faith in
resurrection, its faith in the renewals of the process world, and
so makes possible the onward course of the poems. The letter
is meditative (and instructive like Williams' "A Tract," addressed to Maximus' townspeople) and turns on the flower
ceremony first briefly remarked in "On first Looking out
through Juan de la Cosa's Eyes." This ceremony involves what
most concerns Gloucester *and* Maximus. But though it is the
ritual center of his poem, it is not now, as he would have it in
respect to *Ethos*, the ritual center of a polis.

The poem opens in the midst of an on-going action, for there
are no "beginnings" and "ends," only the process indicated by
the process of the poem, the openness of its beginning and end.
It resumes some essential themes of earlier poems, such insistences as care, attention, risk, negative capability, heroism.
Focal here is the Fishermen's Memorial, Leonard Craske's
"Man at the Wheel," which Maximus considers a "bronze
idol," a misrepresentation of "what a fisherman is. . . ." For a
fisherman, he says, "is not a successful man/ he is not a famous
man he is not a man/ of power. . . ." He is, instead, a man of
achievement, characterized by the virtue of negative capabil-

ity, the necessary condition of resurrection in the poem. The fisherman "works without reference to/ that difference [of day and night, life and death]"; he lives fearlessly in the process, accepts its laws and the mystery of sea-change (evoked by echoes of *The Tempest*). This mystery, witnessed in the flower ceremony, is what the poem enacts.

Dropped into the Cut, "the flowers tear off//... the flowers/ turn/ the character of the sea...." The flowers turn, and turn the *character* of the sea, whose outward, destructive tides now turn beneficently inward. And with this turning,

> The drowned men are undrowned
> in the eddies
>> of the eyes
>> of the flowers
>> opening
>> the sea's eyes
>
> The disaster
> is undone

Undrowned, undone: these verbs of action, negating action, like "unrocking" in Crane's "Paraphrase," do much of the work, are verbal equivalents, themselves miracles of transformation. Crane is also present in echoes of "Voyages" and in the sea's eyes, a provocative image in Marsden Hartley's "Eight Bells' Folly" (1933), a painting commemorating Crane's death. The inset lines eddy in the motion of their backward-forward meaning, for the eyes may also be the eyes of the flowers, and the opening flowers may also open the sea's eyes, which we learn later is the case: "there are eyes/ in this water// the flowers from the shore,/ awakened/ the sea...." Care and attention and the ritual of flowers are efficacious; they open the sea, not only its eyes of sleep but the door of its tomb. "Opening," set off by itself, is the great miraculous action, again like "night's opening" in Crane's resurrectional "Lachrymae

Christi"—and the tomb's opening reminds us of "At Melville's Tomb," another poem of Crane's in evidence and here repudiated.

The ritual, enacted in the poem, is one of resurrection, and that, to cite "The Twist," a previous poem of turning, is the veracity in this day's sun. The flowers, "received as alien," return on the tide, and death, also alien, "this gross fact," re-turns, re-turns. "In this upset" both contribute to his feeling that "the sensation [of transformation] is true," that trans-formation, as Heraclitus said (*says* in the present of the text), is the cosmic miracle: "all things are exchanged for fire, and fire for all things."

Maximus is aware of the gross fact of death; it has always preoccupied him. In the second part of the poem, he recalls the geysers at Yellowstone that he had seen on his trip West in 1938, the trip on which he strained his heart. They evoke for him "death the diseased/ presence on us, the spilling lesion// of the brilliance/ it is to be alive," his own condition of life, as "The Story of an Olson, and Bad Thing" tells us. This, as well as the ceremony, brings to mind his father's death, obliquely referred to in his appreciative reflection on burial at sea:

> When a man's coffin is the sea
> the whole of creation shall come to his funeral,
>
> it turns out; the globe
> is below, all lapis
>
> and its blue surface golded
> by what happened
>
> this afternoon: there are eyes
> in this water

Death is no longer fearsome; it is return to source, as in "Pacific Lament," to "the whole of creation"; and, as the alchemical references indicate, it is completeness, wholeness, *that* trans-formation. Even more, this funeral rite awakens the sea to see, awakens the father, again recalled by an echo of *The Tempest* ("Full fathom five thy father lies . . ."). And for good reason when we remember the epigraph of *Call Me Ishmael*:

> O fahter, fahter
> gone amoong
> O eeys that loke
> Loke, fahter:
> your sone!

The sea-change Maximus desires involves his father's recognition, an answering, in Whitman's sense, of the universe, an "awakening" to the beneficence ("goodness over and under us") that overcomes negation and restores trust. By working this miracle, the poem (Maximus' flower) does not "rectify" death. It rectifies Maximus and allows him to continue.[69]

This is evident in the last poem, "April Today Main Street," where Maximus disregards chronology in order to end with spring and, in considering an earlier April, in 1642, when Gloucester was refounded by the Massachusetts Bay Company and made "to stick," declares his own intention of sticking with the poem. Again we find him at his work, moving within his environment and looking for evidence. Walking is the mode of *The Maximus Poems* as much as of *Paterson* or Thoreau's excursions; walking is the meditative exercise, and for Maximus it is an excursion into past-and-present, a past made present, past and present so interfused that everything he sees or hears has significance. On this April day, with its "mean easterly," he meditates again on the contrast of past and present, on the outcome of John Smith's vision of the fishing "mines," the true wealth of New England. Smith, he says, imagined

> the Indies
>
> lying just
> offshore to be drawn up

> on silk lines & glowing hooks
> fishermen in palanquins, robed women
> watching, holding children
> on the shore, a daisy world, the silver ore
> codfish.

The patent "to promote/ the fishing" secured the wealth but
not the daisy world. Even with its association with his own
tansy world, Maximus judges this world for its innocence and
impossibility. The evidence, in this instance Osmund Dutch,
shows the process of getting wealth that encouraged immigra-
tion, secured the success of the new town, and led on to inward, continental migration. This process, facilitated by grants
and subsidies, is a representative fact. It recalls subsequent
economic history, and its measure is the present (Vinson's
Cove now a parking lot), when, with the westward movement
completed, movement has reversed direction, raising for Maximus the disturbing question with which the poem ends: "the
128 bridge/ now brings in// what,/ to Main Street?" This question recalls an earlier judgment—that the "newness/ . . . was/
. . . dirtied/ by second comers," that we can now "carry cinders/
in [our hands] for what// American was worth"—and it recalls
the dismay which now has been overcome.

"April Today Main Steet" brings Maximus back to present-
day Gloucester, the Gloucester he had addressed in "Letter 1."
He has moved from harbor to city. He is integral with his
world. As poet-historian he walks at greater ease in his place,
his activities having given it to him, enabled him to inhabit it.
Though he judges it harshly, he is not as estranged from it as
he was at the start. Having recovered the past and brought it
into the present, he may be said to have refounded his city.
He has not, as he wished, compelled it to change, but he has
kept his eye on the polis and in his own activity demonstrated
a stance more favorable for the future than that of Ahab and

the merchandise men. His skillfully woven poem proves his
love of Gloucester ("love is not easy"), the love requisite to
form ("love is form") that he has done so much in his twistings
and turnings to release, and the effort ("that which you can
do") which underwrites polis. For the reader, to whom Maximus transfers his energy, the poem is polis, its space a meeting-
place, its form the image, as Olson says in "Apollonius of
Tyana," "around which any people concentrate and commit
themselves. . . ." It is that much anyway, a considerable poem,
in which he names Gloucester and makes it stick. And in the
further exploration it proposes, in its subsequent installments,
it will also become, to cite "Apollonius of Tyana" once more,
"an image of health in the world."

> The Poimanderes: now I see what was up,
> a year ago, chomping around these streets,
> measuring off distances, looking into
> records, disconsolately
> making up things to do—finding myself peeing
> under a thin new moon on Dogtown and noticing
> rills in the March night

IV–VI
*The Rills of
March, and
Alchemies
of
Resurrection*

Maximus begins again in this volume because the tropic
faltering that is so much an insistence of the previous poems
has been accounted for by history. History has brought him to
impasse and for the time being exhausted his historiographical
impulse. Though history remains a term of articulation, the
poems now find primary articulation in terms of myth and
geology (earth-history). Now Maximus employs "the idiom of
mythical thinking."[70]

For what history denies, myth justifies: *tropos,* the hunger
for being and the push to stand forth, the potencies of Mother
Earth that precede Olympian rule and the imprisonment of

Typhon. With myth Maximus can interpret the dream of June
17, 1958, that is clearly decisive for his work:

Everything $\overset{\text{issues}}{\underset{\text{comes}}{}}$ fr the
Black Chrysanthemum
& nothing is anything but itself
measured so. . . .[71]

With myth he can include in his mappemunde, Peloria, the
serpent-monster to which he himself now gives birth. With
myth—Olson calls it the "archeology of the soul"—Maximus
can undertake the "turning to the hidden oneness" and so press
beyond historical founding to *the* origin (*begründen*) told in
cosmological myth.[72] Historiographical concerns, accordingly,
yield to mythographical—the poems record a comparable
search in mythology and frequently Maximus transposes
mythic material in them, treating it as hitherto he had treated
historical document. This search is the enabling means, *ta'
wīl*, to use the Ismaili word Olson happily seized on, the spiritual exegesis by which, in another definition of the word (as
verb: "to lead back to the origin"), one accomplishes the work
of individuation, the redemption of "the Great Return."[73]

  In the course of his work, Maximus remarks the change from
history to myth by reversing the terms of the title of an earlier
poem. "History is the Memory of Time" (#27) now becomes
"my memory is/ the history of time." History is perspectival,
always limited by the necessary selectivity of the historian,
but myth, the memory of the collective unconscious, is everpresent (eternal) and includes all time. This explains why
Maximus, in turning to myth, perhaps more than he realizes,
advances the poetics of eternal events treated in "A Later Note
on Letter #15." Such a poetics is admirably served by the
spatial techniques already employed, and what is at issue for
Maximus is more theoretical than practical: how to accom-

modate Jung and Whitehead, which in fact he does when he
says that dream is part of any occasion:

> . . . the dream being
> self-action with Whitehead's important corollary: that no
> event
> is not penetrated, in an intersection or collision with, an
> eternal
> event

Here the significant term is "eternal event," a portmanteau
term merging "eternal object" (from Whitehead) with the kind
of event Maximus has in mind when he speaks of Dogtown as
"this/ park of eternal/ events. . . ."

  For Whitehead an "eternal object" is an element of a past
occasion that necessarily enters into the actualization of a
present occasion. In Maximus' formulation it is exemplified by
archetype: when an archetype intersects an occasion we have
an "eternal event," eternal by virtue of the ever-presence it
enables us to experience. Dogtown is a park of eternal events
because all of the original creative action told in myth may
still be realized there—the realization being the overwhelming
one that the earth is *still* alive, a reality very much in process,
eternal. (Olson noted in his copy of *Leaves of Grass*, "Great is
the Earth, and the way it became what it is;/ Do you imagine
it has stopt at this?")[74] The westward migration of myths and
mythic figures—"Old Norse/ Algonquin" is the briefest example—is one of the ways in which Maximus, perhaps going
beyond Jung, wins consent to the continuing energies of the
world and to eternal events. Juxtaposition and configuration
are his chief means, as in the following where Dogtown (hence
Gloucester) because of comparable geographical elements becomes a first city like al Ubaid of prehistoric Mesopotamia:

> off-upland
>   only Ubaid

gets "in"
       to riverine
         (Squam   [Annisquam][75]

And among many eternal events, the following poem is notable not only because of its brevity, but because it is an open on-going verbal act in keeping with process, telling of Phryne, an avatar of the Great Mother, who continues to have for us the wonderful presence she had for the celebrants at Eleusis:

thronged
to the seashore
to see Phryne
walk into
the water

Here the source is Athenaeus' *The Deinosophists*, and in this instance Maximus does not transcribe but recreates (the title "A Maximus Song" helps) the spirit of Athenaeus' account of Phryne's acquittal when her judges, overcome by her beauty, thought her "a prophetess and priestess of Venus." Athenaeus goes on to tell the incident at Eleusis and Phryne's modeling both painting and statue of Venus. All of which, with the spacing and occasion of Maximus' poem and an earlier entry on Gen[evieve] Douglas lying on a kelp bed in the water off Cressy's Beach, recalls, only to make good, the condition lamented in the first volume of *The Maximus Poems*:

Venus
does not arise from
these waters. Fish
do[76]

Finally, the density and frequency of eternal events should be noted because they require that we learn to read in an appropriate manner—and undertake our own researches in myth—and because, by cumulation, they contribute to an overwhelming (book-size: maximal) realization of eternal event. We may describe this by citing Whitehead who sometimes uses "event" simply to denote an occasion or actual entity and sometimes to denote "a nexus of actual occasions inter-related in some determinate fashion in some extensive quantum. . . ."[77]

The mythic method of these poems is not the one advocated by T. S. Eliot in "Ulysses, Order, and Myth"—the "manipulating a continuous parallel between contemporaneity and antiquity . . . [to the end] of controlling, of ordering, of giving a shape and significance to the immense panorama of futility and anarchy which is modern history." Myth for Olson is not a means of order; that would contravene his open poetics. As Charles Altieri points out, myth in such a poetics is not a frame of reference but a way of participating in process, a way of experiencing and coming to just those recognitions that for Olson are the ground of eternal events. Olson explains in *Causal Mythology* that myth holds for him "more of a poet's experience than any meaning the word 'mysticism' holds" and that it offers him (as some of his poems offer us) "the activeness, the possible activeness and personalness of experiencing it [Earth] as such." He told Charles Doria that "one wants a phenomenology in place, in order that event may rearise," and by following his own advice to attend to place, this is what he provides in his most brilliant poems.[78] As necessary as *ta' wīl*, the spiritual exercise of myth, is the complementary activity of coming into the geological and culture-geographical knowledge of place. By platting it—by walking it and reconstituting its history—Maximus now intimately discovers Dogtown, a park of eternal events.

"Letter, May 2, 1959" in the first volume of *The Maximus Poems* tells the exhaustion of historiographical impulse and redirects the subsequent work. Here Maximus complains that the sea smells and the river is unmellowed and that "it's earth

which/ now is strange. . . ." In a concluding verse, much of it
resumed in the initial poems of the present volume, especially
in "MAXIMUS, FROM DOGTOWN–II"—

> the Sea—turn yr Back on
> the Sea, go inland, to
> Dogtown: the Harbor
>
> the shore the City
> are now
> shitty . . .

—he tells his despair ("the present/ is worse give nothing now
your credence") and enjoins us to do what he will do, "start all
over" by stepping off the Orontes and making good an ignorance of myth:

>   . . . step off
> the Orontes onto land no Typhon
> no understanding of a cave
> a mystery Cashes? . . . .

Now Cashe's Shoals figure in the new poems but are of less
consequence than the pun on cache—Maximus will seek the
hole in the Earth that opens to the mysteries—and the pun on
Mt. Casius, which, in conjunction with Typhon, names a central motif of this volume. Mt. Casius, near the mouth of the
Orontes (Orontes in Arabic means "rebel," and the river is
sometimes called "Typhon"), is the place where Typhon, a
terrible dragon born of Earth and Tartaros, in the last battle
with the gods, injures Zeus and thrusts him into the Corycian
Cave. As Maximus will remind us, Mt. Casius is the "Hurrian
Hazzi," that is, the place in the earlier Hurrian-Hittite cognate
myth of Ullikummi where this (diorite) stone giant, Maximus'
most naked instance of tropic force, is given his sky-assaulting
task by Kumarbi. Maximus himself bears all this in his name—
Cassius Maximus Tyrius.[79] The Orontes, finally, also marks
the place of the East African rift, when in Mesozoic times the

Earth, as Olson remarks in commenting on the picture of
Gondwanaland on the cover of this volume, "started to come
apart at the seams." In these ways "a mystery Cashes" relates
to beginnings of incredible, cosmo-geological magnitude.

The double task of beginning at the beginning (stepping off
the Orontes) and of searching out cosmological myth has a
single end. For Maximus the necessary work at our juncture in
history is nothing less than service to the Great Mother, to
Earth herself as a physical thing, the familiar body from which
we are estranged—service to the matriarchy that myth tells us
preceded the patriarchy of Zeus. To this end, he identifies with
Typhon (and Ullikumi: "I stand on Main Street like the
Diorite/ stone") and assumes Typhon's cultural task: to re-
assert the claims of Nature over against Culture, creation over
against order, the unconscious over against the conscious. We
recognize this task when Maximus speaks of the battle of
Typhon and Zeus as "the Civilized War" and, following N. O.
Brown, likens Zeus to the "Boss" who cleverly recruits his
enemies to his own service; and we are reminded by it that a
deep urging of *tropos* for Olson answers to resistance to authority (*imposed* order) and that from the time of his emergence
not only fathers but the state provoked it.[80]

The geological and mythic events Maximus rightly connects
declare the necessary upheaval of beginnings, of on-going creation. "The war of Africa against Eurasia," he announces in the
opening poem, "has just begun again. Gondwana. . . ." In the
rift of continents, history may be said to have its beginning
because subsequent migration responded to it ("The Jews [all
the Semitic peoples, whose cultures were transmitted to
Greece; "arabesque" also plays on this]/ are unique because
they settled astride/ the East African rift"). And so we live
again, in the words of "Letter, May 2, 1959," in a time of combustion. Yet, for all the evident rebelliousness of Maximus,
his work, both private and public, is restoration of wholeness,

individuation on the one hand and "Republic" or polis, balance of powers, of creativity and order, on the other. In a Dogtown poem, where the measure is the present when "species has replaced man/ and nature's gone away to furnaces men shoot/ bodies into, and our love is for ourselves alone," he tells us, modestly and generously, that

> I walk you paths of lives I'd share with you
> simply to make evident the world
> is an eternal event and this epoch solely
> the decline of fishes . . .

In the beginning—and ever after—was the Mother in whom beginning is always possible, and these installments of *The Maximus Poems* comprise the book of the Mother, celebrate that possibility. Though Maximus recalls his mother and admits that "a mother is a hard thing to get away from," his concern with the Mother is transpersonal.[81] In these poems the symbolic action (in Burke's sense) involves the double motion of descent and ascent Maximus refers to in "The Poimanderes": the sinking into nature of the divine figure of Primal Man and the subsequent ascent of the soul.[82] The primary motion involves the recovery of tropic source and the creative act of making love to Earth. There are many instances of this, the most notable perhaps in "Maximus, at the Harbor" where "Okeanos tears upon Earth to get love loose" and Maximus tells us, as he does in a simpler earlier statement, "there is One!/ One Mother/ One Son. . . ." Yet this tropic rage for union is inseparable from the spiritual desire for ascent; it is the manifesting or standing forth by which one creates the "Perfect Child," the self-begotten individuated or redeemed man Maximus so much wishes to become.

The leap, which in turn is the rift, enacted in the first poem and noted in its title ("Letter #41 [broken off]"), redirects the poems from history to myth. By beginning with #41 when he had concluded the first volume with #37, Olson enforces a

break and signals the new departure in his work. This is also
evident in the altered formal character of the book: in the
larger format, the wide margins of empty space that frequently
frame the poems, the inclusion of working notes and blank
pages (fertile emptiness: the essential condition),[83] the super-
cession of letters by daybook or journal entries, the absence
of pagination, and the indifference to established serial order
(we find, for example, "Maximus Letter # whatever" and the
unexpected appearance of "Letter 72"). For the most part the
poems are looser than those in the first volume and seldom as
long, as "complete" or "finished." The very title of the book
confirms its selective nature. Nevertheless the poems are set
down chronologically, frequently grouped together and sometimes brilliantly juxtaposed. They proceed on the three fronts
of the present, the past (history), and myth, the last predomi-
nant, and what seems interruptive of any line of development
is necessary to remind us of the fact that all fronts are always
in motion. Sometimes they come together, as in "for Robt
Duncan, / who understands / what's going on. . . ." They demand that we read them sequentially as a development, as the
enactment of a search. This search, or way, is spiral, according
to Jung whose account of the activity of the unconscious in the
work of individuation suggests the (a) structure of the poems.
Motifs recur, "rotate or circumambulate round the centre,"
as, for example, in Maximus' use of three Algonquin legends—
that of the evil woman who lusted after the snake in the pond,
that of the woman who had her joy in fucking the mountain,
and that of the man with his house on his head ("his head is
heaven"), stages, clearly, of a psychic process in which the
terrible mother becomes beneficent.[84]

   If we read the poems in this fashion, we will find that both
the excitement and pleasure of the work resides less in single
poems than in their totality. To read these poems requires a
labor in libraries not incommensurate with Olson's. This is

one of the ways of participating in them that Olson asks of us. It is also one of their uses, since he would have us have this necessary knowledge, have us follow the course of his reading and remake our minds. The poems in which his reading is conspicuous constitute a periplum, a chart of the coast to be checked against our own experience. The scholarship of *The Maximus Poems* is not there to embarrass us; their poet is not the possessor of "the mind of Europe," but a seafarer who traces his lineage to cartographers and voyagers. For him coasting, much considered in this volume, epitomizes the hazards—both physical and intellectual—of nakedness. The reward of these *Maximus Poems* as history may be, as it seems in part to have been Maximus', the conclusive locating of B. Ellery. But the greater reward, concomitant with a realization of eternal events, is the recognition Maximus himself notes in "tesserae // commissure"—the recognition that the pieces fit, that the book is not rubble but a mosaic.

The resumption in March, "the holy month" when the "year rebegan," also signals the new beginning, as does the new moon, of birth and growth, mentioned in the first poem.[85] This poem, a prelude to more important Dogtown poems, is central to the entire volume. The blocklike verse paragraphs immediately call up the cover (Earth and Ocean, the unity of landmass before continental migration) only to remind us that Earth, with Ocean a primary agent in these poems, is alive: that the great forces that set continents in motion also find release in storms, like the St. Valentine's Day storm of Maximus' youth referred to here, and in volcanic eruptions, like the geysers at Yellowstone he witnessed on his trip West, and, since Jung is referred to in "he said the volcano any of us does/ sit upon," in psychic explosions, eruptions of the unconscious.[86] The poem, as it initiates a new development for Maximus, recalls an earlier leap (rift) at the time of the storm, the occasion of writing his first poem, of great moment in "The

Twist," that poem of tropic awakening. This poem, and its ambivalence, is recollected again in "Kent Circle Song" in the imagery from *Hansel and Gretel* (fairy tales are mythic), and the ambivalence remains throughout the poems, creating the difficulty Maximus has in managing his allegiance to both the terrible Mother and the good Mother (anima).[87] The leap the poem declares involves the work inevitably begun in the first volume but now the overriding concern—the work of psychological transformation, the alchemy of resurrection (to use Corbin's term) by which he would reshape the self; the work, as this and subsequent poems indicate, told not so much in terms of base elements as in terms of *the* elements, of geological transformation and correlative creation myths.

This is the only poem in which Maximus mentions his size. This helps us identify him with Merry in the next poem and perhaps led him to identify with giants, and is significant now because it explains his gracelessness and the consequent ridicule, and probably warrants the wry comparison with continental magnitudes ("Like, right off the Orontes?" Maximus asks).[88] The ridicule is also an important aspect of the poem because in both instances it comes from women, the first taking force from the second ("the new moon/ makes fun of me"), that is, from the Great Mother. Considering the momentousness of Maximus' situation in this poem—he has just returned from Dogtown, is aware of the geological forces that produced it; he has seen "such shapes . . . *in the universe*" (my italics) and knows the continents are moving—considering his more than millennial sense of time and his sense of the incredible agencies at work in earth and human history, his playfulness is humble response to his recognition of the Great Mother who rules the world.

Dogtown is the geographical center of this volume of *The Maximus Poems*. This wild still little inhabited area above

Gloucester is a moraine, an upthrust of granitic rock that
occurred at the time of deglaciation. The geological action of
that time is itself important, serving as it does as a personal
and mythic correlative of creation:

> the earth was down from the weight of the ice
> upon it
> and great beds of water flowing under carried detritus
> was my kame [pun]. . . .[89]

So considered, "Mother Dogtown," as Maximus calls it, is the
entire world—a notion supported by the picture on the cover
as it contrasts with the chart of Gloucester harbor on the cover
of the first volume. Dogtown is Maximus' "2nd town," and as
a park of eternal events is associated by him with "God the
Dog// . . . His Tongue/ Hangs, dropping/ Eternal Events. . . ."
It is a sacred place, like Walden, where Maximus not only in-
vestigates the lives of former inhabitants but finds in the
"watered rock," in the rills of March, evidence of the kind that
Thoreau found at the railroad cut—evidence assuring him that
he "stood in the laboratory of the Artist who made the world
and me," that "Nature . . . again is mother of humanity."[90]
Not for nothing does Maximus speak of the country roads
there as "paradise alley."

Two cosmologies chiefly support this view of Dogtown, the
Greek told in *Theogony* and the Egyptian in the Heliopolitan
and Memphite Theologies. They are not unassociated and
Maximus uses both from the beginning, though the Theogonic
dominates the first Dogtown poem, "MAXIMUS, FROM DOG-
TOWN—I," and the Memphite a later poem, "The Cow/ of
Dogtown."[91]

"MAXIMUS, FROM DOGTOWN—I" belongs with the initial group of poems (pages 1–18) in which Maximus establishes
Dogtown as the earth-ground-center as against heaven—establishes the primacy of Earth-Mother-Black Chrysanthemum-

Lotus, concluding with the fact that if Mother is polis ("the City is Mother—// Polis . . ."), Dogtown, not Gloucester, may well be the capital. For Maximus, at this stage of development, the *aer* (air) of Dogtown is of more concern than the *aither*. In distinctions taken from Jane Harrison's *Themis*, which she in turn took from E. J. Payne's *History of the New World called America*, he tells his preference for the *metarsia* rather than the *meteora*, for the "weather" of "the lower region of earthy mist," which the moon frequents, rather than the upper heavenly region of the sun. The *ta meteura* (*meteora*), he notes somewhat later, will have to wait: "after the weather the/ meteors [heavenly bodies]. . . ." Now, perhaps alluding to Payne and reversing his sequence, he will be the American showing "from heaven the Ladder// come down to the Earth/ of Us All, the Many who/ know// there is One!" If we may appropriate a phrase from Whitman without making light of Maximus' task, he strikes up for the Great Mother, overwhelmed, as he might well be, by reading Erich Neumann's important book.[92]

The proem with which Maximus introduces "MAXIMUS, FROM DOGTOWN—I" is another beginning and, like the telegraphic shorthand of the schematic "MAXIMUS, FROM DOGTOWN—II" which quickly follows it, announces the major themes of the entire book. In it Maximus takes us back to Hesiod, to the very beginning of *Theogony* where Hesiod tells of the creation of all things: "at the first Chaos came to be, but next wide-bosomed Earth, the ever-sure foundation of all. . . ." Maximus picks up the narrative farther on and both freely adapts the translation to his own more felicitous speech and works into the narrative elements from Heraclitus and from his own dream (of June 17, 1958):

The sea was born of the earth without sweet union of
    love Hesiod says

But that then she lay for heaven and she bare the thing
   which encloses
every thing, Okeanos the one which all things are and by
   which nothing
is anything but itself, measured so

screwing earth, in whom love lies which unnerves the
   limbs and by its
heat floods the mind and all gods and men into further
   nature
                      Vast earth rejoices,
deep-swirling Okeanos steers all things through all things,
everything issues from the one, the soul is lead from
   drunkenness
to dryness, the sleeper lights up from the dead,
the man awakes lights up from the sleeping

Maximus' use of Hesiod, here and elsewhere, is subversive. He
is not about to celebrate the Olympian victory. The phrase
"Vast earth rejoices," for example, does not follow in Hesiod,
as it does here, Okeanos' intercourse with his Mother (an
aspect of creation not in Hesiod but in Neumann's account
of uroboric beginning in Egyptian mythology);[93] rather the
phrase follows the strife of Earth and Heaven, and Cronos'
assent to carry out Earth's wish to emasculate his father. Maximus celebrates Earth but even more Okeanos (the son-father,
hence father of himself) who, according to Jane Harrison, is "a
potency of the old order . . . the enemy of Zeus. . . ." Okeanos
is clearly preeminent, becoming for Maximus the One of Heraclitus ("The one is made up of all things, and all things issue
from the one"), at once the power of love, the tropic force of
proliferating nature, and the power of mind ("the thought by
which all things are steered through all things") that leads the
soul, again in Heraclitean terms of wet and dry, sleeping and
waking, through an alchemy of resurrection.[94] This aggrandizement of Okeanos is significant because Typhon, with whom
Maximus identifies, is his surrogate, another potency of the

old order, and because it tells the secret of the dream of the
Black Chrysanthemum—that Maximus is himself the source
of himself.[95]

The cosmology introduced in these verses enables us to
understand the "watered rock" of Dogtown and the rills of
March. Maximus gives us the geological reason—these are
"the rocks the glacier tossed"—thereby suggesting the forces
involved in Merry's fight with the bull. At the same time, join-
ing Greek and Egyptian elements, he explains the cosmology
in detail:

> "under" the dish
> of the earth
> Okeanos <u>under</u>
> Dogtown
> through which (inside of which) the sun passes
> at night—
> > she passes the sun back to
> > > the east through her body
> > > the Geb (of heaven) at night

> Nut is water
> above & below, vault
> above and below

A diagram in *Before Philosophy: The Intellectual Adventure
of Ancient Man* helps us visualize this cosmos:

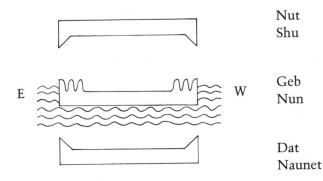

Nut
Shu

Geb
Nun

Dat
Naunet

Earth (Geb) is a dish floating on the primordial waters (Nun), and Nun, like Okeanos, is the water that encircles the world ("which encloses/ every thing," in Maximus' words) and defines its boundary. Earth and heaven are divided by Shu (air), who also upholds the sky-goddess Nut, represented as arching the earth, a celestial cow, whose "four hundred breasts" are the stars, appropriately, the Milky Way. Nut is the Great Mother. Neumann says that she is "identical with the primeval water" and forms, with Naunet, "the Great Round of the feminine vessel"; and he goes on to say, in a passage Maximus carefully attended, that "Nut is not only the daytime sky but also the western devourer of the sun that passes back to the east through her body. . . . Thus Nut is water above and below, vault above and below, life and death, generating and killing, in one."[96]

The latter point about the double nature of the Great Mother is of most importance to Maximus. For Merry is just such a "braggart man" as he is in the proem. (Maximus may have felt as Olson did when first experiencing the sacred mushroom, that he "was literally tak[ing] a bite straight out of the creation. . . .")[97] And what he wisely learns almost immediately and exemplifies in the story of Merry and the bull—the bull is the agent of the Great Mother, the destructive masculinity of the uroboros—is the need, in the desire to recover the source, to put away presumptuous masculinity, the arrogant claim of dominion over the animal world. Otherwise, Maximus, who like Apollonius of Tyana feels so strongly the need to return to place, to know the mysteries, will, like Merry, only discover them, and the Mother's beneficence, in death. Then, he says in the moving concluding verse indebted to the Rig-Veda—

> Then only
> after the grubs
> had done him
> did the earth

> let her robe
> uncover and her part
> take him in[98]

The cosmological schema Maximus employs readily answers to Olson's figure for myth in *The Special View of History*, the double cone, whose axis is the vertical of the self:

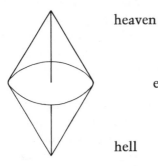

heaven

earth

hell

We should recall now what he said then—"It is with EROS that mythology is concerned"—and also note, by way of distinguishing this volume from the last, that Maximus' interest centers mostly on earth and hell. In this poem he emphasizes "<u>under</u>" and "<u>subterranean</u>" and the "Soft soft rock"—

> my soft sow the roads
> of Dogtown trickling like from underground rock
> springs under an early cold March moon[99]

And in "MAXIMUS, FROM DOGTOWN—II," his configurations tell this insistence on "chthonic femininity": Dogtown is the "<u>under</u>/vault—the 'mother'/rock," the rock is coal of the Pennsylvanian Age, and is the still burning heart of love, the "Throne of Creation" at the bottom of things—in sum: the Black (Gold) Chrysanthemum, origin, source.[100] Or, as he adds immediately in the following poem, Dogtown is the "padma," the pure gold lotus, in Zimmer's account, "the door or gate, the opening or mouth, of the womb of the universe."[101]

The Great Mother is the overwhelming presence of these early poems, where Maximus tells his rediscovery of her, as well as the presence of the entire book. He recognizes her in terrible Medea (himself a Jason in search of the Golden Fleece) and in the destructive Indian woman "who-Lusted After-the/ Snake-in-the-Pond. . . ." He sees her in the waters off Cressy's Beach, recollecting her various forms, as sea animal, as the Lausel woman (plate 2, in *The Great Mother*), as Andromeda (acknowledging that he is not yet Perseus). She is the agent of the miraculous, the bountiful transformation so wonderfully told in the Algonquin legend of "He-with-the-House-on-his-Head," and because he has found her he no longer puts up with Lady Luck or with "<u>heimarmene</u>," bitter necessity. (Does this recovered faith in her beneficence account for the placement here of "Maximus to Gloucester, Letter 27 [withheld]," that powerful assertive poem on the nature of his poetic task, instructing the reader to consider the poems not as a "strict personal order" but as "a complex of occasions"?) She is, of course, the primordial goddess, not the anima, and Maximus throughout the poems seems to prefer her in her original physical rather than spiritually transformed form. The Lady of Good Voyage is his Saint Sophia, or anima, but he would have her the "Vierge/ ouvrante," the Virgin who, according to Neumann, is in fact the Earth-Mother who contains within her the Father and the Son. The Lady of Good Voyage in "The Frontlet" is the "Virgin/ held up/ on the Bull's horns"; she is lifted into the light by Dogtown, and that is the "secret." How significant *under* is! Even the way Maximus puts the following equation reveals it:

> Homo Anthropos
> —and Our Lady: Potnia,
> and Poseidon (Potidan

The redeemed or individuated man must find the anima, but his successful search depends on a prior relation like that of

Poseidon, the violent lover of the White Goddess ("Potidan,"
a synonym for Poseidon, denoting the White Goddess' chosen
lover). Maximus expresses his wish in a prayer to Our Lady:

> mother-spirit to fuck at noumenon, Vierge
> ouvrante

And in the "River" poems of the initial group, the geography
and geology tell it:

> Into
> In the fiord the diorite man obtrudes Obadiah Bruen's
> island on his nose. Into the granite this inlet
> of the sea to poke and jam the Cut and fight
> the sand off and the yelping rocks, the granite
> he rolls as Dogtown throws its pebbles and Merry
> lay among them, busted[102]

Olson's reading is so much his morning work—and so much of
the fabric of the poems—that in terms of it we can mark his
"progress" and even distinguish the volumes of *The Maximus
Poems*. The indispensable books of the present volume are
those that favor the task, first announced in "In Cold Hell, In
Thicket," of arching again "the necessary goddess." Among
them are the books on Greek religion and mythology by Jane
Harrison, those impressive studies subverting the established
patriarchal view as one finds it, say, in her contemporary H. J.
Rose's *A Handbook of Greek Mythology*, and the books by
Carl Jung and Erich Neumann, chiefly the *Psychology and
Alchemy* of the former and *The Great Mother* of the latter,
that call us back to the Great Mother and treat the "healing"
process of individuation. The title of Neumann's book says all
that needs to be said about it, and Jung's introductory comments are enough to suggest its importance to Olson. "Alchemy," Jung says, "is pre-eminently concerned with the seed
of unity which lies hidden in the chaos of Tiamat and forms
the counterpart to the divine unity." It is not concerned with

the unity of father-and-son but with the unity of the mother-and-son, with the "*serpens mecurii*, the dragon that creates and destroys itself and represents the *prima materia*." Alchemy was originally a corrective to Christianity, and it is a corrective for Jung and Olson who wish to restore "the primordial matriarchal world . . . overthrown by the masculine world of the father."[103]

That the serpent has surfaced in these poems is evident at the start in Maximus' aggrandizement of Okeanos—whose characteristics ("entwined/ throughout/ the system") he associates with the sea-serpent that at least from Indian times has been reported inhabiting the waters of Gloucester. Much of Book V, the well-knit Phoenician section of the poems, establishes the pre-Achaean origin of Typhon and treats the genealogy-migration of this "blue monster." The connection already made in the first volume between Gloucester and Tyre is resumed here ("128 a mole/ to get at Tyre") and an early poem gives the controlling idea in its title: "<u>View</u>: fr the Orontes/ fr where Typhon." Subsequent poems, especially the one on Peloria (page 87) and "after the storm was over" and the immediately related poems (pages 94–98) "travel[s] Typhon/ from the old holdings" to a

> grapevine corner
> to shake off his cave-life
> and open an opening
> big enough for himself

Here Maximus alludes to Vinland (see the earlier reference in "Wyngaershoek hoik Grape Vine HOYK the/ Dutch/ & the Norse") and the mail route that in former times took him to "Grapevine Road & Hawthorne Lane" in East Gloucester, and to the Cut, a place of more significant activity. These genealogy-migrations—among them is one devoted to the Great Goddess—are part of Maximus' search for the historico-mythical

beginning which he presses back as far as al Ubaid ("a black-
haired previous people/ dwelling among reed-houses/ on
flooded marshes?") and the Cabiri, the mighty Near-Eastern
gods of fertility in the service of the Great Mother. And one of
the brilliant results of this work and his associative imagination is the lovely poem in which he adapts Pausanius' description of Lerna in order to give us a Gloucester that worships the
Great Mother and the Typhon-begotten Lernean monster:

> 1. Beginning at the hill of Middle Street the city
>   which consists mostly of wharves & houses
>   reaches down to the sea. It is bounded
>   on the one side by the river Annisquam,
>   and on the other by the stream or entrance
>   to the inner harbor. In the Fort at this entrance
>
>   are the images of stone and there is another
>   place near the river where there is a seated
>   wooden image of Demeter. The city's own
>   wooden image of the goddess is on a hill
>   along the next ridge above Middle Street
>   between the two towers of a church called
>   the Lady of Good Voyage. There is also a stone image
>   of Aphrodite beside the sea. 2. But the
>   spot where the river comes into the
>   sea is reserved for the special
>   Hydra called the Lernean monster,
>   the particular worship of the city,
>   though it is proven to be recent
>   and the particular tablets of Poseidon
>   written on copper in the shape of a heart
>   prove to be likewise new.[104]

This is the sacred geography of the harbor section of the
city, where eternal events also occur.

The most important and dramatic involve the "Lernaean
mysteries," the uroboric relationship of the mother and the
son, the divinities of this fatherless place near the Cut "where

the river comes into the/ sea. . . ." The first, occasioned by
eating the sacred mushroom, tells of Maximus' struggle and
failure to raise up and transform the "beast," the Maternal
Uroboros:

> I forced the calm grey waters, I wanted her
> to come to the surface I had fought her,
> long enough, below. I shaped her out of
> the watery mass
>
> and the dragger, cleaning its fish,
> idled into
> the scene, slipped across the empty water .
> where I had placed
> the serpent, staring as hard as
> I could (to make the snow
> turn back to snow, the autos
> to come to their
> actual size, to stop
> being smaller,
> and far away. The sea does
> contain the beauty I had looked at
> until the sweat
> stood out in my eyes. The wonder is
> limitless, of my own term, the compound
> to compound until the beast rises from the sea.

This remarkable poem takes point from the preceding miraculous story of the man-with-the-house-on-his-head. This for-
tunate man sets his house down on "a hard-wood ridge near a
good spring of water" (an approximation of Dogtown) and
awakens to find all manner of good things, a paradisal morning
world in which "he was a partridge and it was spring." The
mother is good and, unasked, gives bountifully. But Maximus,
having fought her below ("the sea-serpent" in a manuscript
version of the poem) and having even given her determinate
shape, now in this winter-time forces her—would, as he says

in the manuscript version, compel her to change ("Backward I
compel/ Gloucester/ to yield").[105] Of course she does not yield
to the masculine will which, as Maternal Uroboros, she incloses, and Maximus, in the related poem that follows, must
chart a different course:

                              by the way to the woods
     Indian   otter
     "Lake"   ponds   orient
          show me   (exhibit
          myself)

Like the man-with-the-house-on-his-head, he turns to Dogtown, he follows "in paths untrodden"[106] to a less demanding,
less conscious but more rewarding relation with nature, a relation which both the Indian story and the chart suggest is akin
to Thoreau's.

   The second event, in "<u>Maximus, at the Harbor,</u>" is prefaced
by historical documentation about the "previledged place/
call[ed] the Cutt. . . ." This poem, among the best in this volume, draws on Hesiod's *Theogony* and Corbin's study of the
Persian alchemy of resurrection. If anything, it is more forceful
than the earlier poem, as perhaps it should be since Maximus
now identifies with Okeanos. Because it is longer and Corbin
provides a scheme, it is also more insistent and explicit about
the rage that moves Okeanos. The verbal violence of this poem
enacts elemental rape; love is indeed "stud," and the barba-
rism/bestiality of beginnings stands revealed. But the violence
is prompted by the tropic rage to manifest oneself (actually
manifest one's thought) reiterated in the explosive keyword,
apophainesthai. If this violence is justifiable as more than
cosmo-psychological description, it is so because Okeanos
rages "to get love loose," to make it the all-pervading cosmic
force, and because his rage is not merely instinctual but is
moved by thought ("the thought of its thought is the rage").

Okeanos is moved by the "magnificant Angel" that precedes
one and leads one back to paradise, to one's celestial self.[107]
His rage is prompted by the desire for redemption. He wants
"the Perfect Child," the self-generated Anthropos who, Corbin
says, will lead us back "to the celestial archetype in which it
originated." In its "progressive rise," the soul returns, moves
back to origin—which may explain, in the manuscript version
of the previous poem, Maximus' wish to compel Gloucester
(the sea-serpent) "backward," and it may explain the seeming
confusion of the following marginalia in *The Great Mother*:
"Sea-Serpent, our Lady or Woman herself." [108]

These are poems of psychic hunger, of impatience with the
uroboric condition and desire to get on with the *work* of redemption.[109] Maximus very early expresses this when he says,
"TO HELL WITH, like/ —& UP heimarmene"—heimarmene
here taking special significance from Zosimos' account, cited
by Jung, of the Son of God (the Anthropos, the Angel) who
leads "the soul forth from the dominion of Heimarmene" into
the realm of light.[110] An early notation, identifying the historical and mythical work of the poems, puts the difficulties
to be overcome:

   B. Ellery   Cinvat Bridge   aer

Maximus has not yet placed B. Ellery, and in his preoccupation
with "aer," the earthly realm of weather, is troubled by his
desire for "aither," for the heavenly things to be had when, in
the Persian explanation, the earthly soul, on the Day of Judgment, meets its Angel, its celestial self, "on the road to the
Cinvat Bridge. . . ." [111]

"Maximus, at the Harbor," the prominent concluding poem
of Part IV, is followed by two briefer poems, one mythical, the
other historical, both concerned with salt. The historical poem
is the deposition of John Watts, a factor, who appropriated
some salt stored on Ten Pound Island. The mythical poem—

> brang that thing out,
> the Monogene
> the original unit
> survives in the salt

—declares a victory of deliverance. Maximus first mentions
the Monogene in "MAXIMUS, FROM DOGTOWN—II,"
where his spelling of it accords with the reference to collagen,
his scientific equivalent of the alchemical *prima materia* that
contains the seeds of life.[112] Jung tells us that Monogenes, the
creator, is the Son of God (another image of the Anthropos),
and that the Monad in which he dwells is the "Mother-City,"
the "metropolis" (*padma* or lotus) Maximus speaks of here and
in the notation on page 18. At this point, then, Maximus survives the uroboric condition, and even as he is sustained by it
is the self that through its own creative agency he hopes to
become. Again, this is the secret. "Who therefore knows the
salt and its solution," says an alchemical text, "knows the
hidden secret. . . ."[113]

Two of the finest poems in Book VI address this fatherhood.

The first, near the beginning of the installment, realizes
what some poems sometimes merely assert or note in their
configurations. "Out over the land skope"—I give it the title of
its opening phrase—is epiphanic, and may take its power from
the fact that it joins one of Maximus' earliest landscapes with
his present experience of light. Graphically it is a spacious
poem that fills the space of the page, and its widely placed lines
and verbal groupings provide a visual equivalent of its stately
declarative speech.

> out over the land skope view as from Alexander Baker's
>   still
> stonewall orchard pasture land-bench over the River
>   looking
> to Apple Row and the Sargents other side the scoop out of

the surface of the earth a lone woman sat there in young
skirt the gulls use it in early morning to drop mussels
on the low-tide rocks

                Dogtown to the right the ocean

to the left

        opens out the light   the river flowing

at my feet

        Gloucester to my back

    the light hangs
    from the wheel of heaven

          the great Ocean
          in balance

                the air is as wide as the light

Hesiod said the outer man was the bond with which Zeus
    bound Prometheus

          the illusory
          is real enough

the suffering
is not suffered

        the foreknowledge
      is absolute

           Okeanos
           hangs in the father

           the father
           is before the beginning of bodily
             things

The initial lines move quickly, sweepingly, opening the view.
"Skope" not only evokes the act of viewing, which is the essential fact of landscape, but allies it to other times, reminding us
that we are witnessing eternal events. The landscape calls up
an unfinished poem of 1940 that begins, "Between the river
and the sea I sit writing,/ The Annisquam and the Atlantic,"
and concludes with, "Over all the gulls"—gulls whose flight

we can attain to only by love.[114] The present landscape belongs
as much to Maximus' past as to the present: at some time he
saw there, as he now recalls, an anima figure, "a lone woman
sat there in young/ skirt," and it is now, as always, a resort of
gulls, his tutelary bird.[115]

The lines that follow extend the skope, opening it to us so
that we see the entire "wheel" of the sky and feel that "the air
is as wide as the light. . . ." Not only does the act of seeing open
this wonderful space but light itself seems to be the accompanying agency: "opens out the light" may also be read "the
light opens out," for light is active here, transforming *aer*; it
"hangs" from the heavens and pervades the harmonious still-
ness, the mandalic circle inclosing the "flowing" river and the
"balance[d]" Ocean (Okeanos, no longer enraged). To use
Gaston Bachelard's indispensable word, Maximus experiences
"cosmicity."

And because he does he tempers his hostility to Zeus. In the
long line that marks this division of the poem Maximus transposes Zosimos' doctrine of the Anthropos, with its advice to
liberate the "outer" physical man by means of the redemptive
work of becoming a man of light. This work modifies his allegiance to Mother Earth; it turns him heavenward, to spirit, the
realm of light. Now Okeanos, who is a son of Heaven as well as
Earth and who in the Pelasgian creation myth is the father of
all things, is one with the light, "hangs in the father," and the
father, as Maximus affirms, is origin, "is before the beginning
of bodily things. . . ."

The alchemy of this poem restores the unity of father-and-
son. This union figures prominently in the second poem, its
title again given by the first line, "to enter into their bodies,"
the line itself taken directly from another essential book,
Henri Frankfort's *Kingship and the Gods*. It directs us to the
Memphite Theology and chiefly its claim, as Frankfort says,
"for Ptah as Creator."

to enter into their bodies
which also
had grown out of
Earth

—this is Maximus' transposition of the conclusion of Frankfort's summary of the Egyptian text that establishes the "sole
creatorship of Ptah": "it had started by stating that the gods
came forth from Ptah, objectified conceptions of his mind,
[and] it ends by making those gods 'enter into their bodies'
(statues) of all kinds of material—stone, metal, or wood—
which had grown out of the earth, that is, out of Ptah." [116] The
way in which Maximus employs such texts requires that we
read fully and understand their contexts; in doing this, we discover one of the things Maximus found congenial in this theology: that Ptah creates through "utterance of thought" and
exemplifies the fact, as Olson noted in *The Great Mother*, that
"the outstretched tongue [phallic in character, Neumann says]
is a sign of power. . . ." The diorite stone, standing on Fort
Place, is also a poet who appreciates the fact that the proud act
of language, of logos, must be deeply rooted. [117]

But this is not the direction Maximus takes in this poem.
The creative act that interests him concerns his own conception, which is also his self-begetting. He tells this story in
terms of Father Sea and Mother Dogtown/Our Lady (referring
to "The Frontlet," an immediately previous poem); and again
transposing from Frankfort, he retells, as might a child dis-
turbed over his own making, the incident of Horus commanding Isis and Nephthys to save Osiris who is floating away.

My father
came to the shore
the polyphony
came to the shore

he was as dust
in the water

    the Monogene
    was in the water, he was floating
    away

                    oh I wouldn't let my Father
            get away
                        I cried out
            to my Mother
            "Turn your head
            and quick"
                        & he came
            to the shore
            he came to the
            City
                    oh
            and I welcomed
            him
            & was very glad

That the father is also the Monogene, the agent of redemption,
compounds the childhood anxiety that gives this poem such
dreamlike force. The puns are as direct as they are brilliant,
and the final line ("& was very glad") is affectively right, having
behind it Olson's usually happy response to dreams involving
his father.[118]

This poem belongs to a large cluster of poems concerned with
myth. Its Memphite Theology prefaces "The Cow/ of Dogtown," which follows it. Even as it marks the turning to the
Father in Volume III—parts of Book VI might well have been
included in Volume III—it secures for Maximus a double allegiance. His need for the Mother is unquestionably great, and in
these poems he serves her well. But he does so, it seems to me,
burdened by the confession he makes in Volume III, where,
with relief, he says that his dealing with his father "was so
loaded in his favor as in fact so patently/ against my mother
that I have been like his stained shingle/ ever since. . . ." Ac-

knowleging this and recognizing that Maximus continues to praise the Goddess, we must consider the development of the poems in the light of Jung's remark on the "strange symbolic wanderings" of the unconscious.[119]

The Memphite Theology permits Maximus to celebrate both Mother and Father, Nut and Ptah. Much of "The Cow/ of Dogtown" is transposition of Nathaniel Shaler's geological description of Dogtown, which Maximus recognizes as an eternal event, as the emergence of Primeval Hill from the primordial waters of the Nile:

> Nut is over you
> Ptah has replaced the Earth
> the Primeval Hill
> has gone directly
> from the waters
> and the mud

What the poem effects—and what makes it effective—is the present sense, with respect to sky and light, of sustaining presence ("Nut is in the world"):

> The top of Dogtown
> puts one up into the sky as free-
> ly as it is possible, the extent of
> clear space and air, and the bowl
> of the light equalling, without at all
> that other, false experience of mountain
> climbed, heaven.

Here—how right the unassuming language is—Maximus has become the man-with-the-house-on-his-head:

> One would sit here
> and eat off checker berries, and blue-
> berries in season—they are around
> the place, at this height,
> like cups and saucers, and one moves around to
> eat them, out of one's hands,

not by getting up but going from
place to place on one's own behind

Yes, as Maximus says, "one could stay here with the sky/ it feels like as long as one chose. . . ."

Somewhat later, Maximus in another important Dogtown poem (on Gravelly Hill) tells us that he sits overlooking the town "like/ the Memphite lord of/ all Creation. . . ." Yet, even so, he is chiefly concerned with Earth as "active" and with the "Hellmouth" at her boundary: "Here you enter/ darkness." The paved hole in the earth is "Hell's mouth/ where Dogtown ends." Thus, in the deepest descent of the poems, we come to Tartarus, which figures prominently in the "one big crash-pole of a poem all solid Hesiod," as Olson called "[MAXIMUS, FROM DOGTOWN—IV]" in a letter to Joyce Benson.[120] And we come back to Typhon, the son of Earth and Tartaros, whose rebellion Zeus "in the bitterness of his anger" punished by casting him down to Tartarus, "his father's/ place. . . ."

There is solid Hesiod in this long poem, but not all of its materials come from *Theogony*. The poem is speculative, Maximus' deepest meditation on origin, and also draws on Egyptian, Norse, and Hindu myths as well as Whitehead's *Process and Reality* and Hermann Weyl's *Philosophy of Mathematics and Natural Science*. Two related things concern Maximus here: the priority of elements in creation and his ambivalence over fathers. We detect the latter in "our father who is also in/ Tartaros chained in being," early parodic lines giving praise to Typhon at the expense of Zeus, and lines that suggest the importance of Tartarus and the desire for deliverance. Although Maximus acknowledges the Great Mother ("'Earth' mass mother milk cow body") he believes there is a "more/ primitive" source, and this is "appetite," or "hunger" (*Ginnungagap* in the Norse cosmology), and that out of this "mouth," this creative space, Earth appeared, "our dear fatherland the Earth/ thrown up to form a cairn [a Primeval Hill]. . . ./"

This cairn points heavenward, and Earth is "spouse of Uranos. . . ." But what of Tartaros (Tartarus), with whom Earth
also mates? Maximus does not so much consider Tartarus beyond Okeanos, that is "outside/ the ends and source of Earth,"
as "<u>underneath</u>," at the "foundations of Ocean," at the "roots
of Earth. . . ." It is "below," and below, he believes, "is a factor
of being. . . ." (As the diorite stone he is bottomed there.) This
accords with his findings about priority: Hunger, Earth, then
Tartaros, so that "Tartaros/ was once 'ahead' of/ Heaven/ was
prior to. . . ." Now Tartarus, where the Titans and Cronos as
well as Typhon are imprisoned, is a factor of being because
what Zeus would put outside his ordered world are "those
who/ strain/ reach out are/ hunger"; Zeus would deny tropic
force, the magnificent energies Maximus evokes in the extensive physical description of Typhon and the account of his
battle with Zeus. And two things support his celebration of
this feral hunger for being: that it moves these "imprisoned
original/ created—all of the first creations/ of Earth and
Heaven" to find the "'way up'" the ladder of redemption, and
that in the priorities of creation Love was not far from first and,
more important, certifying his identification with Typhon,
"accompanied Tartaros/ when with Earth in love he made/
Typhon. . . ."[121]

Maximus finds a first father and one to his liking. And because he does and moves in his meditation from hostility to
love, he finds the creation, in poetry and cosmos, good. In the
small poem immediately following and concluding this longest
sequence of mythological poems, he says:

> I looked up and saw
> its form
> through everything
> —it is sewn
> in all parts, under
> and over

Okeanos "steers all things through all things"; Nut is "above
& below"; and Love, which is form, is likewise a pervasive
cosmic presence.

Book VI continues for some twenty-five pages or more, its sew-
ing somewhat loose, its energy almost spent. There are notable
poems like "why light, and flowers?" which celebrates the
Lady of Good Voyage and perhaps Maximus' success in self-
transformation. He seems to know the Earth Mother's lap and
the mysteries to be found "in the hole in the earth," the "$1.37
worth of change" to be had there, that sum calling up "the
reciprocal 1/137 one of the two/ pure numbers out of which the
world/ is constructed. . . ."[122] And he has himself become a
father who shows his children "where to dig."
    There is the sense of reaching an end. B. Ellery has been
placed, and with "The River Map," he tells us, "we're done."
The title reminds us of mappemunde which is in fact the case,
since "River Map," as Jung explains it, is a drawing revealing
the laws of the world order, made, according to Chinese legend,
by a dragon who dredged its signs from a river.[123] This map is
a mandala, and with it Maximus tells the wholeness he has
achieved. The poem expresses a wonderful sense of the per-
manence of his erotic landscape of being ("the firmness of the
Two Hills"). For the time being the process is still. Now the
tropic force of the river ("neap or flood tide" evokes its youth-
ful turbulence in "The Twist") is in respite:

> nothing all the way
> of the hollow of the Diorite
> from glacial time to this soft summer night
> with the river in this respite solely
> an interruption of itself

Such surcease, too, is an eternal event.
    The end, characteristically, is a departure, a new beginning:

"I set out now/ in a box upon the sea." Like all the mythic and
historical seafarers in the genealogy to which he belongs, like
Ishmael, too, at the end of *Moby-Dick* and Whitman at the end
of "Passage to India," Maximus is once more at sea. In the symbols of analytical psychology he has again launched the ego
upon the unconscious and undertaken in the Mother Vessel
the transformative journey in which the old personality dies
and a new one is born. [124] The rebirth he seeks is of the wonderful miraculous kind already witnessed in the flower ceremony at the Cut, and we remember especially his sense, again
in evidence in this installment, of "goodness over and under
us. . . ." This transformation is also associated with the father,
which is true in the present instance. In one of the earlier versions of this entry, Maximus says:

> I navigate now without authority. Turn, great
>   sun, your disc upon me
> I must cut myself adrift, cut off
> my bull's horns, go where I have refused
> be not the special son of my mother,
> the evidence of my father, the pleasure
> that he had a son, go out into the
>   abandonment
> I have so carefully neglected . . .[125]

Maximus accepts the risk because he knows, with Emerson,
that abandonment is the way of life, the condition of an open
universe and the open poetry by which we navigate it. Using
the primary figure of self and world, Emerson reminds us that
"the life of man is a self-evolving circle, which, from a ring
imperceptibly small, rushes on all sides outwards to new and
larger circles, and that without end." [126] Without end. As
Creeley says, in an essay on autobiography, the mode of *The
Maximus Poems*: in tracking your life "you begin at any point,
and move from that point forward or backward, up or down—

or in a direction you yourself choose." [127] In putting to sea
Maximus is now bound forward and up, toward the shores of
light.

Maximus is his father's son. He prefers alchemies of spiritual **VII and**
descent-ascent to those that propose the priority of the Great **After**
Mother. For all of his love of Earth—compelling to the end and *An Actual*
finally preemptive—his consciousness is patriarchal, starting, *Earth of*
as Neumann explains, "from the standpoint that the spirit is *Value*
eternal *a priori*; that the spirit was in the beginning." As Maximus says in the previous volume, "from heaven the Ladder//
comes down to the Earth. . . ." And his reference there to "The
Poimanderes" (the *Poimandres* of Hermes Trismegistus, the
paradigmatic text, offers the kind of alchemy of resurrection he
appreciates in the Persian angelology and the Taoist *The Secret
of the Golden Flower*) tells us what we now conclusively learn:
that for him the Great Mother is not ultimate source, that she
is not the origin but the nature to which he descends, the darkness he redeems in his subsequent ascent to light. "Books VII
and After," as Olson called Volume III, is the book of the
Father, a celebration of light. [128]
   The most obvious sign of this transformation is the motif of
the inverted lotus:

> Imbued
> with the light
> the flower
> grows down
> the air
> of heaven

Olson inscribed these lines on the title page of Chapter II of
Jung's *Psychology and Alchemy*, where the epigraph from
Virgil reads, "easy is the descent . . . but to recall thy steps and

pass out to the upper air, this is the task, this is the toil!"[129]

The flower now grows down from the "patriarchal heaven" (I quote Neumann).[130] Its roots are in the "Outer Předmost," a kind of heavenly Paleolithic soil, Maximus' designation for a finite, physical cosmos:

> I believe in God
> as fully physical
> thus the Outer Předmost
> of the World on which we 'hang'
> as though it were wood and our own bodies are
> hanging on it

The flower is the tree of life, Yggdrasill, inverted again, and all of us, like Odin, hang from it. Or, more exactly, God the Father is tree, himself maternal, source and sustainer, as in Maximus' pun-pointed entry a few pages on:

> The Return to the Mail-Bag, or
> The Postal Union
> of the Son with the Father

Viewing himself in the mirror, Maximus, aged fifty-two, recalls the picture of himself (Olson) as an infant standing protectively held by his father in his father's mailbag.[131] Father now is womb, uroboros, the heavenly Okeanos Maximus sees when he looks "up." And what he wishes most—what ascent offers—is return: reconciliation, union with that source, some way other than rebellion for the exiled son to know his paternity. (We remember, in *Call Me Ishmael*, the section beginning "He suffered as a son. He had lost the source. He demanded to know the father.")[132] The effort, as the last line of the entry indicates, must be his own.

He needs also an acceptable tropism, the heliotropism this alchemy provides. In no other volume of *The Maximus Poems* does Maximus so carefully attend the rising and the setting of the sun, and acknowledge his allegiance, his "love's obei-

sance," to Helios, "the Father Plant & Day-Sun of/ life. . . ."
Now, he says, he faces the sun like an Arab at least once a day,
usually at sunset. As Olson explains in *Poetry and Truth*, "I
mean [by tropism], obey yourself and in obeying yourself kneel
or lean to the sun, or whatever that heliotrope, like, is." An
echo here tells us that, with Melville, he is addressing a central
issue of his life—"And if we obey God," Father Mapple says
in *Moby-Dick*, "we must disobey ourselves; and it is in this
disobeying ourselves, wherein the hardness of obeying God
consists." Now he can both obey himself and kneel to the sun
because the tropism of his being is heliotropic: the "tropism in
ourselves is the sun." The son who sits in his own darkness is
of the sun. He has "a helio inside [himself]," and so possesses
the light with which to *"light that dark. . . ."* And this, Olson
remarks, is to "come to whatever it is . . . any of us seeks," to
the goal most briefly formulated in the title of an early lecture:
"The Sun, or, Self."[133]

This is but one of several distinctive aspects of what, clearly,
is a concluding volume. Now Maximus completes his mappemunde by extending his excursions to Cole's Island and
Walker's Creek, to West Gloucester—west having its immemorial association with death. The desolation that followed
Betty Olson's death marks this volume. So does the presenti-
ment of his own death ("I go off/ a last time/ to leave this gate/
of my life/ & of the city"). As Ferrini remarked, commenting
on these last lonely years, Olson "had that hunch about time
he knew so well."[134] Evil, too, is conspicuous: Fenrir, the
wolf, now appears, "a principle in creation," and Maximus, in
this appropriation of Norse mythology, acknowledges strife,
"the War/ of the World/ . . . endlessly poised. . . ."[135] There is
also a new hero, a "War Chief," Enyalion who serves human
measure ("the law of the proportions/ of his own body"), and
whom Maximus assimilates to Tyr and Shiva, like the former
enabling the capture of the wolf by forfeiting his hand, like the

latter liberating the world from tyranny by destroying the
Three Towns. This play of opposites, of good and evil, is necessary to a full account of the world (and psyche) and accords
with the resumption in this volume of the political concern of
Volume I. Formally and mythically the last volume is closer
to the preceding volume; it overlaps it. But in important ways
it returns to Volume I: it recovers the original political intent
of refounding or renewing the nation, begins, in fact, with
Maximus' present situation in "gloom on Watch-House Point"
and his wish to "write a Republic"—no longer to work immediate change, but by writing at least, by doing what *The Maximus Poems* have done, begin, as he says at the end, "the initia-
tion/ of another kind of nation."[136] This is one of the important turnings in which the work completes itself. Others are
the return to the locale of Volume I—more than ever Maximus
inhabits the harbor—and with it, a return to his childhood and
youth.

It is notable too that Maximus himself disappears in this
volume and Olson comes forward. There are a few Maximus
poems but Olson, the signatory of several poems, is fully
present as never before, the "plague" of his own "unsatisfying
possible identity as/ denominable Charles Olson" cancelled for
us by the very declaration.[137] Later on in the last explicit
Maximus poem—"Maximus of Gloucester"—he tells us

> It is not I,
> even if the life appeared
> biographical. The only interesting thing
> is if one can be
> an image
> of man. . . .

Yet, unquestionably, this is the most biographical volume, and
is especially moving because it is.

Olson admits us to his life not only because the transforma-

tion that has taken place (is taking place) has released (releases)
his love but because in the absence of friends he needs us:

> And no one
> to tell it to
> but you   for
>   Robert Hogg, Dan Rice and
>   Jeremy Prynne

We share his loneliness, as do the former inhabitants with
whom he has lived so long:

> no one in the world
> close to me, alone in my home where a plantation
> had been a Sunday earlier than this been
> proposed, it is Osman (or Osmund) Dutch's
> name, and Gallop whom I am closest to[138]

And lacking a polis, he inscribes his name with theirs on a
weather shingle. He tells us of his despair in the prayer (there
are now prayers) to Great Washing Rock, where, with the approach of his fifty-seventh birthday, he remarks, "so many
years/ on the lookout and no further than here. . . ." He even
reveals himself utterly abject, the destiny of his spirit un-
flagged ("unflags": a dreadful negative) because "almost for the
first time,/ so has suffering offended/ the earth/ of my being."
And we see him, no diorite stone on Main Street,

> Hunched up
> on granite steps in the part dark Gloucester
> and ghettoes gone cities and an infantile people
> set loose to create what was ground
> and is now
> holes

Offsetting this is a brighter glimpse of Olson the sun wor-
shipper

> having [his] lean Muslim-American supper of
> two cheeseburgers a thin milk shake
> called a <u>frappe</u> Gloucester & a black coffee

And usually the despair is mitigated by irrepressible energy, by the verbal force that, for example, in the poem on being shut in for days by a blizzard, turns desperate emptiness into hunger for everything, the creative desire of *Ginnungagap*. In another instance, his appropriation of Creeley's work, particularly "I Know a Man," saves the situation:

> I said to my friend my
> life is recently so hairy honkie-
> hard & horny too to that ex
> tent I am far far younger
> now than though of course I am
> not twenty any more, only
> the divine alone interests me at
> all and so much else is other-
> wise I hump out hard &
> crash in nerves and smashed
> existence only

Yes, as he says, the divine alone interests him.[139] He is "wholly absorbed/ into [his] own conduits," caught up in "great sweat[s] of being. . . ." "I have arrived at a point where I really have no more than to feed on myself," he says in *Causal Mythology*, with *Poetry and Truth* one of the essential glosses on his last work.[140] This is the Olson who now figures most, a spiritual seeker who takes us into his monkish life, who tells us he has "sacrificed every thing" in "this attempt to acquire complete/ concentration." And though he is much more re-strained in the poems, this is the Olson of *Reading at Berkeley*, a man in need of confession, freed at last by telling what had been hardest for him to speak—that he had wronged his father, had been Fenrir to his Tyr, had harbored evil as well as good.

This volume begins with a scatter of poems. They quickly
establish Maximus' local ways, preoccupations, social views,
beliefs and the fact that, now in the gloom on Watch-House
Point, he has become the watchman of whom we ask—who
asks himself—"what of the night?" The drama of this volume
concerns the darkness of his closing years, the despair and dismay, both private and public, Maximus conquers; its difficult
victory is one of reconciliation and harmony, and, with them,
renewed hope.

The first poem of any size ("Main Street/ is deserted") recovers the heights of the previous volume. Again we are in the
world of light, where, as Maximus says, "the power in the air/
is prana. . . ." Though it is spring again, Maximus now sits in
the ice at the top of the Poles, an upthrust comparable to Dogtown that overlooks the Annisquam River. He is at the top of
the world, like Bulgar, the composite mythic character of his
creation whom he places at the North Pole. Bulgar, a patriarchal figure with some matriarchal characteristics (his sweater
was made by "one of Demeter's pigs," he wears a skirt), is connected with both ice and light, with the wintry landscape of
much of this volume and with the aurora borealis. Like Horus,
he has four sons and hides them in Set's thigh, Set, too, according to Jung, who notes also that the highest Babylonian
gods have their dominion in the northern heaven, having the
Pole for his region. Almost every element of this configuration
speaks for the quaternity and union of opposites represented
by the mandala. And as the goal to be achieved, it has for
Maximus the additional significance of representing the end of
the human migrations he has done so much and continues to
trace. It is a completion, in a new center, and yet it may be,
as "NNW, Novoye/ Sibersky Slovo" reminds us, the dire end
in "Stefansson's ice. . . ."[141]

At the moment Maximus does not consider such linear
finality. In the poems that follow he is happily at work.

His brief entries point to ascent; even history, the origin of
Gloucester, suggests the origin in (and reunion with) the
father. In the blossoming apple trees of Dogtown he recognizes
"Paradise," a thematic notation of his *Paradisio*. He is moving,
as he has it in a late schema, from the "initiatic cosmos (cosmology)" to the "world of nature," to the "celestial world
(theology)."[142] For the time being the gloom of Watch-House
Point lifts: now past achievement ("having descried the nation") yields to future resolve ("to descry/ anew: attendeo/ &
broadcast/ the world"). And he does attend immediately, in the
lovely poem on the star-nosed mole, where the image of the
mole as "a flower dizzy/ with its own self" prefigures his own
wonderful celestial disorientation. A cluster of important
poems (pp. 28–42), in resuming old themes, proposes new
ones. William Stevens appears again, now linked with Ousoos,
the Phoenician, and Maximus considers him the founder of
"Troy/ on this side of history. . . ." And Stevens, who in the
first volume of *The Maximus Poems* was associated with
Olson's father, provides the occasion, in "Stevens song," of the
enabling confession: how "the dirty filthy whining ultimate
thing// entered" and he, the son, "was// a dog," was Fenris,
when his father "Tyr/ put his hand// in Fenris/ mouth. . . ."
This is the context in which, in the succeeding poem, he introduces Bulgar; the context of "Astride/ the Cabot/ fault,"
where Maximus speaks of the NNW direction of continental
drift and announces his high purpose, resonant of Pound's, "to
build out of sound the wall/ of a city";[143] and the context of
his praise of Enyalion, whose far place he associates with
Ousoos and Bulgar, and who, in the subsequent poem on John
(Wanax) Withrop, which evokes the despair of volume one ("7
years & you cld carry cinders in yr hand") is the prototype of
the "men/ [who] cared/ for what kind of world/ they chose to
live in" and in his American avatar reminds Maximus that

"Good News/ can come/ from Canaan. . . ." "Signature to Petition," a poem finally using John Watts in a large way, discredits utopia, but the possibility spoken in the earlier poem indicates the restoration of Maximus' spirit.

Then, March 28, 1964, the crisis of Betty Olson's death, when the Dog, instead of salivarating eternal events as he did in March, 1961,[144] salivarates "Space and Time," the conditions of limitation, and Maximus finds his "own living hand" in the wolf's mouth. God the Dog has become Fenrir. This disaster, so briefly noted, takes force from the earlier passage on Fenrir and Tyr where Maximus remembers the dream first told in "ABCs (2)" ("what bloody stumps/ these dogs have, how they tear the golden cloak")—remembers and, in the very details he now presents, makes it premonitory:

> tore the bloody cloak then
> literally tore the flesh
>
> of the conjoined
> love I was
>
> a dog who had
> bitten into
>
> her body
> as it was joined
>
> to mine

The diminished verse of this time is enough to tell Maximus' loss but in "Maximus to himself June 1964," he eloquently tells it in images that recall the earliest elements of his poetic enterprise:

> no more,
> where the tidal river rushes
>
> no more
> the golden cloak (beloved
> World)

> no more dogs
> to tear anything
> apart—the fabric
> nothing like
> the boat (no more Vessel
> in the Virgin's
> arms
> no more dog-rocks
> for the tide
> to rush over not any time again
> for wonder
> the ownership
> solely
> mine

No more. The refrain recalls another poem of desolation, Poe's "The Raven," but everything in the *Maximus* poem questions Poe's poetics and philosophy of composition. How brilliantly he employs this refrain, making it the initial outcry of grief, always varying it, modulating it into "nothing." And each time a significant image follows the refrain—the tidal river, the golden cloak, the boat in the Virgin's arms, "time" itself. The most important is the first—"where the tidal river rushes"— taken, like the golden cloak, from "ABCs (2)." For this poem not only recalls the deep psychic concern of Olson's poetics, but suddenly becomes a necessary gloss on his work in the last volumes of *The Maximus Poems*. With these volumes in mind we now fully realize the importance to him of discovering "who they are who lie/ coiled or unflown/ in the marrow of the bone"; and we understand the great sweat of being in which he now reverses the stages of rhythm-image-knowing-construct:

> Bottled up for days, mostly
> in great sweat of being, seeking
> . . . .

> to construct knowing back to image and
> God's face behind it turned as mine
> now is to blackness. . . .

The tidal river is most important because Maximus insists on
it, uses it to inclose his previous objects; because it, too, is
precious, the image of *eros-tropos*, of miraculous process, of
redemptive agency; because once again in these poems it is a
prominent feature of the landscape. But now the tide itself is
bereft, there are "no more dog-rocks" for it to rush over. Maximus is no longer the masterful Odysseus steering between
Scylla and Charybdis:

> And the boat,
> how he swerves it to avoid the yelping rocks
> where the tidal river rushes

In the melodramatic terms of the first *Maximus* poems ("the
wondership stolen by,/ ownership"), he now possesses only
"the ownership." No Nike dazzles him. Ownership is negation: he is left alone with all the detritus of culture, the rubbish of creation, he has tried to redeem.

There is substantial truth in Charles Boer's assessment of
Olson's loss: "Your life was suddenly, incredibly, broken apart.
You would never be able to put it back together again."[145] Yet,
in these poems he did put his life together again. That is perhaps *their* most significant achievement: having the poems—
having his life in them—saved him. And *his* achievement:
always the stunning fact of imagination, that when it is great
it refuses the demonism it knows so well and remakes a world,
of benign auspices, where it is possible to live. At times in his
struggle for light, and certainly at the end, Olson repossessed
the wondership.

In the handful of poems written during the first year or so of
loss, there are signs of recovery. *Tropos* reasserts its value:

the sky,
of Gloucester
perfect bowl
of land and sea

And previous material—the sea serpent, Typhon, Okeanos—necessary to a tropic or resistant posture, reasserts itself. Maximus may represent his woe by adding an oven to the head of "The Man-With-The-House-On-His-Head," but refuses that image of the Way and its association with Dogtown by furiously declaring himself Ocean's Perfect Child, even Zeus ("I am the one from [for?] whom the Kouretes/ bang their platters"). In time, "The Wolf/ slinks off":

Fenrir's
mouth
salivarating.
And my arm
on my own body,
my own hand
mine

Here "mine" recalls the earlier poem of loss (and prefigures the repossession claimed in the last line of the book: "my wife my car   my color   and myself"). But this possession of loss is positive because it cancels his filial identification with Fenrir and makes him Tyr.

There are other signs of recovery in the two historical poems that immediately follow, not only in the gathering verbal energy, the fullness of talk, but in Maximus' renewed interest in the second Gloucester, which secured the dream of discovery:

The 2nd Gloucester was a fastening, of around 40 men
    and families,
to hold the future until the future made back to the spot,

course almost due West from Biscay, where fishing
    Europe found her
floating, an island floating in the Western Sea

Still another sign is his repudiation of Otto Rank's theory of
the evolution of the patriarchal nuclear family ("When I was a
Blue Deer," Maximus says, "Viola Barrett was my mother")[146]
and his insistence that procreation is a secondary function, of
little importance in comparison to what he now asserts and
claims for himself—

if man does not spill out his being so, if he hath not the
    axis,
unwearingly revolving in the act of initial creation—
    not the
reproduction of nature alone . . .

Perhaps the best evidence of Maximus' restoration is
"COLE'S ISLAND" where, with wonderful equanimity, he
tells of meeting Death ("My impression is we did—/ that is,
Death and myself, regard each other"), and Death, a country
gentleman—

Maybe he had gaiters on, or almost
a walking stick, in other words much more
habited than I,
who was in chinos actually and
only doing what I had set myself to do here[147]
& in other places on Cape Ann

—Death becomes a recognized part of his landscape, the
stranger we inevitably meet if we walk, as Maximus says he
often does, in the woods. And after the interval of several
months during which Olson taught at Buffalo, and it is again
March, there is the confirmation of two poems. The first,
"Sweet Salmon"—

from the coldest clearest
waters. Cut the finest
on the bone.

> Rose
> directly from the stream straight into my greedy
> throat. And breast. A home
> for life. Wise Goddess
> of the straightest
> sapling

—employs Celtic myth to celebrate the life-restoring gifts of
wisdom and inspiration.[148] The second, "The Festival Aspect,"
is also celebratory, a great prophetic poem of the new year. It
announces, in terms of Hindu myth, a universe sustained by
truth and once more a unity; a universe in which Shiva will
destroy the Three Towns and Ganesh overcome all obstacles;
where, "When the World is one again/ . . . the Flower will grow
down" and "the earth/ will be the light, the air and the dust/ of
the air will be the perfume" and "the gloire / will have returned"; where there will be no anger and "we shall all stand,"
as Maximus tells us he now does, "on our heads and hands,"
with our feet in the air.

  These poems are perhaps the first of those that record the
attainment of "satisfaction." I use Whitehead's term because
it designates the termination, the completeness, of an actual
entity's becoming, the "complex feeling involving a complete-
ly determinate bond with every item in the universe. . . ."[149]
It is an appropriate word for the kind of closure Maximus feels,
for the sense he increasingly has of being physically at home
in Gloucester. In the poem beginning "Physically, I am home,"
he insists on his relation to Earth, on the excellence of sea-
level, and manages to have this "perfect/ 'ground'" as well as
the Heavens by interfusing his terms. Not only is "Heaven"
the mind drawn to Gloucester, it is the night:

> Night
> is the air
> of Heaven. In one place [Gloucester]
> —in the place where God rests—

the Earth glows, in the light
of Heaven

Notation in the poem ("look" View Point// skope// "Height")
reminds us, even as the place of attainment is reversed, of the
opening out of light in "Out over the land skope," a poem of
satisfaction in the previous volume. And this earlier touch-
stone is also the measure of attainment ("Foreknowledge Absolute" introduces it) in "Tall in the Fort," were Maximus tells
us he feels "all the world// close" and "all that one cares for/
proven// and come true. . . ." *All*. With how much he invests
it! With as much as Creeley does, for example, in "The Picnic":

> Time we all went home
> or back
> to where it all was,
> where it all was.

And this is what Maximus achieves in "Celestial Evening,
October 1967," when, losing space control, disoriented like
the star-nosed mole, he is overwhelmed by the "full volume of
all [the universe]" and of "all history existence places. . . ."
"It all/ comes in," he says, and in wonder he attends

> to turn & turn within
> the steady stream & collect which
> within me ends as in her hall and I
>
> hear all, the new moon new, in all
> the ancient sky

So the *gloire* returns, and he has, as he did not have in March,
1964, "the bright body of sex and love/ back in the world. . . ."

Other turnings mark Maximus' turning from death, the turning of the earth itself, "life again here in the North," as he says
of the winter solstice, "saved/ by the tilting of the ecliptic
once more in its favor. . . ."[150] Like Thoreau at Walden, Maxi-

mus on Watch-House Point ("Out here on the end of the land")
attends the seasons, and now in the winter of 1965–1966, the
solstice at hand, anticipates "confidently" the "promise" of
spring: "another/ year of spring to come and Dogtown unlock
her frozen/ bushes and roads. . . ." For him, this "annular-
Eternal" event may even redeem the nation since "its Limit
now reached," it "turns now to its Perfection." And again, like
Thoreau in "The Pond in Winter," his work is to "go [out] on
the frozen being and . . . take the marks and bearings." This
he would gladly do in the "Winter's brilliance with the sun
new-made" and himself delivered from death ("I also re-arisen
. . . from December's/ threat") and with "Love all new within
me ready too to go abroad." Yet like Thoreau, who knew the
desperation of winter, Maximus admits his own. In the newness of the snowy world, "in this light, and on this point"
where he says he can conceive of no hindrance, he is "damned
. . . in death. . . ." The shadow of its evil falls on his soul—and
to such an extent that he imagines the end of the world, when
Fenrir devours Odin, and cries out in the title of a poem,
written on hearing of the death of a writer, "IF THE DEATHS
DO NOT STOP/ WE'LL HAVE NO EARTH OR YEARS
LEFT." He does not deny that "March now has been added so
I have to live a 2nd month of fear & Hell each year. . . ."

Still this winter is resplendent and provides the occasion of
some of his best landscapes. No other volume of *The Maximus
Poems* and no other section of this one is so much devoted to
landscape. This is another reason—and Maximus' excursions
is one more—to recall Thoreau, though it is Fitz Hugh Lane,
Thoreau's contemporary in that great age of landscape, who is
conspicuous here. A native of Gloucester whose self-designed
house on Duncan's Point still commands the harbor, Lane
(1804–1865) was the preeminent nineteenth-century painter
of its sea- and landscapes. Olson knew his work well—the
largest collection is a short walk from Fort Square—sharply

reviewed the first monograph on it, and wrote out his own
appraisal and praise in two poems other than those in *The
Maximus Poems*, one of which entered art history when John
Wilmerding included it in his second monograph on Lane.[151]

View is the central word in his considerations of Lane, and
when he first mentions him in the previous volume we begin
to see the magnitude of its (and his) significance. The juxtaposition of "Lane's eye-view of Gloucester/ Phoenician eye-
view" spells *periplus*.[152] Lane saw Gloucester, often from a
rowboat in the harbor or from the vantage of Rocky Neck, in
the way Phoenician sailors saw the coasts of the seas they
explored. This brief notation places him in the succession of
voyagers and discoverers in which Maximus places himself.
(The cover of Volume III is Winthrop's *periplus* of the coast
of Massachusetts from Gloucester to Marblehead.) In terms of
Maximus' concern with migration, this makes Lane one of the
last "first" people, people in whose experience things are seen
freshly, firstly. In his unpublished review of Wilmerding's
Fitz Hugh Lane (1964), Olson says that Lane belongs with only
four other Americans, none of them painters, all of whom saw
freshly: with Stephens, who "first brought the Maya to men's
attentions," with Prescott and Parkman, who "each saw the
North American continent as a view, and a different one from
the only prior and original such possibility," and Noah Webster, whose dictionary "permitted the English-American language to become the re-issue of the initial European experience. . . ." Olson especially prizes views, as he says of Lane's,
"without any foreignness to [them]," and so reaffirms in terms
of landscape his cultural position, his American point-of-
view.[153] (Much of the point of a last poem is in the title:
"From My Own old/ View point.") He even strengthens his
early position when, in writing of Lane in "An 'Enthusiasm,'"
he says that "he was one of the/ chief definers of the American 'practice'—the word is/ Charles Pierce's for pragmatism—

which is still the con-/ spicuous difference of American from
any other past or any/ other present. . . ."[154]

In relation to landscape, *view* is also a measure of both
Maximus' recovery and the completion of his task. When we
remember "Lower Field—Enniscorthy," Olson's first attempt
"to bring the land into the eye's view," we appreciate how
much he has achieved: not only the balance in interrelated-
ness of self-and-world and the creation of a local cosmos ("a
portion of land which the eye/ can comprehend in a single
view"), but, because of them, homecoming, place, being
("Physically, I am home").[155] And if we contest this he has
every right to say again what he said in the poem on Gravelly
Hill, that "if this is nostalgia/ let you take a breath of April
showers/ . . . reason how is the dampness in your nasal passage"—or, in the present instance, yourself take up a position
and a viewpoint like his in his "eerie," with its "six tenement windows," on Fort Point. Olson turned to Lane because
no artist, beside himself, was so devoted to Gloucester. "I
come (home-wise) of Gloucester," he said, "(as he does blood-
wise . . .)." No one, he felt, had been so responsive to the geography, the climate, and the light of the place and had seen what
he saw and we may still see—"the sky,/ of Gloucester/ perfect
bowl/ of land and sea. . . ."[156]

But Lane brought him home in still another way, to his
father and to light. Olson's father was himself a painter who
had painted these scenes. In one of the poems of this winter
season in which Lane figures, Maximus remembers how his
father set off "with his water-color box to paint. . . ." Then
memory overwhelms him and he rehearses at the greatest
length in *The Maximus Poems* his father's defeat in organizing
the Postal Union and castigates "this filthy land/ . . . this foul
country where/ human lives are so much trash"—this land, he
says with his deep immigrant's bitterness, "which never/ lets

anyone/ come to/ shore. . . ." Yet he had in fact come to shore
because, as he so touchingly tells us, his father had already
come and had secured it for him:

> The love I learned
> from my father has stood me in good stead
> —home stead—I maintained this "strand" to
> this very day. My father's. And now my own[157]

As for light, Lane was the preeminent Luminist. His practice
was "American." In *American Painting of the Nineteenth
Century*, Barbara Novak considers him the exemplar of an
indigenous tradition related to Emersonian transcendentalism
in its fidelity to things and recognition of their animating
spirit. Olson himself approvingly notes "Lane's specificity &/
'place,'" the way he establishes "objects as definitions as exact
today as they/ were then"; he knows the way in which Lane
creates the space of his palpable light by showing "distances/
back of each other"; and, above all, he appreciates his poetry of
light, the best testimony of this being, "'light sits under one's
eyes . . .'" a poem of this time:

> When I think of what Fitz Lane didn't do
> painting all this light which almost
> each day is enough, at least at twilight,
> to rouse one as a change of air does
> to the direct connection our lives bear
> to the mathematic of Creation surrounding us,
> I love him more for his attempts pre-
> Hawthorne to draw in silk the pinks and
> umbrous hills and rocks surround
> on their reflexive & reflexing
> Harbor—light sits under one's eye
> & being as the saucer to the in
> the instance of this evening high al-
> most exactly perfect half moon al-
> ready going westward too[158]

This brilliant poem is tribute to Emerson as well as Lane and is, I think, remarkable enough (and so patently intended) to stand beside Emerson's famous passage in *Nature* on the transparent eyeball. Emerson, too, we remember, is abroad in the twilight and roused to the direct connection his life bears to the mathematic of the surrounding (environing) Creation, that phrase itself reminding us of Emerson's profound appreciation of the fact that "the world [is] throughout mathematical" and of Whitehead of whom Olson, dying, wrote: "The spiritual is all in Whitehead's simplest of all statements: Measurement is most possible throughout the system. That is what I mean. That is what I feel all inside. That is what I love."[159] (*All* again, and the trusting spirit of "The Praises.") Barbara Novak, who points out the importance of measure in the creation of Luminist light, connects Lane with Emerson, remarking that of all the painters of his time, "he was the most 'transparent eyeball.'"[160] Now Emerson, in crossing the bare common, "enjoyed a perfect exhilaration." He tells us that "Standing on the bare ground, —my head bathed by the blithe air and uplifted into infinite space,—all mean egotism vanishes. I become a transparent eyeball; I am nothing; I see all; the currents of the Universal Being circulate through me; I am part or parcel of God." The experience is mystical, but no less so than the circulation of light in the spiritual alchemy of *The Secret of the Golden Flower*, which by this time Olson endorsed. And he would have approved this ego-denying Emerson, the Emerson who repudiated the Plato who "clapped copyright on the world," the Emerson who saw in "the tranquil landscape . . . [a] somewhat as beautiful as his own nature," and who said, in the sentence Wilmerding uses as an epigraph in the first monograph on Lane, "There are days which occur in this climate, at almost any season of the year, wherein the world reaches its perfection."[161] This is what Olson's poem, itself a landscape of light, tells us, and that for him, as for

Emerson, process matters; that his landscape, with its moving
moon, is not, like Lane's, frozen, arrested, static. "Light does
not circulate in a painting by Lane," Novak says. "It does not
unite with air and atmosphere to create . . . a feeling of
action." [162] This is very want Olson has in mind when he
thinks of "What Fitz Lane didn't do." This is not said in censure, for Lane did much: he brought him home to place and
tradition.

Viewing, for Maximus, is a meditative exercise. His landscapes give the feeling of action because both mind and scene
are in motion—and often give, as in "December 22nd," a feeling of tranquillity.

> The sea
> is right up against the skin of the shore with a tide
> as high
> as this one, the rocks
> stretched, Half Moon Beach
> swallowed (to its bank), Shag Rock
> now by itself away from
> the Island, the Island
> itself a floating
> cruiser or ironclad
> Monitor, all laid out on top of the water, the whole
> full landscape a
> Buddhist
> message, Japanese
> Buddhism and maybe,
> behind it, exactly in these tightened coves, Chinese
> Buddhism, fullness and
> pertinax, sharp drawn
> lesson, the rocks
> melting
> into the sea, the forests,
> behind, transparent
> from the light snow showing
> lost rocks and hills

which one doesn't, ordinarily,
know, all the sea
calm and waiting, having
come so far

The Buddhist character of this landscape, so much insisted on,
is as much the result of its meditative quality as of its sharp
drawing, the quick exact verbal strokes of its lines, the careful
placement of nouns (beach, rocks, forests, hills) in terminal
visible positions, the telling junctures ("rocks/ melting/ into
the sea . . ."), the quiet participles (melting, showing, waiting,
having), and the *yugen* of the extraordinary sprung by the ordinary in the last remarkable lines. This, moreover, is the
essential landscape of this winter season: the harbor, and Ten
Pound Island ("the Island, the Island"), the fixed center of the
light of the golden flower.

On Sunday, January 16, 1966, it is unspoken, but we know
it there in the harbor world of the sunset's "Golden life, golden
light. . . ." As Maximus suggests, it is a guardian, like the
Monitor—and a few days later, in a different light, it reminds
him of post–Civil War America. For it is "America," the island
floating in the Western Sea. Most often its size and floating
aspect evoke a ship, as in the most remarkable of the Island
poems, that of February 7, 1966, where he likens it to the
Queen Mary, an attribution, of course, calling up the other
queens (Euronyme, Aglaia) he associates with "this Jewel/
. . . still & white/ in today's sun. . . ." As ship, Ten Pound
Island is in tow to Shag Rock, "going forever," he says, but
never moving: "Is here. Fixed,/ forever." As *jewel*, she is the
jewel in the eye of the sea-serpent reputed to have sailed
around her. Her attendant, Shag Rock, is equally important—
"my Rock," Maximus says, spelling out an earlier notation
("The Cormorant/ and the Spindle/ which marks Black
Rock")—

> my Rock, by which I have 'gone',
> always 'gone', always thank God have 'left'
> "Gloucester", Shag Rock, the property of
> shag   the rule and roost of my
> own black duck, look at it, today!
> right now hurting my eyes she's so studded in the
> glittering direct sun over her

And what does that *aglaia* teach? What is it, as Maximus says,
"my Island/ has taught me"?

With quick associative leaps he tells us in a long passage
that clearly marks a determinative spiritual turning. It involves four elements, the first an alchemy of resurrection
which serves as his own soul's admonition (the soul's emphasis, Emerson said, is always right). In the *Liber Platonis
quartorum*, a philosopher is cited as saying: "I went about
the three heavens, namely the heaven of composite nature,
the heaven of disciminated nature, and the heaven of the soul.
But when I sought to go about the heaven of intelligence [the
highest], the soul said to me: That way is not for thee. Then
nature attracted me, and I was attracted." [163] The juxtaposition of the soul's declaration ("That is no way for thee") with
"10 Lb Island" and the dream of his father, the next element,
is brilliant:

> 10 Lb Island,
> always there in front of me, to which my Father
> in a dream [as well as in fact] had rowed me,
>   the lower process
> in this kind of work   tide, in her revelation, recovered

The father, to whom he has given his allegiance, is here the
agent of his love of nature—of the Goddess—and, again in the
philosopher's words, has taught him "the lower process," a
redemptive process, too, as the association with the tide indicates. In what follows, Maximus reports his spiritual progress,

the successful circumambulation of the Three Heavens he
connects with the victory over the Three Towns; and then he
goes on to say that he had planned "to walk around the higher
world," to take a short cormorant's flight to it, when the soul
intervened and literally de-spirited (dispirited) him:

> how could the heaven of the soul itself say
> 'That is no way for thee' how could I
> be left
> as the cormorant
> with no more flight than
> our own Rock?

For the cormorant, as he observes, is reputed to take flight only
once a year and does so with difficulty "just at water-level, and
lands,/ almost as soon as in flight. . . ." And if that's all that
he is permitted, "where," Maximus asks, "have we gone? and
what is the 'prison' the soul says/ you shall stay in?" To which
his *viewing* gives the stunning, conclusive answer: "It is none,
my Island/ has taught me." Prohibited the highest heaven,
"you suddenly have nothing but matter," Olson says in *Poetry
and Truth* in commenting on this alchemy. But it is matter
itself that is efficacious, that in preventing, enables "your
being to have its heaven." [164]

Toward the end of the volume Olson depicts the moonlit
seascape at low tide, as Lane had, and celebrates both Lane and
what "Lane/ too/ saw. . . ." And what Lane saw, though not
with Olson's intensity, was the "still handsome & efficacious/
environment"—

> The Island, the River, the shore,
> the Stage Heads, the land, itself,
> isolated, encased on three sides by
> the sea and water
> on the 4th side, Eastern Point an arm

> such as Enyalion's to protect
> the body from the onslaught of
> too much and give Gloucester
> occasion, give her Champlain's channel
> in & out (as her river
> refluxes), a body of land, hard on granite yet
> arched by such skies favored by such sea and
> sweetened in the air so briar-roses grow
> right on her rock and at Brace's Cove kelp
> redolents the air, jumps the condition and strain locus
> falls or emerges as the rain on her or the sun

The only difficulty in this splendid tribute to the entire environment of Gloucester is *strain locus*, a term from Whitehead, troublesome enough but compounded by Olson's uncertain reference. Strain locus has to do with the duration of an enduring object—with its momentary rest—and also with the character of the object as a systematic whole depending on its geometrical rather than physical content. In the philosophy of organism it belongs with the real extensive connection of things, presentational immediacy, the possibility of measurement, and the satisfaction of the final phase of concrescence (growing together). In the context of the poem the term confirms Olson's immediate sense of Gloucester as the locus of his feelings, his focal region or space, as a complete enduring object and at the same time an object not (never) at rest, always alive, a body like his own, forever in the process, the downpour of (benevolent) elements. And efficacious: we are indeed "in the presence of the only truth which the real can have. . . ." [165]

The work of these winter months enabled the remaining poems. Reconciliation with his father is the momentous event, involving for Olson two related matters: the fullest ex-

planation of the cause of his despair over America and his acceptance of the vocational choice that now, as at the beginning
of his career, he alludes to in the legend of "Gassire's Lute." [166]
He will continue to speak his outrage, his wish, for example,
to unclutter the efficacious environment by removing to the
cemetery or the moon "these poor stuffed people,/ & their
hopelessly untreated children. . . ." He feels at times that
Gloucester "is out of her mind and/ is now indistinguishable
from/ the USA." But political dismay no longer overwhelms
him. It is true, as he says, that he once lived in Washington,
"the/ capital of this great poor Nation," but his fate was not to
be king—the king in "Gassire's Lute" lives on too long and his
son perforce becomes a bard—but to become a poet; a poet,
moreover, who, he now happily finds, is part of "the World
again," and lives "in a world on an Earth like this one/ we few
American poets have/ carved out of Nature and of God"; a poet
who concludes another survey of his environment by telling us
to "Love the World—and stay inside it." He is involved, he
says, with "these things instead of Kings," and later he adds a
note to the initial entry on Watch-House Point that dissipates
the gloom. It begins with the poetic task—formulated again
in terms of the "ABCs" and requiring the will to act of "The
Kingfishers"—of constructing "an actual earth of value"; it
ends with a notation of the occasion of the poem—"Reading
about my world. . . ." [167] One of the concluding poems says it
(all) in terms of *topos, tropos, typos:*

> the Blow is Creation
> & the Twist   the Nasturtium
> is any one of Ourselves
> And the Place of it All?
>   Mother   Earth   Alone

When younger poets ask him why his poetry "doesn't/ help
anybody," the answer is: "The black cormorant,/ not the gull
["building high" in Crane's *The Bridge*]/ possesses/ my eye-

view." His prayer to his father is "Secular Praise" announcing the resumption of his task, "to create Paradise/ Upon this Earth. . . ." An "end to Hell," he says, "/ —end even to Heaven. . . ." *Earth*. We believe him when he says, "I am going to hate to leave this Earthly Paradise. . . ."

The fullness and fulfillment he now feels is accompanied by a sense of ending. Much of the work he does—that on migration, for example—completes his investigations. Although he is still concerned with the first, or Indo-European, migration, the second, or Norse, is of greater interest to him because it brings him home, and not only to Gloucester but to Neolithic times. He appropriates the legend of S. Cornély to Gloucester and to his (and Lane's) attempt to "lay the Nation in its/ activity"; and he is pleased to learn that a Beothuk Indian canoe is in fact a "Pleistocene/ 'boat.'" Migration feeds his hope for the future, as in the poem of the rose of the World, where he says it is a constant of history, the endless pursuit of animals, plants, men, and gods, for a better environment, for a "new center." And it feeds his hope by taking him back to Gondwanaland, when the world had not started to come apart at the seams, when "Earth Herself was One," and the Atlantic was merely a pond and Cape Ann touched Africa at "Cape Jolly" (Cape Juby). In a poem on his Portuguese neighbors, in which he cites Greek and Norse myths of creation, he tells of the mid-Mesozoic time when Gloucester was Terceira and began its still-continuing drift westward; and recognizing the eyes of the Guanches in those of his neighbors, he knows that "my City she too came from the/ Islands [the Canaries]. . . ." Migration prompts this sense of origin, but also the sense of continuity and flow. It is the largest manifestation of Whiteheadean process, assuring him that

> there is now no break in the
> future, a thing does flow etc and
> intensity

is the characteristic throughout
the system. . . .[168]

And it explains, as he tells us, his persistence in raising
"monuments/ by this River. . . ."

All things flow. Of this he is the poet, none perhaps so much
taken with the "transitions" Emerson valued. His landscapes
are moving pictures ("As eddies work tideswards drawn/
toward the River pulling as the sun does the Fabrick apart").
He is "Charles . . .// of the Process," and his eye as well as body
takes excursions. He is a walker, coming, he says, from the last
walking period of man, and the great excursion of June 5–6,
1966, bears this out. This long expansive poem fills the space
of the page, the graphic evidence of his being at home in his
world. It enacts a nighttime ramble-meditation-writing-of-the-
poem. It is all motion and truly celebrates, as he says in its
defense, "the processes/ of Earth/ and man." Moon, tides, wind
—it is about them, and the turning, the refluxing that both sets
him free and, as he says elsewhere, redeems the town of the
rubbish of creation.[169] This poem calls up all the previous
poems of the tidal river, poems of forces full and forces spent,
of death and of resurrection. And now the great orange moon
free in the sky contrasts with the "swollen" moon of an earlier
time, evoking Whitman's "Out of the Cradle Endlessly Rock-
ing" only to deliver a message of imperturbable love ("I/ with
out wish & full of/ love").

Love and death are the signatures. In another noctural poem
of tides and turning winds he contemplates his own death,
imagining it in a story he himself invents of Homer dying at
Smyrna, having spent the day watching two boys fish. Sometimes he thinks of cataclysmic death, of volcanic eruption and
tidal wave, even, on another December day, this time in
Germany, of Ragnarok (the "terror the sky itself is falling the
End/ of the World Tree has come!"). But the Tree of Life,

Tiubirka, the shaking sacred birch tree, persists, survives the
snow, and tells his own restoration. So does a poem as notable,
on the poppy.

> When do poppies bloom   I ask myself, stopping again
> to look in Mrs. Frontiero's yard, beside her house on
> this side from Birdseyes (or what was once Cunningham
> & Thompson's and now is O'Donnell-Usen's) to see if
> I have missed them, flaked out and dry-like like
> Dennison's Crepe. And what I found was dark buds
> like cigars, and standing up   and my question is
> when, then, will those blossoms more lotuses to the
> West than lotuses wave like paper and petal by petal
> seem more powerful than any thing except the Universe
> itself, they are so animate-inanimate and dry-beauty not
> any shove, or sit there poppies blow as crepe
> paper. And in Mrs. Frontiero's yard annually I
> expect them as the King of the Earth must have
> Penelope, awaiting her return, love lies
> so delicately on the pillow as this one flower,
> petal and petal, carries nothing
> into or out of the World   so threatening
> were those cigar-stub cups just now, & I *know*
> how quickly, and paper-like, absorbent
> and krinkled paper, the poppy itself will, when here,
> go again and the stalks stay like onion plants oh
> come, poppy, when will you bloom?

At the end he lives "underneath/ the light of day. . . ." He
knows the *gloire*, and God's face is no longer black. Dawn is
the time when "men [fishermen]/ are washed as gods in the
Basin of Morning," but, even so, he lives in the sunset, when
the light in the West, as he says in the title of the poem, is
<u>"Golden Venetian Light From/ Back of Agamenticus Height</u>
<u>Falling/ Like Zeus' dust All Over the River & Marsh as/ Night</u>
<u>Falling</u>. . . ." This is the light of consciousness that Whitehead
says is intermittent, usually coming at the end of the process

of actualization and accompanied by satisfaction. It is the golden flower itself, growing down the air of heaven; the golden cloak, the beloved World restored.

Olson said in *Causal Mythology* (the mythology of effica-ciousness and manifestation: his fundamental truths) that the spirit of the world had always figured for him as a woman. The last entry of *The Maximus Poems* begins with the first of his restorations—"my wife"—and accounts for the love that, with the light, radiates this book. "Love makes us alive," he says, and here, more than elsewhere, he is alive and bestows his love. In telling of Fenrir's defeat, he tells the wholeness—the well-being of being—that moves him to love: "This living hand, now warm, now capable/ of earnest grasping. . . ."

Earth is the Goddess. In another concluding entry, Olson is "Enyalion of/ brown earth," the hero whose *imago mundi* is "an actual world of value." One's picture of the world, Olson says in *Causal Mythology* is "initial": "We have our picture of the world and *that's* the creation." It is initial because, as he explains in terms Bachelard would have acknowleged, it is a spontaneous product of the imagination, and because, having this tropic source, it presses for initiation: "the initiation/ of another kind of nation. . . ." The hero who now fights the bosses "goes to war with a picture in his mind"; he is not political in the way Maximus may be said to have been at the start, but radical in the most fundamental way, making, in Emerson's phrase, a silent revolution of thought, giving us a new way of seeing (being); another image of possibility. As Olson says in *Causal Mythology*, he wishes "that the earth shall be of another vision and another dispensation."[170]

It is by way of myth, as the penultimate poem shows, that Olson has done (does) this. Here he is stone, ground, of the earth, in a sense already buried ("My life is buried . . ."); here he finds himself in "Tartarian-Erojan, Geaan-Ouranian/ time," at the beginning, the origin. He has achieved "nakedness," not

only the fresh perception of the New World but the perception
of earth as it was perceived at the beginning of time in the great
cosmogonal myths; and he has learned "the language of being
alive."[171] Like Apollonius of Tyana he has "made his birthplace capable of verticality. . . ." He has learned with Thoreau
that "there is a truer account of [America:nature:place] in
mythology than in any history of America," and in Gloucester
has demonstrated, as no one since Thoreau has, the value of
place, what it means to possess an actual earth and to be physically at home.[172] He might have said with Lawrence, in
Apocalypse, that "we ought to dance with rapture that we
should be alive and in the flesh, and part of the living, incar-
nate cosmos." Hostile to neo-capitalism he might well have
said that we should "destroy our false, inorganic connections,
especially those related to money, and re-establish the living
organic connections. . . ." But instead of saying, as Lawrence
does, that we should "start with the sun," he would, even with
his reverence for Helios, say "start with the earth"—the earth
"that fathers and mothers us all. . . ."[173]

If the penultimate poem tells us that, in initiating another
kind of nation, Olson has completed his "Republic" and that
Good News has come from Canaan, the last entry tells us, in
allegorical terms not unlike Thoreau's on his losses, what he
has in a lifetime lost and repossessed. His wife, as we have
seen, is the *anima mundi*, the Goddess; his car, the masculine
mastery in the world that he had difficulty achieving; his color,
earth brown, the "evidence of truth," the "Fruits/ or the Four
Rivers of Paradise"; himself ("myself") the sun, the Self, not
Maximus but Olson; in sum, a life without estrangement that
has reached the condition of poetry.[174]

Epilogue:
Violets; and Bridge-Work

THERE ARE many measures of *The Maximus Poems*. Perhaps
the most obvious is that it makes good the very thing Olson,
in his earliest criticism, objected to in reviewing Babson and
Saville's *Cape Ann: A Tourist Guide* (1936)—the want of
serious attention to Gloucester and chiefly to the "significant
centre . . .—the fishing industry, its myth, even its economics."
Olson, like Frances Rose-Troup, gave Gloucester "place in the
genetic world." He made it stick; and, as Warren Tallman says,
"in and through [him] it begins . . . to shine on its hill again."
It is as much a place possessed—an inalienable possession—as
Walden Pond.[1]

One reason for this is that in completing the symbolic action
begun in *Call Me Ishmael*, Olson spelled out his obsessive
words (*space, myth, fact, object*) and notably achieved the
project he had spoken of to Ferrini in *Origin #1*:

> the only object is
a man, carved
out of himself, so wrought he
fills his given space, makes
traceries sufficient to
other's needs[2]

By filling his given space and thereby making it place, he made
traceries that we find useful.

Of the seven essential human offices, Olson performed especially those of teaching, giving pleasure, and consoling.[3] For
him, as has been remarked of Jane Austen, the true relation
between people was pedagogic—and it was chiefly in the generous way of his teaching that he gave pleasure and consola-

tion.⁴ Such pedagogy—an antonym for demagogy?—is one of his conspicuous New England traits. Kenneth Burke, whom I cite on the essential offices, replaces "console," his initial choice for the last office, with a word that better explains its function: "pontificate; that is, to 'make a bridge.'" This reminds us that Maximus, in the first instance and always a teacher, is also a Pontifex Maximus. When asked why he went to another culture to get his myth, Olson replied, "I just thought I bridged the cultures."⁵ Bridge-work, as for Crane, was his work. There is much to connect. He makes (restores) connections, and this gives us hope.

But Olson's pontificating is not of the transcending kind Burke chiefly has in mind in treating Emerson. The symbolic action of Olson's work follows the path of descendence rather than transcendence. It does not provide a bridge from here to elsewhere—to a realm beyond, higher, heavenly: transcendent. Nor does it rely, as such bridging does, on generalization. Whether imaginatively or physically, in visionary flight or westward expansion, it resists such restlessness and willfulness. Instead it bridges down and back, from here to beneath ("to a hard bottom and rocks in place," Thoreau said; to Olson's "Ragged Arse Rock Earth"), to the everpresent archaic fundament, to particulars, *things* that have meaning not by way of subsumption but because they exist through themselves—because, at bottom, in his cosmology, as in Whitehead's, things stand forth, "there is nothing in the real world which is merely an inert fact."⁶ Olson is one of the pioneers of *back*/*down*, a direction of increasing significance in the American imagination. He provides a measure of his own achievement, when writing in 1956 of Williams' *In the American Grain*, he said that "the Pelasgian [synonymous for him with "archaic"], & exactly geographically as of Arkadia, is an American's 'home,' his original departing point" and that Williams "was on the truest path an American can follow if

he wishes to go back by the feel of his own texture to his starting place." Williams, he thought, simply didn't go back far
enough, take the steps from Eric the Red to Arcadia.[7] He did.

This pontificating may be put in another way. At the end of
his lecture on *Causal Mythology*, Olson said that he wanted
to use the "papal blessing" that, as a Catholic, still impressed
him. He wanted to bless the city and the world, the *urb* and
orb that figure so prominently in his discussion. Now earth for
him is an *orb*, a "*One*," a thing "knowable" and "seizable,"
as "familiar to me," he says, "as the smallest thing I know,"
and, like every thing, alive with its own meaning.[8] Earth is not
the world, that is, the whole of creation, the universe. It is only
a part of the universe, as perhaps we have begun to realize in an
age so much concerned with both space and ecology. To see it
in this way, or to see it, as Olson does, as Mother Earth, is to
acknowledge dependence on something living, finite, and de-
structible. Conversely it is to acknowledge and so respect a
marvelous bounty. *An actual earth of value*—to have given us
this is indeed a pontifical blessing, an immeasurable gift. In
Olson's poem, as in Whitman's, we may find that a poem is
more than its meaning:

> Have you practis'd so long to learn to read?
> Have you felt so proud to get at the meaning of poems?
> Stop this day and night with me, and you shall
>   possess the origin of all poems;
> You shall possess the good of the earth and sun—
>   (there are millions of suns left;)
> You shall no longer take things at second or
>   third hand, nor look through the
>   eyes of the dead, nor feed on the
>   spectres in books;
> You shall not look through my eyes either,
>   nor take things from me:
> You shall listen to all sides, and filter them
>   from yourself.[9]

Olson gives us the good of the earth (and the sun)—he restores
the priceless things—and, like Whitman, he gives us a way to
know earth intimately. In teaching us to live in the world, he
teaches us, as Whitman had, to live in the body, to know the
world, as Thoreau said, by direct intercourse and sympathy,
with the senses, proprioceptively.

And what of *urb*? *Urb* is polis, and polis is not society.
Olson told Elaine Feinstein, "I find the contemporary substitu-
tion of society for the cosmos captive and deathly."[10] The sub-
stitution is captive and deathly because society, as all of us
know, is not organized, as both cosmos and polis are, in a
living coherent ecological fashion. Present society, itself a
product of the old discourse, does not liberate a beneficent
transference of energy. Because its syntax isn't vital—because
its sentences, in Olson's summary of Fenollosa, are not "gov-
erned by mother earth"—it consumes energy and fosters
entropy.[11] Polis is community, where society is not. Polis uses
people, as Paul Goodman says, as resources; uses them without using them up, in the very exchange of their energies
adding to them. Olson's conception of polis is of this generous,
generating kind: it is the human order of the cosmos founded,
like the cosmos, on the notion of process and necessary vital
exchange. As he said in speaking of the organization of Black
Mountain College, "function, process, change . . . interaction
and communication" is the premise of modern thought; "the
universe—including man and his interests—is . . . in micro-
cosm and in macrocosm . . . the continuously changing result
of the influence that each of its parts exerts upon all the rest of
its parts."[12] Olson's poetics expresses this view and proposes
an ecological model for poem, polis, and cosmos. What happens between things, relations (as Emerson knew), transfer of
energy (enactment: drama) are its prominent features—all
making possible a turning, to play on the *trope* in entropy, that
is not entropic. In bringing cosmos and polis together, in con-

necting them in *cosmopolis*, he defines a new kind of cosmo-
politanism.[13]

This is what Olson had in mind when he said, "I compell
Gloucester/ . . ./ to change. . . ." He would make it the community that Emerson before him had hoped Concord might
become, a generative place. To be made so, I might add, by conversation—a fundamental notion of American social psychology, succinctly expressed by John Dewey: Democracy [polis]
begins in conversation. For an interval Olson found such community at Black Mountain College. Thereafter, community
was what this teacher and talker—consider what it means to
talk to live, the hunger to give and take involved—hoped to
find by establishing lay monasteries and universities (universe-
city: another cosmopolis).[14] In the space of *The Maximus
Poems*, he created a cosmopolis by making Gloucester place,
a navel of the world as perhaps all true cities must be. His first
will, his will to change, was the will to such coherence, to find
and found such a city, an *urb* that had not yet succumbed to
urbanization.

But Gloucester had succumbed. Urban renewal was destroying it even as Olson was writing about it. "Rubbish of creation," his brilliant phrase, recognizes this, and it reminds us,
as his poetics already has, that Olson's vision is not only
ecological in its assumptions (drawn from the earlier ecological visions of the great nineteenth-century New England
writers, from Fenollosa, from Lawrence, from Whitehead's
philosophy of organism) but in its application. With him
ecological consciousness is inevitably ecological conscience,
and stirs the will to change. That is the use to which he turned
"American tales . . . of man against earth."[15]

We must not fail to consider him a nature poet, one of our
best, to be placed in the tradition that includes Thoreau and
Snyder, and we must acknowledge among his poems those,
like "For a man gone to Stuttgart" or "When do poppies

bloom," that explicitly treat nature and merit Frank O'Hara's appreciation of the delicacy of Olson's sensibility.[16] We should also remember his immediate push in response to the "city of mediocrity and cheap ambition destroying// . . . renewing without reviewing [re-*viewing*]"—his "screams" in the Gloucester *Daily Times*, his reminders that "demolition/ and service organization" is "not the same as/ participatory experience. It/ blinds out people into/ mice. . . ."[17] He told his vision in our time of "Tell-A-Vision" when "the true troubadours/ are CBS," and that it didn't do any immediate good didn't deter him.[18] His vision had been formed in response to greater disasters, to that of World War II, which both precipitated present conditions and forced him to review the entire history of humankind, and in that reviewing to find ways (the Way) of renewing.

In the last year of his life, in talking with Herbert Kenny, Olson recalled that he had once been asked why he was writing about a city that was going to disappear. His reply, not to his interrogator but to Kenny, was that he considered Gloucester "a redeemable flower that will be a monstrance forever, of not a city but of City, and stay because she wasn't urbanized." He knew she had been, but he insisted, as *The Maximus Poems* do, that "it's a fishtown, that's all." That *that's all* is everything: cosmopolis. Which is why, in answer to "what do you think the future of Gloucester on Cape Ann will be?" he replied, "An image of creation and of human life for the rest of the life of the species."

This summarizes admirably the Gloucester of his own work, and in elaborating it Olson explained its migratory theme and ecological ultimatum. Gloucester, he said, was "the final movement of the earth's people"; migration ended there; "Gloucester was the last shore. . . ." He had used it "as a bridge to Venice and back from Venice to Tyre, because of the departure from the old static land mass of man which was ice, cave,

Pleistocene man and early agricultural man, until he got
moving, until he got towns." So, he believed, "the last polis or
city *is* Gloucester"—and "man now is either going to rediscover the earth or is going to leave it."[19]

These, we realize with diminishing sense of melodrama, are
the alternatives of human history, alternatives of the kind
Olson confronted in response to the atom bomb and his own
"fatal male small span." For us the inevitable choice is easier
because Olson himself has made it and enables us to do so: to
rediscover the earth. As early as 1947—early, that is, in his
career—he wrote: "It is of nature that we are bereft, the old
mother."[20] His project was to "arch again/ the necessary goddess," to create a poetics and poetry equal to this, one that
restored the function of poetry, which, according to Francis
Ponge, another poet of things, is "to nourish the spirit of man
by giving him the cosmos to suckle." The enabling means is
an open poetics, which, in Ponge's words, requires that we
"lower our standard of dominating nature and . . . raise our
standard of participating in it" and become "not just the site
where ideas and feelings are produced, but also the crossroad
where they divide and mingle."[21] This means enables because
the path (crossroads) the poet indicates between reality and the
soul (self)—to cite Whitman's formulation of the task—is a
pathway to the Way, the source of energy, and because it restores what may be called matriarchal ways of thought. An
open poetics is ecological by virtue of serving the Great
Mother, by standing against the patriarchal consciousness that
estranges us from the familiar world, the actual earth. ("Creation is crucial," Olson said; "If you don't stay close to it you
lose everything.")[22] And it has another virtue of ecological
importance: It reminds us that "acts are value" and that,
having to act, we must, as Olson said at Berkeley, believe in
our action.[23]

Olson himself heartens us by his own demonstration. His

incredible effort to recover a usable past, to make available
the resources of scholarship, to offer a vision (an image of the
world) accords with the idea of the poet he may have acquired
in reading Bruno Snell's *The Discovery of Mind*. If the Greek
poets discovered the mind, he (a learned poet, after all) might
do something equally worthy, equally momentous in human
history. In this sense of the large work to be done, we may find
less outrageous his remark, "the poet is the only pedagogue
left, to be trusted."[24]

We expect too much from poets, even that they singlehandedly
do the work of our time. It is enough if they generate images
and transfer energy, if they set us the necessary tasks, set us in
motion, and give us hope. Olson does this in many ways and
sometimes, as in the following, in ways that appeal to us as
Americans.

1. He said that we were the last *first* people, meaning that in
the course of human migration westward we were the last
people to have the fresh opportunity to use space that the first
people had. Or had had, since we failed this opportunity.
Nevertheless, he persisted in thinking of us as a first people
and tried, imaginatively, to recover for us the space of that
possibility. He learned from Jung that we fill space with our
own projections and that we explore it in order to achieve
wholeness. And so he read the history of the discovery and
settlement of America in this light. We were the *last* first
people in the sense that we had the opportunity to recover the
wholeness that had been lost in the progress of civilization—
and for Olson as for Jung that meant contact with the Great
Mother. In reading *Psychology and Alchemy*, Olson simply
inscribed beneath figure 97, a picture of the "Grand Peregrination" by ship, the words "John Smith."[25] With Jung's explan-
atory comments, this named his (our) work: "an odyssey in
search of wholeness." Such an odyssey, needless to say, differs

from those told in Homer, Dante, and Melville, the last,
Ahab's, putting an end, as Olson said, to the "individual responsible only to himself."[26]

2. Olson's birth and childhood coincide with America's
coming-of-age. His earliest teachers, academic or otherwise,
had engaged—were still engaged—in the most important critical battle since transcendentalism. In this battle between the
modernist Americans and the New Humanists, the factions
that Emerson had called the Party of Hope and the Party of the
Past were renamed by the New Humanists, the defenders of
tradition. The Party of Hope became the Party of Nature, and
the Party of the Past the Party of Culture, Culture having its
Arnoldian meaning. As a result we see more clearly what all
along had been the American critical issue: Nature *vs* Culture.
And we see where Olson, with his push against European Culture, stands.

But what distinguishes Olson from those who precede him
in this debate—and also suggests a difference between the
postmodernists and their modernist predecessors—is his extension of the terms, so that the issue is no longer within the
western tradition but now involves the western tradition as
one of its terms. Western tradition—now American as much
as European—acquires the meaning of Culture, and Nature,
long since lost as the unique advantage of America—we are no
longer "Nature's Nation," in Perry Miller's phrase—Nature is
"backward and outside," the sources or origins wherever they
can be found in all time and all place. Now the issue is world-
wide, of that magnitude of importance.

Nature vs *Culture*. We recall from Levi-Strauss' study of
Amerindian myth and G. S. Kirk's study of Sumerian and
Greek myth that this opposition provides the primary structure of many myths and may be the fundamental contradiction
that myth accommodates. Olson recognizes the ever-presence
of myth in experience. This enables him to recover those times

and places when myth itself arose, and to ask us, in returning
to these origins, to begin again with the primary issue of
human experience.

The whole question & continuing struggle to remain civilized Sumer documented in & out: I imagine you know the
subtle tale of how Gilgamesh . . . was sent the rude fellow
Enkidu to correct him because he, even Gilgamesh, had become a burden, in his lust, to his city's people. As I read it, it is
an incredibly accurate myth of what happens to the best of
men when they lose touch with the primordial & phallic
energies & methodologies which, said this predecessor people
of ours [the Sumerians are the first first people], make it possible for man, that participant thing, to take up, straight,
nature's, live nature's force.[27]

3. Gloucester was once "frontier," a paradigm of the Westward Movement; and it was left behind in its course. Olson
never wrote the long poem on the West that he had proposed
early in his career. He didn't have to because he rehearsed
much of it in the history of Gloucester and found there the
task presented by it: how to stay put, dig in and down. He
awoke in the morning, as he said, "after the dispersion," in a
New England whose urban erosion was of the pattern of previous agricultural erosion. And in the old, misused, and cast-
aside—"the waste and ashes of pioneering," as Van Wyck
Brooks said earlier of the old American towns—he showed us
how to find place; how, in fact, it is more likely to be a place
because it has a history, because human life there has, in whatever ways, altered space.[28] We repossess place in repossessing
the experience of it. *Polis is eyes*: caring and attending are the
best means of urban renewal. It is possible to refound even
with the sacred and profane worn out. By digging in (a) place
we recover not only America but all origin, and in doing this
we remake our places.

Olson traveled much in Gloucester, discovering, as Thoreau

had, that "the nature which inspired mythology still flour-
ishes," and that such discoveries may help us clear away the
junk of history and open the springs of being.[29]

> I told the woman
> about the spring
> on the other side of Freshwater
> Cove which lies
> right on the edge of the
> marsh and is flooded
> each high tide by
> the Ocean which it then
> expells it runs so fast itself
> from its sources and to drink it
> the moment the tide has pulled off even one little bit
> is a water untasteable elsewhere.[30]

Paul Blackburn, "Shop Talk," *Sixpack*, #7/8 (Spring/Summer, 1974), 27.
See Charles Altieri, "From Symbolist Thought to Immanence: The
   nd of Postmodern American Poetics," *Boundary* 2, I (Spring, 1973),
   41; David Antin, "Modernism and Postmodernism: Approaching the
Present in American Poetry," *Boundary* 2, I (Fall, 1972), 98–133.
   3. Robert Duncan, "Some Letters to Charles Olson," *MAPS* #6 (1974),
65–67.
   4. *CM*, 1.

1. The subtitle is from William Rueckert, "Literary Criticism and History:
The Endless Dialectic," *New Literary History*, VI (1974–75), 496, where
Rueckert proposes an ecological model of criticism: "Criticism, in all its
forms, is the actions of the mind upon the grounds of being. A good critic
never litters the grounds of being; he clears them in some way, and cultivates
them so that there can be new forms of being, just as he helps to keep the
springs of action flowing."
   2. *LFO*, 63.
   3. *AM*, 14, 19–20; *Max*. II, 15. Shortness of life and shortness of breath are
related in "The Story of an Olson," and "without breath" is an emphatic detail
of "Pacific Lament," where death by drowning is the imagined action.
   4. I follow Olson's account of his career. Wilbert Snow, his teacher at
Wesleyan, mentions poems that Olson wrote earlier, in "A Teacher's View,"
The Massachusetts Review, XII (Winter, 1971), 42. *Max*. I, 54.
   5. *Call Me Ishmael*: the title speaks also for Olson, and he identifies with
Melville's agony over paternity in a passage (82–85) which provides the best
gloss of "The Distances," one of the great poems on this theme. Here the
homoeroticism in respect to fathers calls up the treatment of Hawthorne and
Melville in *Call Me Ishmael*: "Melville makes little out of the love of man and
woman. It is the friendship of men which is love" (*CMI*, 45). Olson's *Notebooks* record his fearful concern with homosexuality.
   6. ". . . give gifts largely, as a father might": from "In the Hills South of
Capernaum, Port," written at about this time. *AM*, 7.
   7. "Melville & Homer & Shakespeare have been my masters (however
much so many think Pound is)." This denial of Pound, in "Memorial Letter,"
Origin # 20, 3rd ser., (January, 1971), 45, overstates the case.
   8. *RB*, 45.
   9. "Design Etc.," *Standing Still and Walking in New York*, ed. Donald Allen
(Bolinas: Grey Fox Press, 1975), 33.

10. And of course notably Pound's: concern for speech, and composition by the musical phrase.

11. *CO & EP*, 74, 128, 69; *Notebooks* ("April 1945 en route north"); "Want to get the sense of 'I' into Zukofsky's 'eye'—a locus of experience, not a presumption of expected value," Robert Creeley, *Pieces* (New York: Charles Scribner's Sons, 1969), 68, recalled for me by Jeffrey Gardiner; *Max.* III, 212.

12. *CO & EP*, xxiii–xxiv. Again, the concluding phrases argue the need for breath and its assertive force.

13. *CO & EP*, xxiv. For his sexual anxiety, chiefly over homosexuality, manifested, he felt, in dependence on masters, see *Notebooks*.

14. Olson referred to Cagli as "my buddy" (a working-class usage) in Charles Olson, "On Black Mountain," *MAPS* #4 (1971), 33.

15. *CO & EP*, 86, *passim*; *RB*, 44–45. This reading almost immediately followed the trip to Spoleto, and its incredible naked confession may be attributed to Olson's need to place himself in relation to a generation of younger poets, to whom he was uncomfortably father, and to a generation of older poets, who had been father to him.

16. Ann Charters, *Olson/Melville: A Study in Affinity* (Berkeley: Oyez, 1968), 9.

17. Creeley places this poem first in *SW*.

18. *CO & EP*, 67. In this connection, Olson also mentions Yeats, whose artifice is rejected in "The Green Man." With the exception of Williams, Olson rejects the politics of the writers of the Pound era, their antidemocracy and, in Pound's case, the subordination of "critical intelligence to the objects of authority in others." (*CO & EP*, 28)

19. Albert Glover retains this arrangement in *AM* at the expense of the unity of *Y & X*.

20. Olson said in "Poetry and Criticism" (1947), a MSS in the archives, that the "true . . . starting line" for our time was Altamira and explained that the poem was provoked by drawings of Buchenwald, "that compost of civilization."

Yeats also figures in "The K" in the reference to cycles and in the submerged image of the salmon, which calls up "The salmon-falls" of "Sailing to Byzantium."

21. Pound did a series of essays in 1911–12, under the title "I Gather the Limbs of Osiris." That Osiris' dismemberment by Set is associated with Typhon's battle with Zeus should not be overlooked.

22. *CMI*, 117–19; *ML*, 68, 30; *CO & EP*, 97–98. Of *Y & X* it should perhaps be noted that *Y* and *X* are the coordinates of space and time, their intersection the here/now of beginning. They also stand for Olson and Cagli, and their reversal declares their desire to change the previous linear order of history.

23. The tower in this poem is patently Yeats's, and Olson addresses a view of civilization as well as history. The image recalls the Tarot (card 16), with which Olson was familiar. Hart Crane is also present in the poem, chiefly to set off Olson's different response to Mexico.

24. *O* #2, p. 39. This account of the ideal curriculum at Black Mountain College shows the extent to which Olson wished to make it serve his views— how, as educator, he made his push.

25. ". . . there is no one—for form, that is—the equal of E. P. . . ." Olson in

O #2, p. 35. See also Robert Duncan's comment in a letter to Olson: "And we've, both of us, got Grandpa to thank for our way station of the ideogram." Robert Duncan, "Some Letters to Charles Olson," *MAPS* #6 (1974), 59.

26. *CO & EP*, 30.

27. *Ibid.*, 53, 98.

28. Olson copied from the manuscript the opening verses and some subsequent lines. See *ibid.*, 72 ff.

29. Allen Ginsberg, *Indian Journals, March 1962–May 1963* (San Francisco: Dave Haselwood Books and City Lights Books, 1970), 40. Ginsberg does not mention Olson here but is nevertheless indebted, among other things, to "Projective Verse," upon which he comments in Mark Robison (ed.), *Ginsberg's Improvised Poetics* (Buffalo: Anonym Press, 1971), 26 ff., a book dedicated to "Charles Olson, prosodist."

30. The exception is Carol Kyle, "The Mesoamerican Cultural Past and Charles Olson's 'The Kingfishers,'" *Alcheringa*, n.s., I (1975), 68–77.

Guy Davenport, "Scholia and Conjectures for Olson's 'The Kingfishers,'" *Boundary 2*, II (Fall, 1973/Winter, 1974), 250–62, omits Eliot and minimizes Olson's rejection of Pound; Maxine Combs, "Charles Olson's 'The Kingfishers': A Consideration of Meaning and Method," *The Far Point*, #4 (Spring/Summer, 1970), 66–76, treats Eliot but not Pound, as does William Aiken, "Charles Olson: A Preface," *Massachusetts Review*, XII (Winter, 1971), 57–68.

The tendency in glossing the poem without considering its movement is to read it as a symbolist poem—which is to misread it.

31. G. S. Kirk, *Heraclitus: The Cosmic Fragments* (Cambridge: Cambridge University Press, 1954), 250. Olson's meaning is clarified, perhaps, by "to change// is the expectation// we previous immigrants/ tell you" in "Other Than" (1951), where "immigrants" has special resonance in respect to Pound.

32. Olson's etymological interest is characteristic, another aspect of his concern with origins. As etymologist he joins the New England company of Emerson, Thoreau, and Fenollosa. Like them, he traces words to their roots, fastens them to visible things.

33. Pound, who said that his was the finest memory "among the ruins," might better be placed in that tradition. (*CO & EP*, 98) Olson does not mention Neruda in the *Notebooks* of this period, or anywhere else in his unpublished writing, according to George Butterick.

34. Olson copied out part of "The Dry Salvages" in 1945. *Notebooks*, "Washington Fall 1945 I."

35. See Olson, "On Black Mountain," 27.

36. M. L. Rosenthal, *The New Poets* (New York: Oxford University Press, 1967), 162.

37. Olson said in "Issue, Mood" that "The tidy/ fear chaos," a judgment of Eliot, of whom he had written earlier that "tradition is too organized with him, his uncertainty before chaos leads him to confuse authority with orthodoxy." (*CO & EP*, 27)

Wilson's remark is from "The Mass in the Parking Lot," a poem published in *Furioso*, IV (Summer, 1949), 49–51.

The attack on Malraux is somewhat ironic in view of Olson's subsequent proposal to hunt among the ruins. See Charles Olson, "Project (1951): 'The

Art of the Language of Mayan Glyphs,'" *Alcheringa*, #5 (Spring/Summer, 1973), 94–100.

38. This may also call up Eliot by way of "the drained pool" in "Burnt Norton."

39. Kenneth Burke, "Heaven's First Law," *The Dial*, LXXII (January, 1922), 199–200.

40. Olson recommended this essay from Plutarch's *Morals* to his students at Black Mountain College because he believed "*the 2nd AD* holds a dynamic both as of the 'Greeks' as a whole as well as of our own day." *O* #2, p. 43. See also *P*, 9, where he mentions Maximus of Tyre as an example of that "'affective'" time.

41. Olson may also have remembered "old stones that cannot be deciphered" in "East Coker," *Four Quartets*.

42. *Max.* I, 35; Olson, "On Black Mountain," 38; *O* #2, p. 59 ff.

43. *ML*, 22.

44. My italics.

45. Combs, "Charles Olson's 'The Kingfishers,'" 70.

46. Olson refers to this example in criticizing Pound's translations of *The Odes of Confucius* in "I, Mencius, Pupil of the Master": "that in the East the sun untangles itself/ from among the branches." Pound himself uses this ideogram in Ezra Pound, *ABC of Reading* (New York: New Directions, 1960), 21; and Olson copied it from Fenollosa in his *Notebooks*, "Washington Spring 1945."

47. *Max.* I, 35–40; *O* #2, pp. 32 ff., 54, 81–82; *BED*.

48. *SVH*, 47–52.

49. Olson read Prescott in 1941. *Notebooks*, "April 19th 1941."

50. Cholula, historically, is an early event; I use "end" figuratively.

51. Olson may be working from Prescott's "All was now confusion and uproar in the fair city which had so lately reposed in security and peace." William H. Prescott, *History of the Conquest of Mexico* (New York: Modern Library, 1936), 273. The images carry a burden similar to that of "hushed gleaming fields of pendant wheat," in Hart Crane's "Ave Maria," the section of *The Bridge* devoted to Columbus' discovery of America and premonitory of subsequent conquest. Note also the skillful use of end-words.

52. This great poem would have appealed to Olson, especially for Neruda's use of dawn, but it is not easily assimilated to "The Kingfishers," and, if at all, only indirectly by way of Whitman and Crane whom Neruda seems to have assimilated.

53. For Eliot's repudiation of Heraclitus, see Morris Weitz, "T. S. Eliot: Time as a Mode of Salvation," *Sewanee Review*, XL (Winter, 1952), 48–64.

54. Norbert Wiener, *Cybernetics: Or Control and Communication in the Animal and the Machine* (New York: John Wiley & Sons, 1948) is a brilliant work confirming Olson's high regard for Wiener (see *LFO*, 7, 9). There are many reasons for Olson's response to it. It is throughout a model of scientific exploration, all the more impressive because Wiener relates the history of this new field of research and considers its consequences in this "world of Belsen and Hiroshima": "I write in 1947, and I am compelled to say that it [social amelioration] is a very slight hope." (38–39) He also writes it in Mexico.

From Wiener, Olson acquired more than the idea of feedback: Proprioception, for one thing, and steering or rudder control, a significant association for his own image of managing a boat, for another. The idea of feedback, moreover, supports Whitehead's view of the past as necessary material of present occasions and denies the entropic vision of history as decline from the past. For feedback (information) introduces new energy into the system, a congenial idea for someone, like Olson, concerned with energy and its transfer.

Olson's awareness of the significance of Wiener's work is one of the things he shares with Thomas Pynchon.

55. *SW*, 52, 48.

56. Olson copied this from Pound's mss. See *CO & EP*, 74.

57. Pound was attracted to Confucius, Olson says, because Confucius was his opposite. *CO & EP*, 71.

58. Davenport, "Scholia and Conjectures for Olson's 'The Kingfishers,'" 261, notes the echo of Judges 14:14.

59. Heraclitus has a similar view of opposition as the dynamic of existence.

60. *CMI*, 45. That *Call Me Ishmael* finds its way into this context may also be explained by Olson's mixed feelings about Pound's response to it: Pound's concern to get it published but his less than satisfactory comment that he "read [it] with joy—made it unnecessary to read Melville." (*CO & EP*, 138)

61. *O* #2, p. 43 ff.

62. See Charles Doria, "Pound, Olson, and the Classical Tradition," *Boundary 2*, II (Fall, 1973/Winter, 1974), 127–43.

63. To serve Beauty is to resist change. See *Hugh Selwyn Mauberley: "Till change hath broken down/ All things save Beauty alone."*

64. Though not, Olson explained, "to quit, and to make money." See *HU*, 116; *SW*, 63, where Rimbaud is "a proof"; *SVH*, 31, where "Rimbaud had to toss Beauty off his knees."

65. *O* #2, p. 45.

66. *ML*, 90, 26–27, 30. Note Olson's appropriation of "Ez's" manner of speech; and also Thomas Pynchon's sense of this tradition—"hopeless as the one-way flow of European Time. . . ." (Thomas Pynchon, *Gravity's Rainbow* [New York: Bantam Books, 1974], 844.) What Olson told Creeley he expresses earlier in *CO & EP*, especially in "GrandPa, GoodBye."

67. The Mexicans worshipped the sun. Also this calls up the heavily invested "look" of the previous section and thus "A Translation," where habit is rejected, renovation sought, and the injunction is to look to each new day, to the sun. (*CO & EP*, 128)

68. *ML*, 69.

69. Olson might have written this as follows: "there is *ground*, for hope . . . is still *there*, to be used."

1. Robert Creeley, "Preface," *ML*, 5.   TWO

2. *HU*, 65. Also "our small company," as Robert Duncan remarks in a letter to Olson in 1955 ("Some Letters to Charles Olson," *MAPS* #6 [1974], 59) and "the several youngers now appearing in not so many little mags" (*O* #2, p. 35).

For the writers published in *Origin*, see Cid Corman, *The Gist of ORIGIN* (New York: Grossman, 1975).

3. *LFO*, 70, 98; see also 50, 66, 124. The lines cited here are from uncollected poems in *O* #2, pp. 29, 60. Olson said that Black Mountain College was "a true city" (Charles Olson, "On Black Mountain," *MAPS* #4 [1971], 37) and treated Ferrini's *Four Winds*, a little magazine published in Gloucester, as a failed polis (*Max*. I, 17–25).

4. *LFO*, 120.

5. William Carlos Williams, *Spring and All*, in *Imaginations*, ed. Webster Schott (New York: New Directions, 1970), 89; William Carlos Williams, *Selected Essays of William Carlos Williams* (New York: Random House, 1954), 147.

6. *CO & EP*, 82.

7. "Olson's first letter to Robert Creeley," *MAPS* #4 (1971), 8.

8. Reaction is the issue of the important letter to Grover Smith (*HU*, 63–65).

9. *LFO*, 90. This style is deliberate; see *LFO*, 40, 54.

10. *Ibid.*, 130–32. I have in mind Marjorie G. Perloff, "Charles Olson and the 'Inferior Predecessors': 'Projected Verse' Revisited," *ELH*, XL (Summer, 1973), 285–306.

11. See Donald Wesling, "The Prosodies of Free Verse," in Reuben A. Brower (ed.), *Twentieth-Century Literature in Retrospect* (Cambridge: Harvard University Press, 1971), 155–87.

12. Much of the precedent material is available in Donald Allen and Warren Tallman (eds.), *The Poetics of the New American Poetry* (New York: Grove Press, 1973). An instructive guide to those elements of the poetics immediately useful to the new generation of poets is Robert Creeley, *A Quick Graph: Collected Notes & Essays*, ed. Donald Allen (San Francisco: Four Seasons Foundation, 1970).

13. Olson said they were written in 1948 (*PT*, 64).

14. Olson's reading in *Cybernetics* is again evident.

15. See Herbert N. Schneidau, *Ezra Pound: The Image and the Real* (Baton Rouge: Louisiana State University Press, 1969), the essential, revisionist study. Olson's own best treatment of this issue is in "On Poets and Poetry," his reply to Grover Smith, where he clearly shows the relation of symbol to the "old discourse" (rational system and extrinsic form). For example, he dismisses Smith's notion "that images should emerge as 'symbols' in order that there be this objective vision he sets up as success. [For] it doesn't take much thought over Bill's [W. C. Williams'] proposition—'Not in ideas but in things' ['No ideas but in things']—to be sure that any of us intend an image as a 'thing,' never, so far as we know, such a non-animal as symbol." (*HU*, 63–65)

His letter to Robert Duncan, "Against Wisdom as Such," also treats this issue and is especially valuable for the association of Fenollosa ("drive all nouns . . . back to process") and Jung (the poem as a "man-made continuum 'which contains qualities or basic conditions manifesting themselves simultaneously in various places in a way not to be explained by causal parallelisms'"). (*HU*, 67–71)

In "The Post-Virginal" (*AM*, 139) Olson comments on the image as thing, as objective predication: "Keats: the intensity of object. The trouble/ with symbol,// it does not trouble." In *SW*, 60–61, he speaks of the symbol as related to a transcendent world.

Herbert Schneidau, "Wisdom Past Metaphor: Another View of Pound, Fenollosa, and Objective Verse," *Paideuma*, V (Summer, 1976), 15–29, should also be consulted.

16. *LFO*, 121. Considering going to Yucatan again, as against going to New England or staying at Black Mountain, Olson told Corman that he preferred to "go where no anxieties breed . . . where/ i breathe more// easily. . . ." (*LFO*, 79–80)

17. In addition to Eliot, these lines recall Pound (in *Mauberley*), Rimbaud, and Homer. Olson returns to the tidal river throughout *The Maximus Poems*.

18. For example, in "The Story of an Olson, and Bad Thing":

> . . . Ships, ships, it's
> steering now that is, it is
> the biz-i-ness NOW, you
> who care, who can
> endure . . .

The subsequent lines on "single intelligence" make clear the connection with projective verse.

19. *LFO*, 61; *HU*, 71. The fullest examination of this is in "Human Universe," to be discussed later. Now only the following need be cited: "The process of image . . . cannot be understood by separation from the stuff it works on." (*SW*, 61)

20. See Ann Charters, *Olson/Melville: A Study in Affinity* (Berkeley: Oyez, 1968), 87, where Olson also glosses this passage in terms of Whitehead. Robert von Hallberg notes the movement from "concrescence to perception to formal activity" in "Olson, Whitehead, and the Objectivists," *Boundary* 2, II (Fall, 1973/Winter, 1974), 91. Though more complex, Olson's formula is comparable to Williams' descent-ascent—a movement from chaos (unselectedness) to cosmos. For Pound as father, *PT*, 64.

21. Olson judges Pound's entire career in the concluding verses of the poem (*AM*, 53) by alluding to *Mauberley* as well as the *Pisan Cantos* (LXXIV includes material from the earlier poem). Olson rejects Pound's devotion to Beauty and concurs in the judgment in *"E. P. ODE POUR L'ELECTION DE SON SEPULCHRE"* that in trying to wring lilies from the acorns he was "Wrong from the start."

22. William Carlos Williams, "Introduction," *The Wedge* (1944), *The Collected Later Poems of William Carlos Williams* (New York: New Directions, 1963), 4. *Engenders* is a strong verb, calling up "The verb detaches itself/ seeking to become articulate," in "The Desert Music," a poem Olson admired.

23. The last has often been ridiculed in order to depreciate Olson's essay. For its importance, see Robert Duncan, "The Typewriter," *MAPS* #6 (1974), 7–16.

24. Charles Olson, "A Syllabary for a Dancer," *MAPS* #4 (1971), 4, 9; Olson, "On Black Mountain," 31.

25. *SW*, 20.

26. Ezra Pound, *ABC of Reading* (New York: New Directions, 1960), 201, 206.

27. *Max*. I, 2. Here the percussive verse also distinguishes Olson from Pound.

28. *SW*, 28; again, the prose here is percussive.

Part II insists on roots in relation to breath. In this it recalls an essay Olson knew, B. L. Whorf's "An American Indian Model of the Universe," where for the Hopi the "spirit of the Breath" is related not only to the heart but to "the very heart of the Cosmos" and root is the vertical axis. Benjamin Lee Whorf, *Language, Thought, and Reality*, ed. John B. Carroll (Cambridge: MIT Press, 1956 [1950]), 59–60, 64.

29. Ezra Pound (ed.), *The Chinese Written Character as a Medium for Poetry* (San Francisco: City Lights Books, 1969), 15. *Notebooks*, "Washington Spring 1945," contains careful notes of Olson's reading of Fenollosa.

Undoubtedly, Olson was aware in codices—not necessarily Mayan—of the representation of speech-breath as thing, comparable to the "little smokies" of comic strip characters, as the Italians call such represented speech. Speech so represented is both projective and flowerlike (tropic), the latter related perhaps to the pre-Columbian connection of flower-poetry-song.

Olson's statement, "That which exists through itself is what is called meaning" (*PT*, 61) is relevant here.

30. *Origin*, 1 (Spring, 1951), 5. In this letter of November 7, 1950, directed to "Projective Verse," Olson makes explicit the connection with resistance (and "The Resistance") and also indicates the American context of his essay: "we are the last first people (he sd. [in *Call Me Ishmael*]). And that means discovery, anew, of speech."

31. Pound (ed.), *The Chinese Written Character*, 12–13. My italics.

32. *SW*, 20.

33. *Ibid.*, 61.

34. Pound (ed.), *The Chinese Written Character*, passim; Emerson, "Language," *Nature* (1836). Olson cites Fenollosa on the "care of myth" in *CMI*, 14. See also for the relation of Emerson and Fenollosa, Hugh Kenner, *The Pound Era* (Berkeley and Los Angeles: University of California Press, 1971).

35. Martin L. Pops, "Melville: To Him Olson," *Modern Poetry Studies*, II (1971), 62.

In Olson's proposed introductory course on the American language at Black Mountain College, Fenollosa's essay is the basic text. In "Bridge-Work" (*"fr. the Old Discourse to the New"*) Olson singles out Fenollosa. (*P*, 8) Otherwise Olson did not comment on Fenollosa, a compatriot born in nearby Salem, an important figure in the second stage of American interest in oriental thought, and one who truly acquired it and, with it, a repugnance for the "Egotistical Sublime." Lawrence W. Chisolm, *Fenollosa: The Far East and American Culture* (New Haven: Yale University Press, 1963) is the best biographical study. In terms of poetics, Schneidau, *Ezra Pound: The Image and the Real* is the most helpful. Donald Davie, *Articulate Energy* (London: Routledge & Kegan Paul, 1955), is best read historically, as part of the situation Olson confronted, for Davie finds support for syntax in Fenollosa and does not, like Olson, respond deeply to process.

Kenneth Burke's remark is from "Coleridge Rephrased," *Poetry*, XLVII (October, 1935), 52.

36. This is Olson's essential quarrel with Emerson. It should be noted, as Robert von Hallberg points out in "Olson, Whitehead, and the Objectivists," *Boundary 2*, II (Fall, 1973/Winter, 1974), that by the time he wrote *The Special View of History*, Olson recognized a positive value in the shaping/order-making power of imagination. Olson's "Credo" (1949) states his general practice: 1) "get it down as it is"—phenomenologist 2) "to render all abstractions"—objectivist 3) "return to [the] subjective when it has been earned"—vision. (MSS Archives)

37. Allen and Tallman (eds.), *The Poetics of the New American Poetry*, 224, 209.

38. D. H. Lawrence, Preface to *Chariot of the Sun*, by Harry Crosby, *Phoenix: The Posthumous Papers (1936)*, ed. Edward O. McDonald (New York: Viking Press, 1936), 261.

39. *SVH*, 32; *HU*, 125.

40. See Egbert Faas, "Olson and D. H. Lawrence: The Aesthetics of the 'Primitive Abstract,'" *Boundary 2*, II (Fall, 1973/Winter, 1974), 113–26; Charles Boer, *Charles Olson in Connecticut* (Chicago: Swallow Press, 1975), 12–14.

41. Lawrence, "Preface to *Chariot of the Sun*," 257, 258.

42. *ML*, 9–11; *AM*, 72.

43. *LFO*, 129; *HU*, 63.

44. Smith's omnibus review included Brom Weber's edition of Crane's letters ("that pitiable anarch") and Vivienne Koch's book on Williams, as well as recent studies of Yeats and Durrell. See *New Mexico Quarterly*, XXIII (Autumn, 1953), 317–29. Olson's reply is also critical of Smith's academic loquaciousness. All citations from Olson's reply are from *HU*, 63–65.

45. Olson's "new humanism" is not Babbitt's and More's, which for him is very much the "old humanism."

46. *Origin*, I (Spring, 1951), 5–6.

47. *LFO*, 18.

48. Vincent Ferrini, "A Frame," *MAPS* #4 (1971), 50. There are many Olsons and many voices, but Ferrini's choice is a good one if one wishes first to encounter rather than overhear him, as in *CO & EP*.

49. *CO & EP*, 52.

50. *LFO*, 119–21.

51. For Olson's relation with Dahlberg, see John O. Cech, "Edward Dahlberg and Charles Olson: A Biography of a Friendship" (Ph.D. dissertation, University of Connecticut, 1974). For Olson's reading in Van Wyck Brooks and Waldo Frank, see *Notebooks*. Eliot's remark is in Charters, *Olson/Melville*, 10.

52. *LFO*, 98, 101, 9.

53. *LFO*, 10, 2–11; *ML*, 22.

54. *LFO*, 34, 45, 20, 22. The epigraph recalls that of the petitioning son in *Call Me Ishmael*, only now the father speaks.

55. See editorial statements by Russell and D. S. Carne-Ross, *Nine*, I (Autumn, 1949), 5; II (November, 1950), 269–79. Olson himself was later served in a similar way by Harvey Brown and his Frontier Press.

56. *LFO*, 48 ff., 6; *HU*, 156. The sexual reference here and in the earlier remark on "heteros of the States" may be attributed to Olson's identification of Culture, dependence, and homosexuality. In his *Notebooks*, "Faust Buch #1 Washington, Spring, '47," he addresses his own difficulty: "this awhoring after culture on my part is a path by which I continue to be a son, and fail to take up my own perceptions and malehood." Yet, as George Butterick reminds me, Olson uses *heteros* to designate those who belong to the "heterogeneous present." See *AP*, 39; *Max*. I, 10.

In one of the earlier Notebooks, "#4 Cambridge & NY Winter–Spring 1940," he addresses the "Problem of culture" by setting Melville and Thoreau against James and Eliot, the latter wanting "frames, explanations of things, operations of society, politics, and religion into which they could fit themselves."

57. *Nine*, I, 5. Olson connects this tradition to Pound by way of Pound's service to Beauty and *Guide to Kulchur*.

58. *HU*, 156; *LFO*, 2.

59. *LFO*, 48 ff., 4, 9, 10, 100. Of taste, Louis Sullivan says: "Taste is one of the weaker words in our language. . . . It savors of accomplishment, in the fashionable sense, not of power to accomplish in the creative sense. It expresses a familiarity with what is *au courant* among persons of so-called culture. . . . It is essentially a second-hand word, and can have no place in the working vocabulary of those who demand thought and action at first-hand." (*Kindergarten Chats and Other Writings* [New York: George Wittenborn, 1947], 38.) Olson endorsed the conception of *Origin* as a magazine "'for the creative.'" (*LFO*, 51)

60. *LFO*, 12, 46–47; *Origin*, I, 5. See Emerson, *Nature*: "He is placed in the centre of beings, and a ray of relation passes from every other being to him."

61. *LFO*, 44, 45, 50.

"Cid Corman was to get a First Mate . . . he set a pattern for the idea of a magazine." So Ferrini says in telling of his own failure, disclosing, however, that Corman only got First Mate, was never Captain. Ferrini, "A Frame," 52.

Olson's phallic argument eventually embarrassed him. See *Reading at Berkeley*. Terms such as these are familiar in our cultural quarrel with Europe. Emerson called for a native "masculine" art, as did Sullivan, who considered Richardson's Marshall Field Wholesale Store "an entire male." Williams distinguished his work from Pound's in terms of tradition-derived "androgynous" nurture and direct approach to the "supplying female."

62. Robert Duncan, "Early Poetic Community," *Allen Verbatim*, ed. Gordon Ball (New York: McGraw-Hill, 1974), 133–34.

63. *LFO*, 25, 66.

64. Pound did not respond to *Origin*. See *LFO*, 63.

65. *Ibid.*, 127.

66. His version of wringing the neck of rhetoric.

67. In defense of this verse, recall Olson's remark, in "Projective Verse," that both projective and nonprojective verse will continue to "go alongside each other."

68. *LFO*, 2.

69. Ferrini earned his living as a framemaker. An excellent introduction to

his life and work is Vincent Ferrini, *Selected Poems*, ed., with an introduction, by George Butterick (Storrs: University of Connecticut Library, 1976).

70. Robert Creeley, *A Quick Graph*, 68. Among the considerable evidence of Olson's early attention to Crane is an unpublished poem addressed to Crane in *Notebooks*, "Enniscorthy—June, 1946."

71. *SW*, 25, 26.

72. See Dewey Wayne Gunn, *American and British Writers in Mexico, 1556–1970* (Austin: University of Texas Press, 1974).

73. "What we are" calls up "The Kingfishers," and the remarks on discourse a major issue of "Human Universe" and "To Gerhardt . . . ," where Olson says, "For the problem is one of focus, of field as well as the point of/ vision . . . ." The use of Mayan terms is comparable to the use of Mayan myth at the close of "Human Universe."

74. *CMI*, 14, 15; *ML*, 83, 84.

75. Crane was aware that the past, still living in the present, was beneath the surface of "history," and he turned to Mexico after writing *The Bridge*. He knew Williams' *In the American Grain*, where Williams speaks of the need for contact with the Indian world and, in "Descent," a chapter on Sam Houston, declares that "we must go back to the beginning," descend "to the ground." Olson cites this chapter in his continuing argument with Gerhardt in the funeral poem, "The Death of Europe": "I have urged anyone/ back (as Williams asked/ that Sam Houston/ be recognized. . . ."

76. *CMI*, 115–16. The myths Olson cites as well as "The Distances" are evidence of this profound motive. The myth of Kronos castrating his father Uranos is central to "To Gerhardt," where Olson refers to it in his remarks on left- and right-handedness.

77. *RB*, 39; this reading had as part of its occasion Olson's recent visit to Pound; see also *LFO*, 90; *CO & EP*, 83, 99.

78. "E. P. never in his life would have spent the years that Frobenius did pushing around Africa." (*CO & EP*, 103)

79. *LFO*, 90, 69; *Nine*, II (November, 1950), 269.

80. *A Quick Graph*, 223. See also Jonas Mekas, *Movie Journal: The Rise of a New American Cinema, 1959–1971* (New York: Collier Books, 1972), 29: "The soul of a European [Mekas is European] is full of deep grooves, molds, forms of past cultures. He may even die with his grooves, without accepting them. That is his fate.

"It is a different situation in America. Anyone, in any art, who perpetuates molds . . . commits an immoral act: instead of freeing men, he drags them down."

81. The lines on the horse's tail refer to "Montage 5" of Gerhardt's "Brief." Sam Houston descends, Ulysses moves horizontally.

82. See, for birds, *ML*, 9–11; for "contrive," Crane's "At Melville's Tomb."

83. *HU*, 155. Again, an old American argument. Horatio Greenough counseled American architects to "learn of the Greeks to be American." See *Form and Function*, ed. Harold A. Small (Berkeley: University of California Press, 1947), 67. For the connection of the poem to Gerhardt to the Way of later poems, see *O* #5, pp. 56–57; and for the Turko-Siberian lore of the poem, brought to my attention by George Butterick, see N. P. Dyrenkova, "Bear Worship

Among Turkish Tribes of Siberia," *Proceedings of the Twenty-Third International Congress of Americanists* (New York: n.p., 1930), 411–40.
    84. *ML*, 5–6.

THREE   1. *LFO*, 140, 141. Baseball, a pastime at Black Mountain College, supplied the following metaphor:

> art
> is the twin of
> the game: how
> do you dance, now
> base-stealers?

See Fielding Dawson, *The Black Mountain Book* (New York: Croton Press, 1970), 90–92.
    2. *LFO*, 141; *SVH*, 15, 13. "Apollonius of Tyana" is a dance-drama; I speak of it here as an essay only in respect to its considerable verbal character.
    3. *P*, 12; *LFO*, 33.
    4. D. H. Lawrence, *Psychoanalysis and the Unconscious* and *Fantasia of the Unconscious* (New York: Viking Press, 1960), 69. Olson recommended the preface of *Fantasia* to both Creeley and Ed Dorn. See *ML*, 88; *BED*, 6.
    5. *HU*, 17. All subsequent quotations are to this edition.
    6. *LFO*, 2.
    7. *SW*, 62.
    8. *BED*, 8–9; *P*, 10; "The Area, and the Discipline of, Totality," unpublished essay, Archives; *LFO*, 106–107.
    9. Reports of Olson's teaching describe a similar procedure and tonic effect.
    10. Space (geography) is a present record of all the time that has "taken place" within it. Olson may have acquired his sense of millennia from V. Gordon Childe's *Man Makes Himself* (New York: New American Library, 1951 [1936]). See especially the chapter on "Time Scales."
    11. *BED*, 3–11; *ML*, 88.
    12. *Max.* I, 20, 22. The old epics and myths are recognized as models, at least in respect to size and scope. Like *Gilgamesh*, *The Maximus Poems* takes its name from its hero and from the historical Maximus of Tyre, who was especially concerned with a city.
    13. *CMI*, 117.
    14. *Ibid.*, 14.
    15. *LFO*, 57–59. Appropriately, Olson mentions Lawrence in this letter.
    16. The last lines play on Kora in hell.
    17. *O* #4, pp. 61, 55; "Esthétique du Mal."
    18. The crude masculinity of these poems should not be excused by attributing it to the persona or to the patent mythic model. Martin Duberman notes that Olson at Black Mountain had "a stereotypic, almost truckdriver view of 'masculinity.'" Martin Duberman, *Black Mountain: An Exploration in Community* (New York: E. P. Dutton, 1972), 346.
    19. Ann Charters, *Olson/Melville: A Study in Affinity* (Berkeley: Oyez, 1968), 88.
    20. In Emerson's sense of original relation to the universe.

21. *SW*, 27.

22. Robert Creeley, *A Quick Graph: Collected Notes & Essays*, ed. Donald Allen (San Francisco: Four Seasons Foundation, 1970), 67–68.

23. *Max*. I, 132. Olson recalls Hart Crane's "The Tunnel," *The Bridge*, which treats descent, is resurrectional in theme, and contains terrifying images of cosmic birth and abandonment as well as images of beneficent deliverance.

24. *ML*, 41, 67; *SW*, 55; *LFO*, 71.

25. *LFO*, 71, 69; *SVH*, 54–55.

26. *ML*, 41, 67–68.

27. Charters, *Olson/Melville*, 88–89; *ML*, 66–67.

28. *ML*, 40–41. On "human house," see "The Resistance."

29. *LFO*, 46–47; *ML*, 68–69.

30. *ML*, 26–30.

31. *O* #2, p. 12. For his appreciation of Litz, who was in residence during the summer of 1951 ("the only dancer there is, these days, who is moving, forward"), see *LFO*, 53.

32. Olson recalls his early training in *Max*. I, 60–61, where the following verses relate to "Apollonius of Tyana":

> The old charts
> are not so wrong
> which added Adam
> to the world's directions
>
> which showed any of us
> the center of a circle
> our fingers
> and our toes describe

For Finch, see "Dancer and Clerk," *Massachusetts Review*, XII (Winter, 1971), 34–40.

33. See Jill Johnston, "The New American Modern Dance," reprinted in *Salmagundi*, XXXIII–XXXIV (Spring/Summer, 1976), 149–74. This special dance issue, excellently edited by Martin Pops, is the source of subsequent short-title references.

34. Frank Kermode, "Poet and Dancer Before Diaghilev," *Salmagundi*, 43. See also Kermode's *Romantic Image* (New York: Knopf, 1964).

35. Charles Olson, "A Syllabary for a Dancer," *MAPS* #4 (1971), 9.

36. Cited by Olson, *O* #2, p. 26; *LFO*, 102.

37. *Salmagundi*, 51, 78, 80, 82; *AM*, 51; *HU*, 71; *LFO*, 61.

38. *LFO*, 140, 53; see also 55, 61.

39. For Litz's art, see Jill Johnston, cited above. That Litz's "lyrical and personal" solos were reactions to Martha Graham may account for Olson's denigration of Graham in *Max*. I, 35. Olson dedicated "A Round & A Canon," a lovely poem of exquisite movement, to Litz and Harrison. The details of "Glyph" are from *O* #2, p. 13. He also wrote a poem for Merce Cunningham. For a detailed account of Black Mountain College at this time, see Duberman, *Black Mountain*, 334–413.

40. I cite, merely as an example, from the minutes of a faculty meeting. *O* #2, p. 18.

41. All citations may be found in *SW* and *HU*.

42. "Man is a thing which [simultaneously] thinks and dances," a definition Olson derived from the Vedas. See Olson, "A Syllabary for a Dancer," 9, 12.

43. Olson speaks of "Apollonius" as a play. *SW*, 156; *HU*, 44.

44. Mary Wigman, cited by Martin Pops, *Salmagundi*, 12.

45. *BED*, 8.

46. Of course, it may be to Olson's purpose to say, "In what concerns yourself, act as a private man; in what concerns the state, act likewise"—advice that addresses his own situation and accords with the solution expressed in "Letter 9" of *The Maximus Poems*. Apollonius actually says, "Act like an emperor in matters that concern your power, but like an ordinary citizen in matters that concern your person." I cite the most recent and trustworthy edition of Philostratus, *Life of Apollonius*, trans. C. P. Jones, ed. G. W. Bowersock (Harmondsworth: Penguin Books, 1970),128.

47. *O* #2, p. 54.

48. Dawson, *Black Mountain Book*, 90.

49. Philostratus, *Life of Apollonius*, 170. Olson alludes to Pound in remarks on Confucius. The first judges Pound against his own Confucian standard: Apollonius "was Confucian about such things as his responsibility for the body politic." The second suggests that Olson has traveled farther—and spiritually, too—than Pound: for "Kung Fu Tse had not . . . been as far as Tai, the precious mountain."

Pound himself uses Apollonius in *Rock-Drill* (1955).

50. Again, educational policy: "The College has the respect & attention Sophocles had for the human body. (He went each morning to the temple of Aesclepius.) Coming out of the American system—[the body] as a dumb awkward deprived beaten bag and strait-jacket—we take it any one needs to be reminded & re-experience what they were born with." *O* #2, p. 55.

51. *PT*, 43 ff.

52. Olson, "A Syllabary for a Dancer," 14.

53. Verticality is to coherence as horizontality is to dispersion. See *ibid.*

54. See "The Gate & The Center."

55. For the "Double-Backed Beast," the primal parents, see *AP*, 39.

56. *RB*, 45.

57. *Max.* II, 2–6; *PT*, 15–21.

58. Martin L. Pops, "Melville: To Him, Olson," *Modern Poetry Studies*, II (1971), 92, 90.

59. *Max.* I, 1.

60. They are also positively associated with Olson's father.

61. Charters, *Olson/Melville*, 84–90.

62. Robert Creeley to William Carlos Williams, September 27, 1951, in Robert Creeley Papers, Beinecke Library, Yale University; Pops, "Melville: To Him, Olson," 91.

63. *LFO*, 122. See the course description for "History and/or Culture," where Olson proposes to work from the premise that "an attack on event and events from the position of the single man as capable of knowledge sufficient to judge and compel event is the only study equivalent to the fact and motive of event itself." *O* #2, p. 42 [1954].

64. *HU*, 157. Originally published in *The Black Mountain Review* in 1954.

65. *LFO*, 140.

66. Robert Duncan, "Early Poetic Community" *Allen Verbatim*, ed. Gordon Ball (New York: McGraw-Hill, 1974), 135, recalls that Olson didn't permit Emerson to be taught at Black Mountain College perhaps for the reason acquired by Olson in reading Melville: "Emerson/Thoreau: misleading men"; Emerson and Thoreau "acted as if they were in on the original creation & made some corrections" (*O #4*, p. 55). At Wesleyan, Olson had written an essay on Emerson's poetry, and at Harvard had studied with F. O. Matthiessen, whose unfavorable views of Emerson he assimilated. See Wilbert Snow, "A Teacher's View," *Massachusetts Review*, XII (Winter, 1971), 42; *Notebooks*, "#4 Cambridge & NY Winter–Spring 1940."

Later Olson acknowledged the Romantics: "The professors don't know how seriously the Romantic Poets belong to the poets of the present"—for the good reason that "Romantic/Romance has to do with the springs of feeling/ the springs of action" (*O #4*, pp. 54–55). For Olson's connection with Transcendentalism, see *PT*, 55.

67. "And I believe, more than anyone else in our time . . . [what I have] tried to encourage people to believe—is, their own action" (*RB*, 27). Olson's Emersonian lineage has been stressed by Robert Duncan who traces "projective verse" to an American "aesthetic based on energies" as exemplified in Emerson's "Hamatreya"; he also makes the fitting connection with John Dewey's *Art as Experience*. See Robert Duncan, "Notes on Poetics Regarding Olson's 'Maximus,'" *The Black Mountain Review*, #6 (1956), 201–202. It is significant, too, that Emerson has been considered a forerunner of Whitehead. See Harry Modean Campbell, "Emerson and Whitehead," *PMLA*, LXXV (1960), 577–82.

68. Duncan connects *his-story* to *histology*. *O #4*, pp. 40–45.

69. *SVH*, 5–6. Olson's preoccupation here suggests Kenneth Burke's dramatism.

70. See also *LVO*, 83; *BED*; and *Max.* II, 79, where Olson treats this in terms of Whitehead and Jung.

71. *Muthos* and story are oral over against the writing of discourse.

72. The reference to Whorf's article should be followed up, as Olson suggests at the end of the previous section. This article provides the transition to localism and supports Olson's notion of *tropos*. Whorf points out that one's "growth axis" (the vertical and "subjective") is the center from which the "objective" world extends and that occurrences elsewhere, though simultaneous in our sense of time, being distant for the Hopi, are past. Benjamin Lee Whorf, *Language, Thought, and Reality*, ed. John B. Carroll (Cambridge: M.I.T. Press, 1956), 62–63.

73. *Max.* III, 10.

74. Whorf, *Language, Thought, and Reality*, 59.

75. I introduce Sullivan because he is a precursor whose *Democracy: A Man-Search* is concerned with our estrangement and recovery of agency in history. Paul Tillich, whose discussion of the demonic in *The Interpretation of History* Olson mentions, provides a measure of Olson's concern with the beneficent aspect of *tropos*, since the demonic is an essential energy of all

creative act. In terms of Olson's "love is form" (*Max.* I, 1), the demonic is
its destruction.

76. See "The Lamp," *AM*, 221: "only if there is a coincidence of yourself/
& the universe is there then in fact/ an event."

77. *SW*, 62.

78. *O #3*, p. 31.

79. Lawrence, *Fantasia of the Unconscious*, 56; *O #4*, p. 55; Alfred North
Whitehead, *Process and Reality: An Essay in Cosmology* (New York: The
Social Science Book Store [Macmillan], 1929), 135–36. Olson's recollection of
Yeats's remark fits his own poetics: "We come to bring you *images* for your
verse." (My italics)

80. *ML*, 91. That the lectures address Pound is borne out by the following:
"get rid of Logos/Phanos/Melos! get rid of Ez's trilogy! . . . O's replacement:
Actions/Feeling/Sentence" (*O #4*, p. 56), which accords with this statement in
the lectures, "the actionable, or, the very act of the sentence, is the dynamic
which matters."

FOUR
1. *SVH*, 58.

2. *CO & EP*, xxiii.

3. *O #4*, p. 78.

4. Robert Creeley, *Contexts of Poetry: Interviews 1961–1971*, ed. Donald
Allen (Bolinas: Four Seasons Foundation, 1973), 160; *O #4*, p. 79.

5. Olson knew Whitman's work early and well. In 1933 he wrote "Whitman
and Orientalism" for Stanley Williams at Yale, and his copy of *Leaves of Grass*
is heavily marked, one reading as late as 1960. (Archives) Olson praised
"Crossing Brooklyn Ferry" in *O #3*, p. 37.

6. Donald Allen and Robert Creeley (eds.), *The New Writing in the USA*
(Harmondsworth: Penguin Books, 1967), 326–27. See also "Gassire's Lute" in
Leo Frobenius and Douglas C. Fox, *African Genesis* (New York: Stackpole
Sons, 1937), 97–110.

7. *AP*, 39–40.

8. *SW*, 136; "And Ode on Nativity," *AM*, 81–84; *Origin #1*, pp. 53–54. See
the fable of the artist of the city of Kouroo, in Thoreau, *Walden*.

9. Lionel Trilling, *Sincerity and Authenticity* (Cambridge: Harvard University Press, 1972), 8; *LFO*, 106; *O #4*, p. 79, where "personality" is probably
directed at Whitman; Fielding Dawson, *The Black Mountain Book* (New
York: Croton Press, 1970), 88, 107; Gary Snyder, *Earth House Hold* (New
York: New Directions, 1969), 123–25; *O #1*, p. 20; see Olson's concern with
"*root* experiences" and "*archetypal memory*" in *O #5*, pp. 55–57.

10. *ML*, 28; Charles Olson, "Memorial Letter," *Origin* #20, 3rd ser. (January, 1971), 43–45; William Carlos Williams, "Review of *The Maximus
Poems* 11–22," *MAPS* #4 (1971), 61.

11. *SW*, 25–26, 15; see *O #3*, pp. 47, 51, where he says that archetext "has
the character-action of story, and . . . the character-object of image," thereby
fulfilling his desire to "live one's own image, rather than use it simply for
writing." (*PT*, 34).

12. Dawson, *The Black Mountain Book*, 88–89.

13. Ann Charters, *Olson/Melville: A Study in Affinity* (Berkeley: Oyez, 1968), 88. "Acts of form" enters his vocabulary at this time. See *BED*, 4.

14. An event comprises many actual occasions. Williams' previous use of the word follows Whitehead's usage prior to *Process and Reality*.

15. *ML*, 6.

16. *LFO*, 104.

17. *SVH*, 45.

18. Dawson, *The Black Mountain Book*, 99.

19. Olson treats this theme, already of ecological import, in "Troilus," *AM*, 3.

20. *P*, 4.

21. William Carlos Williams, "The American Background," *The Selected Essays of William Carlos Williams* (New York: Random House, 1954), 147.

22. Mircea Eliade, *Rites and Symbols of Initiation: The Mysteries of Birth and Rebirth* (New York: Harper Torchbooks, 1965), xii.

23. Havelock Ellis, "The Art of Dancing," *Salmagundi*, XXXIII–XXIV (Spring–Summer, 1976), 5.

24. *CO & EP*, 89.

25. For Olson's awareness of this, see *RB*, 34.

26. Williams, "Review of *The Maximus Poems* 11–22," 61–65; Williams, *Selected Essays*, 32; George F. Butterick, "An Annotated Guide to *The Maximus Poems* of Charles Olson" (Ph.D. dissertation, State University of New York at Buffalo, 1970).

27. Olson claims Homer as one of his masters in "Memorial Letter," 45. As for Whitman, "And of these one and all I weave the song of myself" (§15, "Song of Myself").

28. Most of the poems in the first and second installments were written at Black Mountain College; only the third was written in Gloucester, where Olson took up residence late in 1957. The number of poems in each of the early installments seems to have been an editorial-production matter decided by Jonathan Williams, a student of Olson's at Black Mountain College and his enterprising publisher.

29. Charles Olson, "A Syllabary for a Dancer," *MAPS* #4 (1971), 11.

30. The poems are dedicated to Robert Creeley, "the figure of outward," for whom Olson wrote "Charles Olson, For R. C." (*O* #6, p. 3). For Ferrini, Olson is the figure of outward; see Vincent Ferrini, "A Frame," *MAPS* #4 (1971), 58.

Outward, as Olson uses it elsewhere, is connected with the ego, with men like Ahab. It is the horizontal direction of dispersion and exploitation to be countervailed by the vertical direction of coherence and creation. See Olson, "A Syllabary for a Dancer," 13–15.

31. *SVH*, 37.

32. The importance of the advertising theme may be seen by reading Northrop Frye's *The Modern Century*, where the structure of leisure [polis] he opposes to the structures of politics and economics is threatened by the media, the "public relations" that now includes propaganda and advertising.

33. See Erich Neumann, *The Great Mother: An Analysis of the Archetype* (Princeton: Princeton University Press, 1972 [1955]), 98.

34. *CMI*, 14; *AP*, 40.

35. *SVH*, 54. Olson spells out the ecological message of Whitman's metaphor.

36. Finding these related in his examination of the dictionary is an example of luck.

37. The lovely verse beginning section one is a measure of relationship as well as an example of Olson's "nature" poetry, of his gift of attending emergence, "the rising of/ the forces," as he says in one of his finest poems, "For a man gone to Stuttgart . . .":

> the flowering plum
> out the front door window
> sends whiteness
> inside my house

The phrasing, as in many of the early installments, owes much to Williams, and the "close music," treated in his essay on Shakespeare's late plays, to Pound, but the greatest debt is to Fenollosa. Note consonantal *fl* and *pl* in the first line, the vowel leading from *o* to *u*, and the pleasant terminal *m*. The line has a smooth processual movement, followed in the next and longest line by the more deliberate movement (duration of the flowe*ring*). Here there is some harshness; the different *o*'s lead on to the most pleasant, and lead to the verbal action: "sends whiteness." The transference of energy is a gift. The very sharpness of the whiteness (a substantive) is in the stress on the long *i*, and the transference, conveyed by the *s*'s, continues into the last line, where the long *i* of "inside" and "my" brings the "whiteness" with it. The movement of the lines and the well-placed initial stressed "out" and "inside," enact interpenetration. ". . . inside my house" recalls the epiphanic moment of renewal in *Walden* ("Suddenly an influx of light filled my house"), house having for Thoreau the sense of bodily being it has for Olson. The poem is an act of attention, demonstrating the stance called for in "Projective Verse." Outside and inside suggest the separation of self and world; the poet is inside himself and there are things outside himself. But the door does not block the passage because he sees through himself (to modify the phrase in "Projective Verse"), that is, shares—is himself moved by—the forces that move the plum to flower. And so in the flowering plum he *recognizes* his own flowering or tropic awakening.

38. Charles Olson, "Notes for the Proposition: Man is Prospective," *Boundary 2*, II (Fall, 1973/Winter, 1974), 4.

39. Honor: "man's splendor" in "An Ode on Nativity."

40. See *Max*. II, 14.

41. *HU*, 131–34.

42. *Max*. I, 123.

43. See *CO & EP*.

44. John Finch, "Dancer and Clerk," *Massachusetts Review*, XII (Winter, 1971), 36–37.

45. *SVH*, 54–55.

46. *ML*, 46; Gondwanaland in *Max*. II is another such geographical/global image of primordial unity.

47. *HU*, 132. For Olson's comments on this poem, see *RB*, 41 ff.

48. *CM*, 5.
49. *RB*, 41, 47, 54.
50. See "ABCs (2)"; Charters, *Olson/Melville*, 86–87.
51. Robert Duncan, "Notes on Poetics Regarding Olson's 'Maximus,'" *Black Mountain Review*, VI (Spring, 1956), 208.
52. Olson, "A Syllabary for a Dancer," 13, 14.
53. *SVH*, 21.
54. *HU*, 137.
55. *BED*, 13.
56. *ML*, 90; *HU*, 143; *SW*, 29; *BED*, 12, 14.
57. *BED*, 10, 7.
58. The reference here is to Edgar Anderson, *Plants, Man and Life* (Boston: Little, Brown, 1952).
59. This seems to be the first letter of this installment that was written on Olson's return to Gloucester, and the hardship may be consonant with his own effort to begin again. See also *O* #6, pp. 61–62.
60. Joyce Benson, "First Round of Letters," *Boundary* 2, II (Fall, 1973/ Winter, 1974),362.
61. C. G. Jung and C. Kerényi, *Essays on a Science of Mythology* (Princeton: Princeton University Press, 1969 [1949]), 6 ff.; *CMI*, 14.
62. Carl Sauer, "Foreward to Historical Geography," *Land and Life: A Selection from the Writings of Carl Ortwin Sauer*, ed. John Leighly (Berkeley: University of California Press, 1967), 367.
63. For Olson's concern with the West and its relation to *The Maximus Poems*, see *O* #5 and #6.
64. *CM*, 29.
65. See *RB*, 43 ("Caesar's dream is true"), a fact probably less disturbing to Olson because Erich Neumann discredited the Freudian interpretation by making the Oedipal situation a necessary and impersonal (archetypal) event in the evolution of consciousness. See Erich Neumann, *The Origins and History of Consciousness*, 2 vols.; (New York: Harper Torchbooks, 1962), I, 182–84.
66. These lines call up the treatment of the antemosaic in *CMI*, 82, where relation to space is the important consideration.
67. Monads refer to Leibnitz, but serve well as an image of isolated egos.
68. See *Max*. II, 129, an image of the Great Round. Olson marked *K'un*: "earth, the Receptive . . . one of the two primal principles, namely the yin principle which is embodied in the energies of the earth," in his copy of *The Secret of The Golden Flower*, trans. and explained by Richard Wilhelm, with a Commentary by C. G. Jung (London: Kegan, Paul, Trench, Trubner, 1945), 19. Archives.
69. The poem may also be read as a yielding to death, as in Crane and Whitman, in order to overcome an overwhelming anguish.
70. The phrase is N. O. Brown's, from his edition of Hesiod, *Theogony* (Indianapolis and New York: Bobbs-Merrill Co., 1953), 15.
71. *O* #3, p. 62.
72. *O* #2, p. 67; *O* #4, p. 81.
73. Henri Corbin, "Cyclical Time in Mazdaism and Ismailism," in Joseph

Campbell (ed.), *Man and Time: Papers from the Eranos Yearbooks*, Bollingen Series XXX, 3 (New York: Pantheon Books, 1957), 147, 150, 167. See also Henri Corbin, *Avicenna and the Visionary Recital* (New York: Pantheon Books, 1960), 28–35.

74. Archives.

75. *Squam*, Indian for harbor in the mouth of a river, secures a prehistoric parallel.

76. See also Jung and Kerényi, *Essays on a Science of Mythology*, 151; Nike, in *Max*. I, 15; D. H. Lawrence, "The Man of Tyre," *The Complete Poems of D. H. Lawrence*, ed. Vivian de Sola Pinto and F. Warren Roberts (New York: Viking Press, 1971), 692–93.

77. Alfred North Whitehead, *Process and Reality: An Essay in Cosmology* (New York: The Social Science Book Store [Macmillan], 1929), 124.

78. Eliot's essay is in *The Dial*, LXXV (November, 1923), 483; Charles Altieri, "From Symbolist Thought to Immanence: The Ground of Postmodern American Poetics," *Boundary* 2, I (Spring, 1973), 633–34; *CM*, 12, 9; *AP*, 51.

79. *O* #6, p. 59.

80. See Brown's introduction to *Theogony*, 20, 22, 43; Charles Olson, "Dostoevski and The Possessed," *Twice A Year*, V–VI (Fall–Winter 1940/ Spring–Summer 1941), 230.

81. For Olson's troubled relations with his mother, see "As the Dead Prey Upon Us" (1956) and "Moonset, Gloucester, December 1, 1957, 1:58 A.M."

82. See Hans Jonas, *The Gnostic Religion: The Message of the Alien God and the Beginnings of Christianity* (Boston: Beacon Press, 1958), 147 ff.

83. *Ginnungagap*: "Space preceding creation, in which the worlds were made." I cite H. R. Ellis Davidson, *Gods and Myths of Northern Europe* (Harmondsworth: Penguin Books, 1964), 231.

84. C. G. Jung, *Psychology and Alchemy*, trans. R. F. C. Hull. Bollingen Series XX (Princeton: Princeton University Press, 1968 [1953]), 28. Maximus seems to have appreciated "circumambulate"; he mentions "Al ʾArabi's/ circumvallum" (*Max*. II, 197), an Islamic account of the process of individuation. See Fritz Meier, "The Mystery of the Ka ʾba: Symbol and Reality in Islamic Mysticism," in Joseph Campbell (ed.), *The Mysteries: Papers from the Eranos Yearbooks*, Bollingen Series XXX, 3 (New York: Pantheon Books, 1955), 155–56.

85. Joseph Garland remarks that "Gloucester has three other seasons [besides summer], plus March . . . ." *The Gloucester Guide: A Retrospective Ramble* (Gloucester: Gloucester 350th Anniversary Celebration, Inc., 1973), xiii.

86. Jung stresses the normality of these eruptions, the "powerful autonomy of the unconscious . . . [the] volcanic outbursts from the very bottom of things." C. G. Jung, *The Integration of Personality*, trans. Stanley Dell (London: Routledge & Kegan Paul, 1940), 12.

87. See, for example, the poems on 138, 139, 146, 159.

88. Olson's size undoubtedly troubled him and may account for his interest in the spurious folk-hero Paul Bunyan. See Notebooks #5, "Gloucester Spring 1940," and also his passport which gives his height as 6'7".

89. This poem on "Stage Fort Park" follows the geological account of Dog-

town in "The Cow/ of Dogtown" and is fitting because both underwent the same geological action.

90. "Spring," *Walden*. Watered rock also has alchemical significance: "the water is extracted from the stone or *prima materia* as its life-giving soul (*anima*)." Jung, *Psychology and Alchemy*, 234.

91. I characterize "MAXIMUS, FROM DOGTOWN—I" in this way because the Egyptian, although prominent, is assimilated to the Greek. At this point Maximus overlooks the primary place of Atum in creation.

92. Olson read Neumann, *The Great Mother* with care and probably read Neumann's equally important *The Origins and History of Consciousness*.

Harrison's distinctions are in Jane Harrison, *Themis: A Study of the Social Origins of Greek Religion* (2nd ed; Cambridge: Cambridge University Press, 1927), 390–92. They are also in the edition of *Theogony* Olson used, Hesiod, *The Homeric Hymns and Homerica*, trans. Hugh G. Evelyn-White, Loeb Classical Library (New York: G. P. Putnam's Sons, 1926), 87n. In the larger movement of the remaining installments, Maximus follows Payne's sequence from Earth to Sun.

93. See Neumann, *The Great Mother*, 217, 221–22, heavily marked by Olson. (Archives)

94. Harrison, *Themis*, 457; John Burnet's translation of Heraclitus, Fragments 19, 59, 64, 73, 74–76, in Olson's source, W. H. Auden (ed.), *The Portable Greek Reader* (New York: Viking Press, 1948).

95. "The self-generating power of the soul is man's true and final secret"— Neumann, *The Origins and History of Consciousness*, 210–11. See also *O #3*, pp. 59–63.

96. Henri Frankfort *et al*, *Before Philosophy* (Baltimore: Penguin Books, 1973 [1946]), 54–56, to which I am much indebted; *The Great Mother*, 221–22.

97. *O #3*, p. 61.

98. Neumann cites Rig-Veda, X, 18, 43: "As a mother covers her son with the hem of her cloak, so cover him thou, O earth." Neumann, *The Great Mother*, 223.

99. *SVH*, 54; sow, water, moon: all emblems of the Great Mother.

100. Jung, *Psychology and Alchemy*, 23, 218, where he notes that carbon, having a valence of four, represents quarternity.

101. Heinrich Zimmer, *Myths and Symbols in Indian Art and Civilization*, ed. Joseph Campbell (Princeton: Princeton University Press, 1946), 90.

102. Maximus' response to *heimarmene* also suggests masculine presumption—his belief in the Father, who will deliver the soul from Nature. For Vierge Ouvrante, see Neumann, *The Great Mother*, 331. For his preference for the primordial goddess, see also *Max. II*, 159, and "The Horses of the Sea," his poem on Our Lady of Good Voyage, who, "like Athena standeth out/ with concerns which are general/ as against those which a mother// . . . is presented with. . . ." Charles Olson, "The Horses of the Sea," *Sparrow 43* (Los Angeles: Black Sparrow Press, April, 1976).

103. Jung, *Psychology and Alchemy*, 23–25. "Healing" is Jung's term.

104. See Pausanias, *Pausanias's Description of Greece*, trans. J. G. Frazer (6 vols.; London: Macmillan & Co., 1898), I, 129.

105. These lines appear in *"Maximus to Gloucester, Letter 27* [withheld]." For the MSS., see *O* #3, p. 58.

106. Olson reread Whitman in 1960.

107. Consider here the appropriateness of Whitehead's "subjective aim."

108. Corbin, "Cyclical Time in Mazdaism and Ismailism," 161–62; Neumann, *The Great Mother*, 23 (Archives).

109. Both Corbin and Jung stress the work involved, which Olson noted in the marginalia of Jung, *Psychology and Alchemy*, 352, 355, is to liberate God (Archives).

110. Jung, *Psychology and Alchemy*, 360–61. Zosimos provides another alchemy of resurrection, one that Jung connects with the Persian (368).

111. Corbin, "Cyclical Time in Mazdaism and Ismailism," 131–32.

112. Jung, *Psychology and Alchemy*, 178.

113. *Ibid.*, 107–108, 257.

114. Notebooks #4, "Cambridge and New York Winter–Spring 1940."

115. See James Joyce, *The Portrait of the Artist as a Young Man.*

116. Henri Frankfort, *Kingship and the Gods: A Study of Ancient Near Eastern Religion as the Integration of Society & Nature* (Chicago: University of Chicago Press, 1948), 28. See also *Max.* II, 158: "Ptah/ man of the earth."

117. Frankfort, *Kingship and the Gods*, 29; Neumann, *The Great Mother*, 169–70; *SW*, 25.

118. Frankfort, *Kingship and the Gods*, 31–32, and for "polyphony," 25; see Notebooks, especially those of 1945, and "Faust Buch #1," Washington, Spring 1947–July 22, 1948.

119. Jung, *Psychology and Alchemy*, 183.

120. Benson, "First Round of Letters," 360.

121. For Olson's gloss, see *ibid.* On psychic hunger, see Jung, *Psychology and Alchemy*, 221.

122. For a gloss, see Hermann Weyl, *Philosophy of Mathematics and Natural Science* (Princeton: Princeton University Press, 1949), 287.

123. C. G. Jung, *The Archetypes and the Collective Unconscious*, Bollingen Series XX (Princeton: Princeton University Press, 1968 [1959]), 359.

124. Neumann, *The Great Mother*, 291–92.

125. A shorter version is inscribed in Olson's copy of James Pritchard's *Ancient Near Eastern Texts Relating to the Old Testament*, where Olson worked especially closely with *Gilgamesh*. (Archives) The version cited is from George Butterick's soon-to-be-published annotations of all of *The Maximus Poems*.

126. Ralph Waldo Emerson, "Circles," *Essays: First Series* (Boston: Houghton, Mifflin and Co., 1903), 304.

127. Robert Creeley, "Inside Out," *Sparrow 14* (Los Angeles: Black Sparrow Press, November, 1973), 3. This essay is an excellent gloss on the undertaking of a generation of poets, and Olson is much in evidence in it. Creeley notes Olson's relevant comment that "the initial sign for the pronoun *I* was a boat . . . a vehicle of passage or transformation," and places the work of post–World War II poets in a Jungian context: "We saw what Jung might call the 'individuation process' enter the nightmare of 'divided creation,' torn from centers of physical reality" (11).

128. Neumann, *The Great Mother*, 58; *Max.* II, 9. *Poimandres* may be read in Jonas, *The Gnostic Religion*, Chapter 7, or, partly, in Corbin, *Avicenna and the Visionary Recital*, where it is related to Persian "recitals." *The Secret of the Golden Flower* suggested Olson's "The Secret of the Black Chrysanthemum," of all of his schema the most inclusive and the essential gloss on the last two volumes of *The Maximus Poems*. See *O* #3, pp. 64–81.

129. Archives.

130. Neumann, *The Great Mother*, 50.

131. The picture is on the cover of Charles Olson, *The Post Office: A Memoir of His Father* (Bolinas: Grey Fox Press, 1975).

132. *CMI*, 82 ff.

133. *PT*, 43–44, 50; *LFO*, 122. *Heliotropism*: how wonderfully it enabled Olson to serve both mother (matriarchy) and father (patriarchy) and justified the tropic necessities of individuation introduced in *Max.* I, 40. There the *fylfot*, connected with Lady Luck, is the swastika, which Jane Harrison notes, is a wheel symbolizing the order of Nature and in its sunwise turning following the way of Truth and Justice, hence giving one the feeling of luck. See Harrison, *Themis*, 525–27.

134. Vincent Ferrini, "A Frame," *MAPS* #4 (1971), 57.

135. For Olson the most important sources of this mythology are Davidson, *Gods and Myths of Northern Europe*, "a beautiful—'lucky'—book," he noted on the flyleaf (*O* #2, p. 73) and Murray Fowler, "Old Norse Religion," *Ancient Religions*, ed. Vergilius Ferm (New York: Philosophical Library, 1950), 237–50. For Olson's comments on Fowler, see *PT*, 50, 53.

136. Like Pound in the *Pisan Cantos*, he may be said "to dream the Republic," to refuse to yield the idea of it. For Pound, this is related to the legend of "Gassire's Lute," which Olson apparently learned of from Pound. (See Notebooks, "Enniscorthy—June, 1946.") For Pound's use of this motif, see Noel Stock, *Reading the Cantos: A Study of Meaning in Ezra Pound* (New York: Minerva Press, 1968), 76–77.

137. His presence makes acceptable the poem written in Berlin—a poem, in any case, thematically appropriate to this volume. Olson discusses his relation to Maximus in *PT*, 34.

138. His relation to history is now especially intimate. See also *Max.* III, 82, 97, 135.

139. See Vincent Ferrini, "The *Theia Mania* of Charles Olson," *Selected Poems*, ed., with introduction, by George Butterick (Storrs: The University of Connecticut Library, 1976), 94–95.

140. *CM*, 4.

141. Olson often wore a sweater, according to Ferrini, "A Frame," 57; C. G. Jung, *Aion* (Princeton: Princeton University Press, 1968), 124; *The Secret of the Golden Flower*, 99–100; for migrations, see *AP*, 67; *Max.* I, 151. Also, in Norse mythology, Buri had Bor, and Bor had three sons.

142. See Charles Boer, *Charles Olson in Connecticut* (Chicago: Swallow Press, 1975), 129; *IO* #8 (1971), 274.

143. The allusion is to Amphion at Thebes, but also to Pound's *The Cantos* (LXXIV): "To build the city of Dioce."

144. *Max.* II, 36.

145. Boer, *Charles Olson in Connecticut*, 19.
146. See "As the Dead Prey Upon Us," *AM*.
147. The use of the middle voice is significant.
148. See also *Max*. III, 187, where the "salmon of/ wisdom" is associated with love and breath.
149. Whitehead, *Process and Reality*, 71.
150. Jung notes that "the year is a symbol of the original man," that the solstice is a turning point, and that in alchemy the work is completed in autumn. Jung, *Psychology and Alchemy*, 192, 199.
151. For Lane, consult John Wilmerding, *Fitz Hugh Lane 1804–1865; American Marine Painter* (Salem: Essex Institute, 1964), and *Fitz Hugh Lane* (New York: Praeger, 1971). Olson's poems are in *AM*, 226, 227–28.
152. *Max*. II, 100.
153. Archives. For Olson's concern with the American language, see John Cech, Oliver Ford, and Peter Rittner, *Charles Olson in Connecticut: Last Lectures* (Iowa City: Windhover Press, 1974).
154. The juncture, dividing "conspicuous," restores our sense of the Latin *spicere*, to look, and insists on what the entire word means, to look closely. For pragmatism, see *PT*, 58.
155. *P*, 4.
156. Archives.
157. See *Max*. II, 137.
158. *AM*, 227, 226; *Max*. III, 118.
159. Ralph Waldo Emerson, *Representative Men* (Boston and New York: Houghton Mifflin and Co., 1903), 85; *Max*. III, 124, 125; Whitehead, *Process and Reality*, 506; Boer, *Charles Olson in Connecticut*, 107; *IO* #8 (1971), 276.
160. Barbara Novak, *American Painting of the Nineteenth Century* (New York: Praeger, 1969), 108, 110.
161. Emerson, *Nature* (1836); *Representative Men*, 77.
162. Novak, *American Painting of the Nineteenth Century*, 121–22.
163. Jung, *Psychology and Alchemy*, 266.
164. *PT*, 56–58. The poem has an unusual, conclusive period.
165. Whitehead, *Process and Reality*, 472–508; *SW*, 45.
166. See Frobenius and Fox, *African Genesis*, 97–110.
167. For Olson's comments, see *PT*, 61–64.
168. The reference is to Whitehead's notion of "fluent energy": "Mathematical physics translates the saying of Heraclitus, 'All things flow,' into its own language. It then becomes, All things are vectors." Whitehead, *Process and Reality*, 471.
169. *RB*, 35.
170. *CM*, 36, 15.
171. Charles Olson, *Pleistocene Man* (Buffalo: Institute of Further Studies, 1968), 9.
172. Thoreau, "Walking."
173. D. H. Lawrence, *Apocalypse* (New York: Viking Press, 1973), 200; *CM*, 14.
174. For Virgin Mundi, see *RB*, 47; *AM*, 223 ff.; *PT*, 12.

1. Charles Olson, review of R. W. Babson and F. H. Saville's *Cape Ann: A Tourist Guide*, in *New England Quarterly*, X (March, 1937), 191–92; *Max.* I, 151; Warren Tallman, "Proprioception in Charles Olson's Poetry," *Open Letter*, 2nd ser., #2 (Summer, 1972), 13. Richard Chase, *The Democratic Vista: A Dialogue on Life and Letters in Contemporary America* (New York: Doubleday, 1958), has Cape Ann for its setting. But Chase, aware of Eliot's relation to Cape Ann, is not aware of Olson's. Neither is John D. Boyd in *"The Dry Salvages*: Topography as Symbol," *Renascence*, XX (Spring, 1968), 119–33, 161.

2. Ann Charters, *Olson/Melville: A Study in Affinity* (Berkeley: Oyez, 1968), 85; *Origin* #1, 53.

3. He did not govern, serve, defend, or cure. See Kenneth Burke, "I, Eye, Ay—Emerson's Early Essay 'Nature': Thoughts on the Machinery of Transcendence," in Myron Simon and Thornton H. Parsons (eds.), *Transcendentalism and Its Legacy* (Ann Arbor: University of Michigan Press, 1966), 4–5.

4. Lionel Trilling, *Sincerity and Authenticity* (Cambridge: Harvard University Press, 1972), 82.

5. *CM*, 35.

6. Chapter II, *Walden*; *Max.* III, 198; Alfred North Whitehead, *Process and Reality: An Essay in Cosmology* (New York: The Social Science Bookstore [Macmillan], 1929), 472; Charters, *Olson/Melville*, 85.

7. *AP*, 83.

8. *CM*, 37, 5.

9. §2, "Song of Myself"; for "listening," see "Projective Verse," *SW*, 25.

10. *SW*, 29.

11. *O* #4, p. 68; see also 50: "a sentence should be *the* ordering of the universe."

12. *O* #2, p. 11.

13. *O* #4, pp. 66–68.

14. See *O* #4, p. 59; *O* #2, p. 65 ff.

15. *O* #5, p. 3.

16. Frank O'Hara, *Standing Still and Walking in New York*, ed. Donald Allen (Bolinas: Grey Fox Press, 1975), 13.

17. *AM*, 229–34.

18. *Max.* I, 71.

19. *O* #1, pp. 7–44.

20. "Imago" (essay MSS., 1947). Archives.

21. "In Cold Hell, In Thicket"; Francis Ponge, "The Silent World is Our Only Homeland," *The Voice of Things*, trans. Beth Archer (New York: McGraw-Hill, 1974), 109.

22. *O* #1, p. 31.

23. *LFO*, 62; *RB*, 27.

24. *HU*, 19.

25. Archives.

26. *CMI*, 117–19.

27. *HU*, 23.

28. *AP*, 40; Van Wyck Brooks, *Letters and Leadership* in *Three Essays on America* (New York: E. P. Dutton, 1934), 117.

Epilogue

29. Henry David Thoreau, *The Journals*, in *The Writings of Henry David Thoreau* (20 vols.; Boston and New York: Houghton Mifflin Co., 1906), VIII, 145. The allusion to W. H. Rueckert's essay, cited in chapter 1, is the least of my indebtedness. I owe him much, most recently the deeply stirring experience of his unpublished paper, "Literature and Ecology" (MLA, 1976), which called many things to my attention, among them Ponge's essay.

30. *Max.* III, 14.

Index